Additional Praise for

Starting with Goodbye

"Lisa Romeo has carved out fresh terrain on a bookstore shelf already tightly packed with grief memoirs, and she's done it movingly and with deep insight."

—JILL SMOLOWE,
author of *Four Funerals and a Wedding*

"Written with great tenderness and quiet mastery, *Starting with Goodbye* is a daughter's love letter to her father, and a welcome reminder that our most intimate relationships don't end with death but are transformed over time if our hearts are open, our spirits are attuned to mystery, and we are willing to carry on a different kind of conversation."

—KATRINA KENISON,
author of *Magical Journey: An Apprenticeship in Contentment* and *The Gift of an Ordinary Day*

"Rich, intelligent, thoughtful, personal and investigative. What stands out is the voice, continuing to probe and wonder, open still to discovering what might be true about this interesting life. Just the kind of character we like to follow around. Intensely emotional without being maudlin."

—BARBARA HURD,
author of *Tidal Rhythms* and *Stirring the Mud*

"This is a brave and vulnerable book, like *The Year of Magical Thinking*. The energy of this book is leaping off the page with internal struggle. The writing moved me — gorgeous sentences. I felt the narrator's presence so strongly and felt so connected to what she was going through, and what she had lost. It so beautifully reflects the 'stuckness' of grief, with a lack of sentimentality that is powerful."

— LARAINE HERRING,
author of *Lost Fathers* and *Writing Begins with the Breath*

"Lisa Romeo's writing is beautifully poetic. Her story is one that all daughters of difficult fathers will want to read."

— SUSAN KUSHNER RESNICK,
author of *You Saved Me, Too.*

"I read this book slowly, mindfully, wanting to do what the author's father exhorted her to do: Pay attention. *Starting with Goodbye* pulls you along with its own sense of movement, heightened and fluid; I wanted to relish it all, and live within it."

— LORRAINE MANGIONE, PHD,
co-author of *Daughters, Dads, and the Path Through Grief: Tales from Italian America*, and professor of clinical psychology, Antioch University New England

STARTING WITH GOODBYE

Starting with Goodbye

A Daughter's Memoir
of Love after Loss

LISA ROMEO

UNIVERSITY OF NEVADA PRESS *Reno & Las Vegas*

University of Nevada Press | Reno, Nevada 89557 USA
www.unpress.nevada.edu
All photographs courtesy of the author unless otherwise noted.
Cover design by TG Design

The poem "Elegy Elegy" © Brian Henry, reprinted with permission from *Static & Snow* (Black Ocean, 2015).

LIBRARY OF CONGRESS CATALOGING-IN-PUBLICATION DATA
Names: Romeo, Lisa, 1959– author.
Title: Starting with goodbye : a daughter's memoir of love after loss / by Lisa Romeo.
Description: Reno : University of Nevada Press, [2017]
Identifiers: LCCN 2017037705 (print) | LCCN 2017047714 (e-book) ISBN 978-1-943859-68-9
    (pbk. : alk. paper) | ISBN 978-1-943859-69-6 (e-book)
Subjects: LCSH: Grief—Anecdotes. | Romeo, Lisa, 1959–
Classification: LCC BF575.G7 R653 2017 (print) | LCC BF575.G7 (e-book) | DDC 155.9/37—dc23
LC record available at https://lccn.loc.gov/2017037705

The paper used in this book meets the requirements of American National Standard for Information Sciences—Permanence of Paper for Printed Library Materials, ANSI/NISO Z39.48-1992 (R2002).

FIRST PRINTING

Manufactured in the United States of America

For Frank, Sean, Paul
(my *menfolk*)

Contents

Illustrations follow page 80

Author's Note

WHAT HAPPENED MATTERS, and this is a story of what happened. But it is only *a* story of what happened *to me,* as best as I can remember, as best as I can tell it so that it makes sense. My excavation of memories was augmented by personal notes, family documents, photographs, and ephemera; but this book does not claim to convey *the* truth. Memory, as I understand it, is colored by the experience of the remembering itself. Others who may have been witness to some events will have different memories: something *else* happened *to them.* To protect privacy, some names, identifying details, and other information has been altered; a very few events have been compressed or merged for clarity.

On the way to this book, some of the material has appeared in short essays and narratives, under various titles, and in different combinations or structures, in: *Barnstorm; Change Seven; Fifty Is the New Fifty; Gravel; Halfway Down the Stairs; Healing Muse; Hippocampus; Litbreak; Lunch Ticket; Pithead Chapel; Purple Clover; Quay; Under the Gum Tree; Under the Sun;* and *Word Riot.*

STARTING WITH GOODBYE

ELEGY ELEGY

The dead keep coming back to us
whether we will their return or not:

in our sleep, when we slip to resist,
in books, and in song, when the voice

shuffles forward to call "I'm still alive /
I win the prize / I'm still alive,"

even though he's not, even though
he knew that his song some day would prove

false, a sometime untrue statement
that no one, not even a ghost,

can retract. Instead, those of us left
are left to notice, and miss, and hurt.

How thin is the human voice,
it cannot keep even the dead

distant, on the other side of any
thing we would call any thing.

— BRIAN HENRY

Prologue

THE LIMOUSINE DRIVER rings the bell at six in the dark morning. I'm thirteen and my parents and I and Laurie, my best friend and next-door neighbor, are off—somewhere, again. We watch as eight suitcases disappear into the trunk, and feeling sassy, I chirp out, "That's right, neighbors, the Chipolones are going on vacation, again." Laurie adds, "Eat your hearts out." My father shushes us, reminding me again that we don't advertise when the house is going to be empty, but we especially don't flaunt our good fortune. And good fortune it is. From the time I am five, we travel, short trips and far, long vacations in the next state or across oceans. We dress up to fly, fly first class, sleep in majestic hotels, eat well, come to love luxury. We travel for no reason, four or six or nine times per year, because we can.

1969

Customs inspection, JFK Airport. August 30.
"How long have you been away?" the man in a uniform asks.

My father says, "About three weeks." His friend Sam nods in agreement.

Simultaneously, I smile, point to my mother and Sam's wife, Suzie, and blurt, "Well, but *we've* been gone for almost two months."

Dad groans. The inspector begins opening all thirteen suitcases, running his hands around the edges, riffling clothing, shaking out shoes. He asks for the women's purses, and for mine too. I slide my little girl purse, the white one shaped like a lunchbox and decorated with passport stamps, onto the counter, and smile nicely at the man.

Inside my little girl purse are twelve gold Swiss watches.

I don't know what I've done, only that Dad groans again, and must now go over to a desk, fill out forms, and pull out his bulging money clip. When he's done, he smiles at me, but kind of funny.

August 13, Rome

We couldn't throw a coin in the Trevi Fountain, because it was being cleaned. Went to see some gardens. Came back to the hotel. Mommy went to the beauty shop, so I played cards with my father.

July 28, Vienna

Daddy took me to the park. Went on rides, played games, ate pretzels, and went swimming in a very cold pool. Also saw the famous Lipizzaner riding school!

July, 24 Munich

Went to the zoo with my father and fed the elephants, while Mommy, Suzie, and Cathy went shopping.

July 20, Amsterdam

Went to church and after Communion, saw Daddy and Sam standing in back of the church. Cathy and I had to stop giggling so Mom and Suzie wouldn't know. They weren't supposed to come to Europe until next month! Tried to watch the moon landing on TV in the hotel, but I was too tired. I'm so glad Daddy is here.

July 5, New York City

Got on ship with Mommy, Cathy, and Suzie. Waved goodbye to Daddy from deck.

1

Last Words

MY FAVORITE PART of any funeral is the eulogy. Perhaps it is strange to *have* a favorite part of a funeral. But, I do.

I like to imagine the speaker—a family member or close friend—pen in hand or fingers poised on keyboard, struggling for the right words, holding each one up, turning it round and round in the late evening light, asking if it fits. Asking if something as insignificant and mighty as words can honor, but not deify, the dead loved person, and perhaps even bring some levity or light to what is dark and serious.

The eulogies I am talking about, the kind I sit up straight and listen to most intently, are sometimes clumsy, rambling speeches, not too highly polished, that bring into focus the dearly departed in ways that do and don't always make him or her sound too good to have been true. Sometimes when I see who is approaching to speak, I'm glad it's so-and-so because I know I'll hear a good story, a real story, or I worry about what so-and-so might say. Either way, I want the storytelling to begin.

The terrible and wonderful thing about a eulogy is that it is not a forgiving genre: One is a composer conducting with no rehearsal and one arm injured. There's typically little time to mull, to think deeply; a eulogy is one of the early tasks in the business of grief, demanding we find the perfectly nuanced space between sentiment and sentimentality without much chance to revise, edit, delete.

You only get one chance.

I got two chances.

I delivered my father's first eulogy, which I thought of then as the only one, in the odd city where my parents had retired and lived for twenty-five years. The setting was a subdued service in a nonsectarian, nondescript funeral home seven blocks from his house in the American Southwest. I delivered the second one back in New Jersey—where Dad was born, worked, and lived for fifty-five years and where I was still living, where I live still—in a quietly elegant Roman Catholic church.

I got it mostly right, but wrong both times, unsure even now if I was talking mostly to myself, to the gathered mourners, or to my father.

I was forty-six and had spent more than forty years writing, privately because of inner need, and publicly as part of all my adult jobs. I approached the eulogy at first *as* a job. On the airplane from my home in Cedar Grove, New Jersey, to Las Vegas, I thought I was merely turning around fast copy about an untimely death. For that, I could draw on a few scraps of experience, all more than twenty years before, all connected to horses. Once, at a Santa Barbara horse show, about ten feet in front of me, an Olympic-level horse named Hai Karate had dropped dead mid-jump over a huge fence, during a Grand Prix. A couple who were horse show judges had perished in a fire. A trainer died in a horse van accident.

I'd written about these events in *The Chronicle of the Horse,* for which I'd been a columnist and contributing writer. The gig allowed me to stay on the horse show circuit myself, competing on two expensive horses, courtesy of my father's polyester money and my mother's eager prodding about living out a once-in-a-lifetime "flight of fancy."

But I was rusty at the job. I was no longer that young reporter, committed to checking facts, getting everything exactly right, making sure my own narrow view was balanced by the bigger picture. It showed.

Anyway, something else was going on.

With the first stroke of the pen, it occurred to me it was the first time that I'd written more than a line or two about my father.

Could that be right? I took a mental inventory. I'd published many personal essays, about motherhood, family life, and my former life as a competitive equestrian (a life my father had once financed), and yet I'd scarcely mentioned him? On a folded-down tray table, at 31,000 feet, above Indiana or Colorado, I was aware that what I was doing, I could never have done during his lifetime: write about a father I didn't know well. This man—who, it would turn out, in death, I would keep returning to—was the same man I had kept turning away from while he was alive. It felt, from the start, like atonement.

I did what I could.

There were moments when I could not bear to look down at the page. Many more when I could not look away.

I slipped the notebook back into my tote and tried to sleep. I dreamt of my past, less world-weary self.

That young woman knew precisely what she wanted and moved boldly in the direction of her dreams. That younger woman thought owning a half-dozen hunter-jumper show horses in eight years was not unusual. She interviewed Olympians with confidence, segued into a public relations career in Manhattan, found her old high school crush and married him. That younger woman's life was easy, safe, and once filled with travel, clothing, credit cards, and cash. She was cushioned by the small fortune her father had made as a scrappy entrepreneur, and she had taken almost all of it for granted. She and her father were not particularly close, and she often thought of him as an old-fashioned dolt, at least when she wasn't happily and habitually leaning on his advice, connections, and ability to take care of life's annoying disturbances.

That confident, carefree, and myopic twenty-something had everything and nothing in common with the forty-six-year-old woman scratching out a eulogy that October morning in 2006. That woman was the nervous mother of two sons, a strong but always fretting advocate for the one child with special needs, a workaholic, a budget-watching worrier in six-year-old shoes scrambling each month to stretch her husband's modest paycheck and her unpredictable freelance income. The woman on that airplane was searching for the right words, pondering how to balance admiration for a father everyone called "a prince among men" and the enigma she knew.

Since then, there have been a lot more funerals, and I have listened to many other eulogies: beloved elderly aunts who've passed in their nineties, the parents of friends, and the friends of my parents—people I remember gathering as couples in our crowded New Jersey living room when I was a child in the 1960s, who sluiced anisette or sambuca into their espressos and told bawdy jokes, the women in bouffant and flips, the men in suits and snazzy ties.

I'll answer the phone and hear the once-familiar voice of the daughter or son of one of those "couple friends," and I know what's coming: the illness or broken hip, the hospital–rehab–nursing home narrative, the information—wake, funeral mass, burial. The next day, I read the obituary at the funeral home's website, and try to guess who wrote it. I read other obituaries too, strangers' stories, drawn to the symmetry: born/died, here/gone. Perhaps I find that in an account of a life already lived (well, or not), I can learn something about how *to* live. So much seems clear in an account of a life that is complete, or at least it appears that way in the dull glow of a computer screen. All of the gray area is another matter, the places where real life existed, in the margins, between the lines.

When those calls come, after I say how sorry I am, and that I'll see them at the services, I hang up, and I think about that son or daughter alone at a kitchen table later that evening, a cup of coffee or tea steaming, a poised pen or curled fingers ready but not ready to strike, the words distant and slippery, or flowing and jumbled. We write what we can at those moments, knowing there is no time to dither, to linger.

Yet to linger is all we hunger for.

————

When I tried to write that first eulogy, I wasn't thinking about the common experience of trying to write something true about a dead parent. I had no idea I would write a second eulogy, and not even an inkling yet that so much more would transpire, that I'd get a second chance to know that unknowable father of mine. But if anyone's grief can have a theme, that was mine, or ours: a second chance.

Heavens knows, we needed one.

In life, I'd mostly ignored him. In life, my father had not evoked strong emotion in me; maybe I mistook what he did evoke in me as something else. I thought all the bickering meant we didn't like one another, but in fact it meant we were *too* alike. The truth was, he had always seen that, had always seen me, and that's what made me squirm. He knew I was like him in fundamental ways; I had always hoped he was wrong.

I was my mother's baby, her last born by eight years, and it was a fact widely acknowledged that we were one another's favorite. I'd often thought, a housewife in possession of a bottomless spending account, a cleaning service, a seamstress, and a standing weekly hairdresser date, was in need of a final female child to treat as a girlfriend. While a father in possession of a fortune was not in need of anyone.

In the days just after my father's death, I began to question my understanding of our family dynamic. I was struck by a yearning so powerful, to know him, to understand his story, to figure out *our* story.

And so, we started talking.

We "talked" more after he died than we ever had before. He (his spirit? my conjuring? my grief-mind? something else altogether?) dropped by for chats: when I was sitting at my dining room table, in the doctor's waiting room, at my kitchen counter dawdling over a cup of coffee after I'd dropped the kids off at school, in my living room late at night when I was reading, on the patio while I was carrying groceries from the car to the back door. We talked, and we were quiet with one another, too. I got used to this, and came to think of the quiet spaces in those visits as part of our "conversations" too.

In our second relationship, we seemed to interact without the strain of his always needing to be right and my always needing to prove he wasn't. But can a relationship really continue, and even get better, when one of the two is gone? At the time, the woman I was—frugal, pragmatic, a lapsed believer, writing a eulogy she thinks of as work— would not have thought so.

I was wrong.

Maybe the eulogy is never finished. Because the relationship is never finished.

2

The Hotel Hospital

WILD NEW THOUGHTS and fabulous ideas arrive in my mind while on airplanes. All the vacations, and the airplane thoughts, dot my memory, like pushpins in a paper map, marking not only where I've been, but how often I knew change was possible. As a child and teenager, home, for a long time, was being away. I learn much of what I will ever know somewhere other than home.

Unlike Frank, my tall husband, who flew for the first time in his twenties and still despises the physical confinement of an airplane seat, I have always been comfortable on planes. I rest, sleep, and dream in flight, and this has been true during the times when my own tall frame is slim and fit and 150 pounds, and when I am moderately overweight, and even during the times when I am obese and need to ask for the seatbelt extension. Airplanes lull me, and I dream. I bask in the mental freedom almost any flight promises. In airplane seats, I can be all of my selves, all of my ages, at once. I read, and I make plans. I remember.

On an August morning in 2006, three months before my father dies, I wait at the gate for a flight that was hastily arranged. The day before, while on vacation with my family, I'd gotten the call that my father was in the hospital after having a stroke. Waiting at the airport gate, I am both a responsible woman and still that little girl, both the dutiful adult daughter and the stretched mother, the seasoned traveler and the discomfited sleepy unplanned passenger. I'd packed haphazardly while Frank was on the phone with the airlines, our two sons sandy and silent, the cousin whose home we were staying at in Manasquan, on the Jersey Shore, making us sandwiches for the two-hour car ride back to our home one hundred miles north. There, I'd unpacked, repacked, and made lists. Lists are my way of warding off emotional disintegration— noting what must be done, and then doing what must be done. Staying busy, always.

On the list: photo shopping.

When I get to my parents' house—a sprawling ranch they had custom built in Las Vegas in 1981 when I had just graduated college and they were retiring relatively young at fifty-five, and relatively well-off—I plan to begin choosing photographs for the collage we will surely hang, when the time comes, at my father's wake. Yes, he is still alive. (Or, at least, as I will discover, someone who resembles my father, who sounds like him and has some of his memories, is moving and breathing in a body that bears a hospital bracelet inscribed with the name *Anthony Chipolone.*)

I think about the sifting of the photographs, this sad yet somehow life-affirming task that lies ahead, soon or later. This is simply me being me—efficient, practical, and product (not process)—oriented. I don't find the anticipatory list-making morbid, or a way of tempting fate. I don't believe in positive thinking; I believe in preparing for the worst and then being enormously relieved when something better happens. I simply reason, he may die soon, and so the photo finding will have to be done. Why not get a head start? Part of this too is my trying to wrest a smidgen of control, to stake some part of the process as mine.

I push my fingers hard against the skin of my eyelids. Inside, instead of black, I see glinty colorful zigs of neon, and so I press harder. The flight is delayed, and so I wait, as I suppose I will be doing every day, for weeks or months, for another call, a phone call that will summon me on this same trip, for that other reason.

When I hear the call for first-class passengers, I remember myself as a twitchy eight-year-old girl in an expensive matching knit dress and coat, holding my father's hand, excited to be on our way to California, Mexico, Miami, everywhere. Maybe it's because I am traveling without my own children that my thoughts reach back to trips from my own childhood, when the other end of an airplane trip meant sprawling suites and fun and room service, instead of duty and fatigue and worrying how Frank will manage and if my kids will brush their teeth while I'm gone.

Eventually the gate attendant calls the rest of us, and I enter the plane, bound for a coach seat, but first glancing momentarily to the left, half-expecting to see my father lounging in first class. I can picture him there, cracking his knuckles, younger, vital. I remind myself to keep moving, and that he is seventy-nine and has had a stroke. That he has mild Alzheimer's. My brother tells me Dad has been remembering all the long-ago vacations, the first-class seats, chauffeured limousines. I'm told he asked an ICU nurse, "Is there going to be a movie on this flight?"

For the first time in a lifetime of flights, I put on the soft sleeper blindfold I'd found jumbled in the linen closet drawer where I store the travel-size shampoo bottles. I clamp on headphones and select classical music, as a friend has suggested, and for the next couple of hours, I do nothing—nothing but sort through the pictures in my memory and think of lists to come, and speculate what it may be like when he is gone.

Several years later, I will learn that what I am doing on that airplane flight is processing "anticipatory grief," common among baby boomers unfamiliar with dealing with the death of a loved one.

But I don't know that yet. I think I'm just remembering.

I remember how my father used to walk around the block, admiring the neighbors' gardens, waving to the kickball teams, nearly every night after dinner, in tall nylon socks and shiny Italian shoes, and how I knew, with the smugness of youth, what a dull old-fashioned man he was. I even withered when someone at school said, "I saw your father out walking last night."

Behind my sleep mask, I see the younger father, on a 1970s Saturday night in our New Jersey living room, the man people said strongly resembled Errol Flynn, a heartthrob from the golden age of Hollywood. He stands against the white baby grand piano, his suit uncreased, smoking and humming "Spanish Eyes," and then he smiles and whistles at me, a gawky thirteen-year-old in Danskin stretch pants. He and my mother are heading out to the New Jersey Textile Industry Dinner or the Polyester Manufacturers Ball. Polyester made him a success, but he only wore the stuff on weekdays. His weekend evening style was sharper, his suits made by a Hungarian tailor in a gritty Paterson storefront. He was never without a pocket square. If the word *dandy* had not gone out of fashion, that is what you might have said about his look— pencil mustache, hair styled, a pinky ring, but tasteful. He ruined me, my father, for every boy in blue jeans and a torn T-shirt who would look my way.

When I was at my parents' house last, a year before the stroke, my father was still himself, lumbering about, complaining of arthritis pain. He also was someone else, someone seemingly no longer able to keep track of his files, checkbook, mail. Mom asked me to search for the legal documents she knew they had, somewhere. She had already searched the desk, file cabinets, and the freezer. A will, medical directives, power-of-attorney—where would my once smart and formerly organized but now befuddled father have put them?

What I found instead were his high school notebooks, stacked and neatly labeled, the one marked "Science 1942" filled with meticulous colored-pencil renderings of the human heart, the muscles in the leg, the frontal lobe of the brain. My father, ordered to quit school in the tenth grade to help his father operate a scrap metal business and support his seven siblings, had wanted to be a doctor; we all always knew this. As a very small child, I once thought he was, at least an almost-doctor. He dispensed medical advice to everyone—some sought, some unwanted. We teased him about it: "Oh, here comes another one of Doctor Tony's diagnoses." He laughed, then. Gazing upon those note-books, the hopeful sweep of his careful script where he labeled the aorta, the Dr. Tony jokes did not seem so funny.

His penchant for self-diagnosis got him in trouble sometimes. When blood appeared in his urine, he attributed it to a new vitamin supplement, and refused to ever try another one, even after the blood continued for weeks and was linked to a kidney infection and had nothing to do with the pills.

Briefly, I consider reading more of the beachy novel I had transferred from my vacation suitcase to my carry-on, but I am drawn to another image in my mind: me, just the night before, sitting on my king-sized bed with my twelve-year-old, Sean, who picks at the pilled lint on the spread, his chewed stubby fingers with spits of fingernails tracing the pattern. My boy is limp with exhaustion and worry for me and for his ailing PopPop, whom he resembles. He grabs my hand, and says, "Don't worry, Mom. I'll help you."

Someday I will probably want to remember my kind young son watching me through hopeful brown eyes (my eyes, everyone says) and too soon playing parent. But I want to forget too. For now, everything seems both blurred and too vivid, churning through my mind. The airplane speeds me closer to more scenes, ones I cannot yet imagine.

Months before I left on this trip, I was having a conversation with Laurie, who also still lives in our hometown. We're close still after forty-two years; despite now holding different political views and religions, we still click. We're married to men who, like us, were each other's best friends since early childhood; our families feel intertwined. But mostly we're still close because we want it that way. We choose it. Over coffee at my house, I tell her—I can't remember why—that when the time comes, my father wants to be cremated, and that I agree. I never want to visit him at a cemetery, I say; he would not really be there. Laurie tells me that she agrees, but at the quiet mausoleum where her father's body rests, she also finds his memory alive, and this makes her happy. Now that he is gone, almost every memory she recalls of her strict and stern father is a happy one. I find myself wondering, as the plane descends, if all memories of the once-loved are automatically transmuted to happy recollections upon their death. I realize I may soon find out, and I wonder, but only briefly, if all the tension between my father and me—that disjointed, argumentative, contrariness we've always both exhibited—will fade then.

At the Las Vegas airport, I step into a taxi and give the driver the name of the hospital, some twelve miles west. The driver's bushy eyebrows twitch upward, a question in the dark hollows of the man's eyes. "My father," I say. A few minutes later, the desert heat makes me woozy, and I steady myself by placing my head on my folded hands on the back of the front seat. The driver reaches his left hand across his body, and rests it on mine, so briefly I almost don't remember it. Then his eyes locate mine in the rearview mirror, and he blinks, slow and long and says, "I know."

In his hospital room I don't at first acknowledge the shriveled man in the bed, as my father—Tony, Big T, Tony Chip—the man who was once lean and limber, whose strong hand I held on trips to an office he had for a while at the Empire State Building, who spun me around in circles with iron forearms under my armpits, whose sturdy legs walked the Washington Monument Mall with me on his shoulders, covered the Miami Seaquariam with me on his hip. The man in the bed is someone else, someone too weak to stand now, because of the arthritis, the stroke, the osteoporosis, the curved back, the hip pain.

I'm strangely pleased to know that he cannot remember this list of maladies; they exist only in his recent memory, which he has intermittently, and mercifully, misplaced. I like knowing that each morning when he wakes, he doesn't remember he is in such terrible physical shape. But then I wonder if each morning there is fresh sadness when he is confounded anew by his weakened, terrible condition.

But he seems preoccupied with other, more pressing matters.

"I want to get up, damn it," he says, when he sees me. Not *hello.* Not *Oh, it's Lisa.* Not *How you been, kid?* the way he usually greets me. "I know my rights, damn it. They can't make me stay here," he growls.

"You have to stay for a while, Dad," I say. "It's a good place."

"It's a dump," he says. Then, more genially, "Give me the phone, I want to call the front desk. I want to switch hotels."

I am to learn that like so many Alzheimer's sufferers, my father is skipping through decades, alighting in different time periods. I imagine that he lingers wherever it suits him, wherever it is most appealing or perhaps most potent. I decide this is a good use of what memory he has left at his command, and I promise myself I will not attempt to drag him through the time tunnel of reality. Anyway, I am too tired to try.

When I call my mother across town, she asks, "Is he himself today?"

How to answer? "Yes," I say finally. "Exactly himself, if you subtract twenty years."

I imagine my mother might be comforted or pleased to hear this, to know that her spouse of fifty-nine years, whose physical suffering is so great his pain meds are dispensed on demand, is mentally reliving some past pleasures.

Later, when she comes to the hospital, I see how it is.

But first, Dad asks about long-dead relatives, talks about houses he has not lived in for forty years, refers to companies he closed down decades before, wonders what to order from room service. My mother cannot walk down the hallway to get him the ice water he wants because her chronically inflamed knee is acting up and this puzzles him and he wants to know, "When did that happen?" She does not respond verbally at first, just draws her mouth into a tight line and focuses out the window, at the floor, in her purse.

"Years ago, Tony. We're getting old," she says finally, and he appears confused.

While he naps, she tells me the towel rod in the guest bathroom at the house is broken, and she does not know whom to call to fix it. The pool man wants to replace the filter motor, but she isn't sure he's being completely honest. And what should she do about my father's Social Security checks, since he can't sign his name anymore?

I shrug. "I don't know," I say. "We'll figure it all out tomorrow."

I'm too tired to think about these things, but I'm not too tired to recognize my internal swell of annoyance at my brother, Gary, who lives a half mile from my parents' house. Why isn't he taking care of such chores and worries? I want to confront him but know I probably won't, at least not in person because I know he's good at verbal sparring and I stink at it, not able to draft, revise, and edit in my head. I'm sad that this sometime volatile brother, whom I once idolized, is someone I've grown distant from and angry with recently as we've squabbled in disjointed, heated telephone discussions about Dad's care and our parents' endless demands on their son. I know he *is* taking care of things, so many small and big things that neither my older sister, Cathy, nor I can do—because we live in Massachusetts and New Jersey and not Vegas—but I can't help thinking that he's not taking care of *everything*. I am nothing if not judgmental.

When my father awakens, Mom asks him about the same three things: the towel rod, the pool filter motor, the Social Security checks. To each, he answers with some variation of *When did that happen?*

Mom's exasperated. *Weeks ago. Last month. Remember?* She still remembers what she ate for breakfast this morning, alone. I see and hear only her frustration at his incapacity, when what I want to see and hear is her compassion. I know, though, that for her, compassion—deep and true and kind—almost always comes later, often much later. In retrospect. I've seen this before. In the moment, my mother more typically lashes out, annoyed, impatient at her poor fortune and at others' inability to take care of everything, to fix, and to do so immediately.

I guess too that this time it stems from fear. Her husband, who has always taken care of everything, whose slow mental slipping away the past year she's been able to frequently hide, has gone and let this terrible thing happen, and she already understands that she's truly on her own now for the first time in almost sixty years.

The next day, my father and I have the first of what I will come to call *The Cash Conversation*.

"I need to have some cash. For tips. When they bring the room service again. Or for the bellman, you know. I don't have any money," he says, appearing both flabbergasted at his own carelessness and annoyed at—the world.

I remember the polite young man who brought up a flower arrangement the day before and how flustered Dad looked, how many times he thanked him and this funny motion he seemed to be making with his right hand sliding at an angle along his protruding hipbone.

"You don't need any money at this place, Dad. Everything is paid for. It's all covered in advance," I say, because I have to say something.

"No, tips are never included," he says, exasperated I suppose because he knows that all our travels should have taught me this valuable travel truism decades ago.

"Yes, Dad," I try again. "But remember when we went on cruises? How it was all included? It's like that here."

He clucks his tongue, and a little spittle runs down the side of his drooping mouth. "A man's got to have some money in his pocket," he says, his voice so mournful, so stripped, as stripped as he is under his thin, wrinkled blue robe.

Lunch arrives, and my father waves at the dietary aide and says, "Thank you ma'am." When she leaves, to me, he says, "See what I mean, I have nothing to give her."

I replay the conversation for my mother and brother later that night over dinner at a neighborhood restaurant. Why did I imagine they would find this sad little story to be sweet? They both frown, shake their heads, and Gary says, "He says that ten times a day. He thinks he's in a hotel. Last week he picked up the phone and wanted to call the front desk to order a car and driver."

"Where do you suppose he wanted to go?" I ask, delighted at the possibilities. "Did you ask him?"

I am the writer in the family, the one who likes to ask those kinds of hypothetical questions, and I forget that the response from my family is often bewilderment, a slow shake of the head. Here, clearly, I am the only one charmed by my father's serendipitous speech. I nearly don't censor my next thought: that his mind has taken him to some more congenial place, a place he knows and knows how to leave, that he's made himself comfortable, emotionally, and that we should be happy for him. Isn't that better than telling him he's got it all wrong?

Gary asks if I'm insane also.

I begin to see that perhaps I am the only one who can afford this charmed perspective; I am the only one who has not grown weary, who has not watched her intelligent husband, her competent father, mentally diminish day by day—before the stroke and the hospital forced us all to confront it. I am the only one who has not reluctantly forfeited yet another scrap of hope each day. I am the lucky one who lives 2,700 miles away and who can and will, in a week or so, leave behind the nonsense conversations, the soiled bed sheets, his wild screams just before awakening, which I have heard about but have not yet heard.

While I feed my father breakfast the next morning, he stops chewing, and pieces of egg drop from his lips as he stares at me, his eyes scary wide.

"Oh, Lisa, my Lisa," he says.

He grabs my hand tight and quick, pulls it to his lips, spilling egg, and kisses my knuckles. When he opens his mouth again, a brace of questions tumble out, the last string of lucid sentences he will ever say to me. "When did you come? Is Frank here? And Sean and Paul too?"

"Dad! Dad!" I choke out through a bloated throat. "Oh, Daddy, hi, how are you?"

I kiss his cheek and begin to splay out answers, about what grades the boys are in back home, who's playing what sport, what's going on in Scouts. He listens, nods, seems to understand, or at least doesn't seem *not* to understand. Then he's quiet and so am I.

A little while later, he squeezes my hand and says, "I'm a sad sack."

"Why?" I ask. I put my right hand on his left shoulder, his bones under the now-papery skin hard against my palm as I search for any remaining nearby muscles to massage.

"I left your mother all alone." His eyes are milky but hold my gaze. "I can't take care of anything anymore."

"No, no, Dad. You took care of everything, just like you always do," I say, hoping he will not belabor this line of thinking, will not get specific about what "anything" means.

I think my words deliver their intended salve. He closes his eyelids, nods slightly again. But maybe he's just tired, and though his face is still, there's a twitch in his hand, and I think I notice his lip curl up a bit on the one side of his face he can still control. I think of a dozen other things I should say, or could say, but it all seems completely beside the point. "What will be, will be," he has so often said to me, when I'm worried over outcomes I cannot control.

He opens his eyes again. "No, it's true. I can't take care of anything anymore."

I remember how I used to calm my sons when they were babies, by lying down close to them and breathing slowly, deliberately, and how they'd eventually still and almost match my measured breaths. I'm too afraid of hurting my father to climb in the bed next to him, so I kneel bedside and bring my face close to my father's and I breathe deeply, slowly, an inch from his ear. Soon, his taut face and rigid limbs seem to melt into the bedclothes, his wild, urgent features go lax against the pillow. For a moment, I have an inflated self-congratulatory sense that I've accomplished something important that only I could have done, that my coming to Vegas was vital to his peace of mind, and not just so that I could one day say I had visited my father while he could still recognize his youngest daughter.

In the car during the ten-mile trips to and from the hospital, in moments of hubris when I am overly impressed with my verbal abilities, I believe I will still get to deliver some poignant lines at some particularly heightened moment, and my father will appreciate my well-chosen words for their elegance and obvious positive effect on him. I even picture my mother and brother listening to me, as I hoist words from the page in my head into the heavy hospital room. I imagine my father saying something intelligent, and me saying something equally intelligent back, the way it often was at the dinner table when I'd visit as an adult and the rest of the family might roll their eyes as if to say, *there they go again, those two, showing off their vocabulary.* That's how I picture it: He will say something profound, and then I will say something profound back, and they will be great words, all of them.

Instead, each day he rouses, seeming distressed, and repeats himself: "I'm a sad sack"

And I repeat myself too: "Nah, you did good, Dad."

Another day, when he speaks, he says, "We have to go to the funeral." His eyes are searching, sunken. He grabs my hand again, the grip weak though insistent.

"Whose funeral?" I ask, wary of the answer.

"Papa died," he says. "Did you tell my brothers and sisters?"

"Grandpa died a long time ago," I say, then admonish myself for the correction. I pat his hand, I swipe my wet cheek, I turn away, and when I look back at him, I have arranged a new smile on my face.

"There are things we have to do," Dad says, "arrangements to make. We have to do it properly." He is using the urgent, boss tone I have heard him use a hundred times with recalcitrant employees, with mediocre contractors, and with a younger, wise-ass me.

I try to intuit what it is about this event, this rite, which occurred twenty-six years before, that is niggling at him. I won't know for another few years that Alzheimer's sufferers still frequently feel emotional pain connected to long-ago events. Now, I wonder what it is about this memory that will not be quieted. Except for the obvious parallels between dying fathers, I come up empty. "Yes, Dad, you did all that. It was a proper funeral. You took care of everything," I say.

Then my father is quiet for a while. Later, he wants to know, "Did Papa die?"

My brother's reaction, when I relay this, is impatient, perhaps disinterested, though I may be misreading it; he's often impatient about even minor things. Perhaps he's just exhausted. He shakes his head and mutters something like, "Right up to the end, it's still all about his old man."

I want to say, no. No, don't you see—it's all about *you;* it's all about sons and fathers and love. But I don't say this because really, what do I know? What do I really know, from the inside, about my father and *his* father? About my father and his only son? What do I know—despite witnessing it once as a child, and now as an adult whose husband and father-in-law are equally yoked—about the dynamics of patriarchal family business that spills over into family, about being father and son *and* boss and employee, and decades-old guilt and the shackled inheritance of paternal duty?

Anyway, maybe it is all just babbling.

3

Hard Days and Hands

THE DAYS DRIFT ON, and one afternoon I am passing the time waiting for a visit from one of the young physical therapists, and struggling again, with conversation. Dad has plenty to say, but in reply I find myself tight-lipped. To his complaints about the food, service, quality of the linens, view, television volume, room temperature, and how long it takes anyone in "this damned hotel," I nod and murmur, "I know," and pat his knee.

Sometimes, he seems to return to himself and asks sensible questions, like whether the landscaper has trimmed the oleander, or if the temperature is still over one hundred. While I ought to be pleased to respond to these "real" concerns with appropriately congenial retorts and pleasantries, I begin to understand those moments are nothing more than a momentary brush with reality, soon forgotten. I speculate too that he could just be repeating back what comes up in the periphery of his hearing as Gary and Mom and I talk in the hospital room while we think he is sleeping.

Still, I latch on to any seemingly cogent, present-day question, and I perk up but also try not to seem surprised. I want it to seem as if our conversation is normal, just like it might have been a week, a month, a lifetime ago. But I bungle this, and my barrage of answers have an opposite effect, scaring him or pushing back on him in an almost visceral sense. Instead of being reassuring, I am probably disconcerting. He seems to recede into whatever protective, shielding shell his dementia has provided. Quickly, I learn not to overreact to the short returns to reality, to be quiet and still in my responses, and to not expect any normal to last more than a few minutes.

One day, Mom is worn out. She isn't whistling while getting breakfast ready, hasn't flung open the shades and curtains with her usual cheery morning buoyancy I've seen her muster even on difficult days.

I convince her to stay behind and rest at home, rather than making the trip to the hospital later. Gary is working an extra-long shift in his casino gaming surveillance position in order to have a day off soon. It's a Saturday, so no medical tests are scheduled, which leaves just me to occupy Dad's time. Outside, it measures a dried-out 110 degrees, while inside his room the air conditioning pours out of vents in frigid waves for which I am both grateful and resentful. For some reason, the chill reminds me of the need to keep dead bodies refrigerated. My father shivers in his Johnny gown, and I keep rearranging the four white cotton hospital blankets around his twitching goose-pimpled legs.

It's a day of what I come to call "seesawing"—he's dipping in and out of several different time periods filed in the catalogue of his past. I am trying to figure out how to answer the question, "Did the shop burn down?" This refers to a devastating 1968 fire ignited (accidentally or on purpose was never determined) during a robbery, a fire that reduced a newly built part of his polyester factory to rubble. It likely involved a bitter former employee, and nearly destroyed my father's typical positive outlook—especially when he learned, a few hours later, that his son had gone missing from his Hudson Valley, New York, military academy high school the same night. (We'd learn later that Gary and his buddies glimpsed flames from their bus windows as they headed to Florida, but of course didn't know *which* flames.)

"Did the shop burn?" he asks again.

I begin, "Well yes, but..." and waver, trying to formulate a response that acknowledges the accuracy of his memory but one that I hope will not foment further distress. But by the time I think of what to say, Dad has already moved on.

"Is your mother keeping up with the shots for her knee?" This reaches back only a couple of months prior, when he'd accompanied her for a cortisone injection.

Whipsawed like this, between eras, I'm working furiously though silently, to avoid making costly verbal errors that could pitch him into one of his lengthy sad spells, during which he might weep and shiver. I am mentally exhausted by 10:30 in the morning.

To fill time, I go in search of a male aide to help me get Dad from his bed into the armchair for a change. My father, never a bulky man, has shrunk in height and depth; on his five-foot, ten-inch frame small sacks of flesh hang where muscles have disintegrated. He is not heavy, but the arthritis and atrophied limbs make him so stiff, he needs to be carried and moved as an unbending unit. Once he is settled in the chair atop a thrice-folded blanket—otherwise, even the padded chair would be too hard for his bony buttocks—and with his catheter tube covered, IV pole properly positioned, and two blankets tucked in around his torso and chest, I drag over a chair and take one of his hands into both of mine.

My father always treated his own hands with care. His nails were never dirty, even when he was still occasionally working on the factory floor, supervising crews baling scrap newspaper and rags, cutting and sorting fabric, separating scrap metals. I have later memories of him walking from the musty warehouse back toward his modest but neat office, a metal nail file flashing. I have another sudden image of his hands from my childhood, professionally manicured, at a time when only very rich or fussy men did so. How elegant his hands were, then. Like Tony Bennett's, mid-song, gesturing ever so subtly, filled with emotion, offering protection.

He always washed his hands long and thoroughly, soaping repeatedly and way up beyond the wrists, and when I started watching television medical dramas, I noticed that was how doctors wash up before surgery. How long, I now wonder, did his childhood dreams, unfulfilled and maybe mocked, persist?

I study his hand, noticing how withered it is, eight decades of toil and task. His nails, once always neatly clipped and squared, are ragged and dirt-flecked, uneven, with rough angles, longer than I've ever seen them. I make a mental note to bring in manicure tools the next day (though the next day I will forget, as I do the day after).

Dad always had rather big hands for his average build—expressive and kind of flat, chalky and wide and not particularly solid to the eye. Even when he was a younger man, the skin on his hands felt loose and fleshy, but sheathed over iron. I remember my hand in his at Palisades Amusement Park and the Munich Zoo.

I remember those hands flung across me on the bench front seat of our early sixties Cadillacs and Buicks, before seat belts were standard.

I remember how his two hands covered my entire back when he'd push me on the backyard swing, and I'd protest "not so hard." I remember how goofy I regarded him when he'd conducted a piece of piped-in music mid-air over the restaurant table in some swanky spot in Switzerland where I'd petitioned to sit in the chair opposite the window with the best view of Lake Lucerne and where he happily sat with his back to the glass. I remember him pointing his finger, his nails tatting the pane, making sure I did not miss the ferry, the steamboat, the sailboat, the yacht.

In the hospital, I try to do what I can with a nearly worn-out emery board from my purse. If he notices his hands today, I am momentarily concerned that their current state will make him unhappy, then I chastise myself for thinking he would be vain enough to be worried over the state of his manicure, when he has more important things to worry about.

Studying those hands, limp in his lap, I remember some peculiar things I used to notice he did with those hands. He had a physical habit of placing his left hand flat against his stomach, and then tucking his fingers into the waistband of his pants or bathing trunks, or his baggy Bermuda shorts, just the thumb looped over the outside of the garment. He would do this while sitting, standing, even lying down. I used to think it was because he had scars in the area, from numerous gastrointestinal surgeries. But my mother says he always had that habit, even as a teenager, and even I recall seeing old photographs of him as a snappy young strapper, wearing perfectly pressed trousers, suspenders, gleaming white shirt, a hat, a cigarette in his right hand, and there is his left hand—against his stomach, inserted at the waistband.

My son Sean does the same thing. Because he's seen his PopPop do it and picked up the habit? Ask him and he says it just feels good. Did my father get it from his father? Or was it just what a lanky gentleman might do with an overly big hand when it was not holding a cigarette or a neatly folded overcoat?

Months from now, after he is gone, I will keep thinking about my father's hands, how they were always moving whenever he was whistling, which he did frequently, and loudly, and melodically; how he waved hello and goodbye in slow motion, his fingers cascading from pinky to thumb, as if trailing across piano keys.

Months later, I will remember how much he liked Sinatra, and how he always said Sinatra's greatest performing strength wasn't his voice as much as his mastery at hand gestures, how he'd bring a song alive through his hands. Perhaps Sinatra's hands inspired an entire generation of young men coming of age in the early forties. One day, after he's gone, I will spend all of an icy winter day watching Sinatra videos on YouTube, and not know why.

Later, months later, while driving to Maine for a graduate school seminar, I will listen to journalist Tim Russert reading from his book *The Wisdom of Fathers,* a compilation of letters from average Americans sharing memories of their fathers. An entire section is devoted to fathers' hands, which will not surprise me.

Later, I will go looking for those hands among the hands that may carry some of the same metatarsal-memory genes. My own fingers are thick like his, but not expressive—too thick, I always lament, for a woman's hand, and my fingertips are rounded and not square like his. For a tall woman, who is usually also fat, my hands are average size; the weight doesn't tend to accumulate there.

I don't get much of a chance to study my brother's hands, though during the glancing few minutes when he holds mine at my father's memorial service, I will notice a stubby roundness and a ropy physical strength unlike anything I ever felt in my father's hands. My father's hands were strong but in a more gentle way. Cathy has piano hands, either perfectly matched to her musical accomplishment on that instrument, or maybe they developed that way to accommodate her passion, begun in childhood.

Sean has long, slender fingers set on a long slender hand, none of the flat fleshiness of my father, but who knows what my father's hands were like as a teenager. This is interesting, because in other ways, this son's body resembles my father's—longish legs and bony feet, an elongated torso. Paul's eight-year-old hands are still little boy hands, but I notice his fingertip pads are wide and his knuckles are pronounced.

In the hospital, I ask my father if he wants me to rub on some hand cream. He shrugs. I do it anyway, but I'm thinking, isn't forty-six too young to be old enough for this? I want to be a little girl again, holding his hand, not noticing if it feels doughy or not, only that it's big enough to offer security. I rub and smooth and massage. He seems to like it, tries once or twice to curl his hand around mine, though arthritis won't let it close.

After the hand cream, he replays the *I'm Leaving This Place Conversation*, which segues into the *This Lousy Hotel Conversation*. I only reply back to a few of his remarks, but the pace and rhythm makes it feel like we're having a real conversation.

"They can't keep me here against my will."

"They're not, Dad. You're safe."

"But I know the law. If I want to leave, I can, you know."

"Of course, Dad, but you know, you're really not strong enough right now."

"Get them to call me a taxi." He points to the hallway. "Where's my suitcase, I want to go."

"Maybe tomorrow, Dad, not today."

"Get your mother, she'll know what to do."

I can't help but react, physically, to this one. I sit up and laugh out loud. First, because it reminds me of the line from *Gone with the Wind* when Scarlett's crazed just-widowed father advises everyone to ask his wife what to do. But more because my father always personally handled everything related to travel, finances, and dealing with authorities, because, he often implied, *women won't know what to do.*

"Well, I know what to do too, Dad."

"Take me home. I want to go home."

"I know, Dad. I know. But for now, you need to be here."

"But *why* can't I go home?"

I want to know this answer too. I want to know why my mother has already said he won't be going home. I want to know why she can't make it possible. Why he can't come home to convalesce, or die, in the five-thousand-square-foot house with four huge bedrooms? Why can't she hire round-the-clock caregivers, which they can well afford? Why, when he is released in a week or so, does he have to go to a nursing home? I leave it.

"How is the horse?" he asks.

I haven't owned a horse for about ten years, but I like that question because it means he knows it's me he is talking to, his younger daughter who begged him for a horse every week, probably beginning around age six, the child he took to the pony rides every Sunday morning, and every November to the National Horse Show, where he splurged on a dozen pricey raffle entries for a free horse.

When I was fourteen, I found a little stable only a mile from home with an empty stall and what I'd soon learn was a reasonable monthly board rate—though at the time, Dad mock-protested that it would break the bank. He groused that one thing would lead to another—expensive tack and show boots, horse show entry fees, more—and he was right of course. But he bought me that first horse (and second, and third...), even allowing me to quit piano lessons (I was tone deaf) so I could spend more time at the stable (where my heart sang).

Before I could drive myself, he drove me to horse shows at 5:30 on Sunday mornings, and I was embarrassed because he stayed in the car and dozed off during the preparations, even though later he got up, got a cup of coffee, and watched me ride. Then, he'd insist I was "robbed" when I didn't get a better ribbon, before heading back to the car to read the paper. How I longed for him to walk around, watch me with my horse, chat with the trainer, run his hand over a muscled flank, a quivering nose, like the other stable dads. Why, I used to agonize, did he always have to be so separate?

The year I turned twenty-one and my horse qualified for the National Horse Show in Madison Square Garden, my father paid for me to stay in a Manhattan hotel for a week (though we lived just twelve miles across the river) and bought excellent first-mezzanine tickets to all my horse's classes. I was miffed, though, that he didn't come down to the cramped stabling area and wasn't more impressed with the celebrities in the audience.

A few years later, when he and my mother drove two hundred miles from Las Vegas to Los Angeles, to watch me in a horse show there, and I got a third-place ribbon, he told my trainer, Victor Hugo-Vidal, a titan of the equestrian world, "The damned judges don't know what the hell they're doing."

He was never the quintessential horse show parent, but he bought me more and more horses and tack and custom-made riding boots, and for the twenty years that I had horses, he never failed, in a weekly phone call to ask, "How is the horse?"

In that hospital room, I don't want to tell him that all the horses he bought me are gone, and I especially don't want to remind him that Cool Shoes—my last and best horse, the horse who'd won a blue ribbon at the Garden, the ribbon that is still hanging in the Las Vegas house—had died at age twenty-seven, out of my sight, retired on a small South Jersey farm I never visited because at the time I was numb with post-partum depression.

While I'm thinking how to respond, the subject changes.

"Where is my ticket? Get me my passport. Let me call the concierge."

"Here comes lunch, Dad. Let's do all that later."

"You call this lunch? It's slop. The room service here stinks."

I nod agreement.

"When is that damned bellboy coming back?"

I think he means the aide who just brought the lunch tray. I hope he doesn't take out the lousy food on him.

"They make me wait, for what?"

After a short while of this, he settles. Then suddenly, he tosses my hands off of his, scowls. I get ready for a verbal assault, meant not really for me, but for the world at large, all the captors and commanders who have co-opted his sense of control these last months.

What I'm not prepared for is the look on his face.

My father, in typical 1960s fashion, rarely got involved in the day-to-day discipline of his children. My mother enforced rules with alternating, frightening bouts of screaming and gentle persuasion, slaps, and innuendo. When something serious occurred, however, requiring my father to intervene, it was his terrifying countenance, more than any thundering threats or despotic pronouncements, that made the strongest, most shame-inducing impression. He'd set his mouth in a scary pink line, let his cigarette burn unsmoked in his hand, and just before he spoke, his brown eyes would seem to turn black, then widen to a size that seemed impossibly big.

Not one of his three children could remain unrattled when faced with that stony, silent, maniacal look, perhaps because it was his only weapon. He never hit, but his stare could wound.

That morning in the hospital, when he tosses my hand out from around his own, adulthood sloughs away and I cower mentally, child-like, and brace as his eyes get *that look,* which I have not seen for decades. Owing I suppose to his gauntness and his pasty pallor, this time the darkness of his eyeballs seems more ominous, and the dimensions to which he can open his eyes make them seem to occupy more square inches on his face than physically possible.

He says something, spits it out in loud, painful gulps as he springs wide his eyes, but I will never be able to remember what. The sight of the enlarged, engorged eyes unnerves me enough that my usual ability to file dialogue, fails. There's something about him *still being a man, god damn it, and when the hell are the doctors going to do something about the pain, and those damned nurses need to stop treating me like a child, and I still know what the hell is going on, god damn it.*

I say nothing in return.

I think: *my father is still in there, somewhere, damn it.*

This disturbs me greatly, to think that, somewhere in his addled mind he really *does* know and understand the terrible state he is in. And it also warms me to think that somewhere is a spark still, of the take-charge, demanding, confident man I have known for forty-six years.

I spend an hour that night in my parents' spotless garage, combing through hundreds of black-and-white photographs my mother keeps stored in a heavy mahogany bureau that once belonged to her father-in-law. The photos are not in any kind of order, but each wide, deep drawer is full and so very heavy. Eight-by-tens in cardboard frames from the Copacabana, the Coconut Grove, and the Sands Hotel overlap with dozens of three-inch square snapshots with curly edges, shot at modest little Lake Hiawatha in New Jersey, at the Jersey Shore, and at Frank Daly's Meadowbrook—the vaunted venue from the 1930s through the '60s that had been Cedar Grove's most famous landmark, where Big Bands and bigger stars performed.

When I consider the people in the squares, those glossy smiling ghosts, it occurs to me that my father needs more of his past, not less. I decide to bring a photograph to the hospital the next day, and I make an effort to secret one in my purse, even though my mother would not notice, because she cannot bear to come into the garage and watch me gathering pictures of her once-dapper and now-disappearing husband.

"Dad, I brought you something," I say the next morning, after he is wheeled back from the MRI room. His severely curved back prevented the technicians from running another scan, and the standing MRI machine scared him, and he tried to lunge back to his wheelchair.

When he first grabs the photograph, he seems confused and is about to hand it back, then slowly his eyes dance, and a smile slices his gray folded skin. He suddenly seems to recognize in the frame that one of the young men is himself, the swell who made my mother swoon, the dapper gent, in pinstriped trousers, pale shirt with the cuffs carefully folded back. Here is the confident, cock-sure, bootstrap young businessman, who could dance a mean cha-cha, win at cards and bocce, front the Moose Lodge fundraiser.

My father's eyes begin to move across the scene, seven men, his two brothers and five brothers-in-law, the *fraternita*. They are assembled on a Sunday afternoon in his parents' Clifton, New Jersey, backyard, bocce balls at hand, a small table in the background holding bottles of homemade wine, beer cans, an ashtray.

Except for one brother, my father hasn't seen any of these men—some, sons of Italian immigrants: some, sons of Italy—in many years. Perhaps he thinks of them all as gone. But for the moment, or maybe all the time in his mind, the fraternita is young again, fierce perhaps. I remark that the old blue 1966 Buick Electra my grandfather once drove, the one passed along to me when I turned seventeen, is visible in the left corner; but my father shushes me, his finger to his lips. For the next couple of minutes, he keeps looking at the photo, and I see his eyes pause, move, pause, as the yellowed nail of his right forefinger taps each of the men's faces.

Standing next to my father is the tallest, the butcher with luxuriant prematurely white hair, who always appeared a little too well dressed and clean to have spent six hours cutting beef. Someone must have told me because one day I simply knew that behind the butcher shop, there was a bookie operation in full swing. But it was not my father who told me. No, my father had said, only once, "It's not our business."

Another of my uncles is there, mild, deferential, happy to go along. When did I learn he had "vices" and was miserably unhappy in his marriage? When a cousin criticized him once at a barbecue, my father said, "Don't throw stones."

Kneeling is the conciliator, the guy who often talked down the fractious frat boys. One story goes that he treated his wife badly until the fraternita showed him what might happen if he did that again. I saw him kissing his wife's hand once, and in the car home later I made some mean-spirited remark, and my father said quietly, "That's not for us to judge."

One brother-in-law, the one who hugged fiercely, wearing the wide smile I remember, is there visiting from Italy, where my father shipped hundreds of boxes of American products, clothing, and packaged food. Some questioned if the stuff inside was sold for profit, but Dad only ever said, "It's hard for them over there."

Then there's the thinker who quoted Plato. My cousin told me once that at home this father screamed verbal abuse and used his belt in response to a B on his kids' report cards. My mother often criticized him, but my father said only, "He expects a lot."

Making a rare appearance at a family gathering is the black sheep con artist, the laggard, who showed up broke with outstretched hands and a new wife every few years. When he died, his widow sent my father the poems he had written. *Softening us up because she wants money,* everyone said, and she did. But my father simply put them in his scrapbook and pulled out his checkbook.

My father's finger never once pauses on his own face, this Uncle Tony, the fixer, whose textile factory and trucking company and recycling plant always had jobs for everyone, whose checks and counsel and well-placed phone calls held up drifting nephews and widowed relations.

When things went wrong, everyone went to Tony for a pep talk, a timely telephone call to a well-placed colleague, a loan, the use of a truck—and often, cash. Sometimes there were strings attached, if my father felt that the person needed a way to earn back self-respect or retain her or his dignity by fulfilling a promise in return. Only a few of us know that this is the same Tony Chip who lost a sizable chunk at a craps table one long night soon after retiring to Las Vegas in 1981, an event I only learn about when considering the subject of nursing home costs versus paying for private at-home round-the-clock care. Not knowing what to say, I said what I imagined my father might have said: "That's all in the past."

My father's eyes linger longest on Silvio, a sometimes shady version of my father, only just a little too clever. I can't find the memory, but I know there must have been a time when I first learned that Silvio took the rap for some minor infraction committed by the family business. That the fraternita decided Silvio had the least to lose, and after that, there were houses where Uncle Silvio was not welcome, but my father always said, "He's my brother. Be quiet."

My father's finger traces his older brother's face. "My brother, is he okay?" he asks.

He is okay, living back in New Jersey, occasionally stopping in at my house unannounced for a cup of coffee. I don't tell my father that Silvio will not visit him in Vegas because he says he dislikes airplanes and because he says he cannot travel easily right now, bum knee and all, but that he manages just fine to drive three hours down to Atlantic City to gamble, bum knee and all.

"Because when Papa died, I promised to take care of my brother," my father says.

I know he only means *this* brother. I know my father was drafted to this "caretaking" job because he was the most financially successful as well as the most sensible. But I think about how he was also the youngest boy, and I am angry (twenty-six years too late) that he was saddled yet again with so much familial responsibility.

Then we have *The Papa's Dead Conversation* again, and then my father and I have *The Cash Conversation* again, and this time I show him that I am slipping a pile of single dollar bills into the top drawer of the bedside stand.

"See, Dad? Now you have money for tips."

I tell myself, so what if it is gone by morning, given to or palmed by who knows who. What is the going rate these days anyway for psychic pain relief?

"That's it, kid," he says. He winks. He circles his thumb and fore-finger in the universal OK sign, then brings his circled fingers to his cheek and twists—the little Italian oomph gesture that means *you're sweet,* or *that's it, that's the way.*

My mother and brother arrive with her long, drained face and his tired bearing, and they transform, ready to do their daily cheerleading.

Mom notices the uneaten lunch. "We need you to get better, Tony," she says. "You have to get strong so you can come home."

Gary chimes in, "You've got to eat, Dad. Mom needs you to get well."

I want to scream. Yes, it would be best if he ate, but I don't think that anything any longer is going to occur because someone other than Dad wants it to. I want to say that it isn't about what *they* want or need, or what's desirable to anyone other than the man in the bed. But by now I know I'm just the visitor here, so I say nothing. Maybe, I understand nothing.

When my father is on the fifth floor getting an X-ray, I tell them about the tip money. I don't say it was the best twelve dollars I ever spent, but that's how it feels. I tell it like it's a fun story, something cute and oh so clever. "You should have seen his face," I say, "he was so relieved."

Gary runs his hand through his thick gray hair, and my mother frowns and gazes out the window. I want them to see the humor in it, and I don't understand until much later that their daily diet of Dad's nonsense nonconversations and their own frustrations had already squashed any inherent humor. At the moment, their reaction makes me want to put my fist through the room's clean, wide window all the way to the Black Mountains in the distance. Instead, I excuse myself and collapse into the blue couch in the visitors' lounge that has become my favorite spot, and I dial home to hear the voices I love on the other end. Sean wants to talk to his PopPop, and Paul asks if his PopPop is getting better, and Frank, again, reassures me that I can stay as long as I need, as long as I want.

In the elevator later, Gary hands me my twelve folded single dollar bills. "Someone will steal it," he says. "Anyway, he'll never know the difference." That's true, I think. Or, maybe not. Either way, I want to scream and explain that this was not the point, something that might be evident even to my eight-year-old, maybe even to a seventy-nine-year-old with Alzheimer's.

We ride down in stilted silence, frustration burning in my ear. I try to remember how much I once adored my brother: when I was seven, on visits to him at military school, when he seemed regal in uniform, when I'd watch him rehearse with his basement band, singing just like Gary Puckett of the Union Gap, when even though he was a newlywed, he still took his thirteen-year-old sister to dozens of New York Rangers hockey games. We'd had good times together even as adults; he and his wife had traveled with Frank and me to watch the Giants win Super Bowl XXI at the Rose Bowl.

But I forget all that; in the moment, I just want to be right. I want to avoid confrontation, even over something trivial. Anyway, my plan is now clear: it is almost time for me to go home. I see now, with no surprise, my bitterness steadily receding, that mother and son, often on opposite sides of my father's recent frequent tirades have, wordlessly and with the self-preservation necessary to survive what is coming, lashed their drifting lifeboats together, and closed ranks. Where I used to be aligned, almost always, with my mother against my father, or with my mother against both my father and my brother, now it feels like it's me and my loopy father against—everyone.

I'm the one who doesn't understand. I am the outsider who can and will escape. I want to.

I say goodbye to my father two days later, in the no-fuss way I like to think he would employ himself. There are no histrionics, no carefully thought-out last words, though I know that it is likely a final goodbye.

I simply say, "Bye Dad, I love you. See you soon."

He kisses me, or no maybe he just allows me to kiss him, and puts one arm up around my shoulder.

The next morning, I have more time than I anticipate before needing to leave for the airport, enough time for a quick run to the hospital. I choose not to go.

On the flight back to Newark, I pray for endings—an end to my father's suffering of course, and also an end to my mother and brother's tenuous vigil and to their overpowering wish to have my father restored to full health. I wish for them an end to the strain of want versus need, hope versus bitter acceptance. I yearn too for an end to my own diffident self-righteousness. I like the boundaries endings provide, giving shape to remembering, to everything.

On the plane, I leap ahead, to the imagined day when I will know how all of this ends, to a time when it may be possible to make something of it, something meaningful. Something that will bring together for me the atrophied hospital patient worried about events thirty years past, and the dandy gentleman pillar from my childhood. Both are already outlining their shapes in my memory, separate and together, past and present. The faded photographs at his funeral will stake out their shapes, too. Shape-shifters.

I make a mental note: tip the pallbearers.

4

What We Talk About When We Talk About Dad

I LEFT NEW JERSEY and my parents for college in Syracuse in 1977 and after that lived in California, then very briefly with them again in Vegas, then in Florida, and Syracuse again. I finally circled around to our native New Jersey and made my way back to Frank, who'd once broken my teenage heart. Once married, we put down roots three blocks from where I was raised. We made annual and sometimes holiday visits to Vegas, first as a couple, then with our sons, and sometimes the boys and I only—so that my parents' large home with swimming pool and a working slot machine became a default destination. But by the time my father is ill, the trips have dwindled: 9/11 travel fears on my part, kids' school and burgeoning activities schedule, our tenuous family budget. Plus, Frank and I want to experience family vacations in places that don't involve walking kids around the periphery of casinos and averting young boys' eyes from billboards.

Living across the country has meant that for twenty-nine years, much of my relationship with my parents has been conducted over the telephone. Most of those phone calls were placed by me to their house—once a week during college, about every ten days when I was a younger adult, and then as they grew older, I'd call more often. Invariably though, depending on the decade, if Dad answered, he asked, roughly in order: *How are you feeling? How is work? How is Frank? How are the boys? How is the car? How is the horse?* Once I'd answered— clipped, one-word responses ("Fine. Good. Okay.")—he'd say, "I'll get your mother." Though I always knew he wasn't keen on lengthy telephone calls with anyone, it was never precisely clear to me if he didn't want to talk to *me* or he sensed, as I feared, and which was sadly correct, that I didn't want to talk to *him*.

But sometimes we did talk for a few minutes about something

I knew might interest him, or vice versa. A public relations client who was annoying me, or one that I was trying to sign. What the new governor of Nevada had done. An upcoming TV documentary I think he'd like: social justice, history, anthropology. Perfunctory maybe, but the stuff I wouldn't mention to my mother as we traded food and shopping notes, her grandsons' antics, family gossip, and complaints about our respective husbands.

One of the last fluid phone conversations of more than a few moments that I remember having with Dad, less than a week before his stroke, was nothing special. I only remember it because I was packing for the Jersey Shore, carrying around the phone switched to speaker mode, and miming "Shhh" to the boys. I think he was warning me to watch for riptides at the beach, to wear sunblock. In response to my nonchalant "How is the arthritis?" I vaguely recall him muttering something like "my hip is killing me, but what's the use of talking about it." I don't recall how I responded, but I'm guessing it was some version of "Well, be sure to ask the doctor about that next time."

The telephone held our family, flung across the continent, together.

My phone call life with Cathy began when I was five and she left for college in Massachusetts, a move my child mind took as betrayal: since I was born when Cathy was twelve, I'd clung to her, and she'd happily acted as a second mother to me. We kept talking when she began teaching and living first in Boston and then in more rural central Massachusetts, chatting easily together over the years—about babies, books, her difficult first husband, her high school students, and when she'd next visit New Jersey—and less easily when she'd urge me to build a better prayer life, or explain that some recent misfortune of mine, like falling and breaking two teeth and cutting up my face, was part of some divine plan.

The calls between my brother and me were once warm and full of easy light banter, especially after I married an equally devoted New York Giants fan, because then for a good part of every phone call I'd hand the phone over to Frank. But those calls grew strained when by necessity they morphed into reports on Dad's health and how our parents were driving him to the brink with their constant demands (*fix the*

VCR, *reprogram the sprinklers, why am I getting this bill?*). Stony silences develop when I can't understand whether my brother is resigned about Dad (*He's just senile.*) or angry with the man (*He needs to try harder!*).

By 2006, I begin keeping my cell phone fully charged, and within reach. I tell my siblings it's the best way to get to me, quickly. Gary grumbles, but Cathy agrees, though neither enter my number—or any number, it seems—into their cell phone contacts but instead carry around little slips of paper with phone numbers scrawled in ink. While Cathy is twelve years older than me, she often seems the one more open to technology, ready to adopt any communication system that will work for us. Maybe that's because she teaches high school students, while Gary takes some pride in being a bit of a luddite. While she's always been motherly toward me, my sister also always recognizes my agency in life; with her I feel seen. It always feels to me that my brother prefers I remain the baby of the family, though perhaps some of that is about casting himself in the mold of our father, a family patriarch.

Our age spread and birth order shows up, here and again, and soon, everywhere. Not only were we raised in different time periods, each sibling grew up—as the psychology books explain—"in a different family." Cathy was born in 1947, into a cautious post–World War II milieu, to twenty-one-year-old parents whose financial future was uncertain. Gary entered a more secure economic environment in the early fifties, his father's business on the rise. But by the time I came along, eight years later, almost everything was different. By then, my father was on the way to wealthy. By the time I'd turned six, my siblings had each left home, for college and military school. In many ways, I was an only, spoiled child. It made a difference.

For weeks after I get home from Las Vegas in late August, I attend to reentering the work of the graduate writing program I had begun in early July. It's what's called "low-residency"—ten days on campus every six months and, in between, intense one-on-one work with a faculty member. I convince the program director to allow me to ditch the cold, remote male professor to whom I am assigned and who, after learning of my father's situation, assigned me to read a raft of books about dead, dying, absent, or distant fathers. I read the books; I hated every word, and don't know that less than six months later, and for years to come, it is those books that will buoy me and sustain me, those books I will return to again and again.

But for now, I want out; I want an adviser who can assess my life at the moment and say: *I have been there, I have done that.* I want the one writing instructor I know who has written through sadness and uncertainty, through mothering demands and midlife, as her own unknowable father withered a continent away. I demand and get that mentor, and I dive back into my work.

Meanwhile, I tour a nursing home near my house, because for one fleeting week, we all naively flirt with the absurd idea that my father can travel back to New Jersey, followed by Mom, a move she's wanted for some time. There, I ask the chirpy administrator what the old folks do all day, after they eat and get their bed-bath, and take their meds. "They talk among themselves," she says. "They have their memories you know."

This strikes me as cruel rather than kind, the assumption that if they can but access good memories, that this might be a solace and not a tantalizing reminder that might wound. I don't want to think about what those memories—of once-rich lives, of kids, careers, vacations, images of the strong people they used to be, the way they once could read the fine print, toss a baseball, write an engineering report, cook for a crowd, coax tulips from a rocky garden, drive cross-country, and make their own beds—might mean to the rememberer, who is unable to retrieve that former self, to reconcile that self with the person in the bed, wheelchair.

My aunt Mary, my mother's fiery, outspoken, rough-around-the-edges oldest sister, whom I adored, once flew out to Las Vegas for a visit—her first and, we all knew, her last. Shrunken in a wheelchair, her Lucille Ball hair by then a dusky gray, Aunt Mary was ravaged by lung cancer after working for minimum wage for fifty-five years in a dry cleaner to support herself and her widowed mother. I recall her wheelchair parked at the edge of the family room, the television being on, my mother busy in the kitchen, my father on his favorite couch. I was reading on a window seat, twenty-two years old, less than a year out of college.

"I'm sixty-four years old, I never even lived, and now I'm going to die," Mary suddenly announced, loud enough for everyone to hear.

No one said a word for a moment. Then my father got up and went to his den, clicking on the TV in there. This didn't surprise me because though he liked Mary, he disliked any talk of death more. My mother yelled out, over the noise of the TV, "No you're not."

I was mute. I wanted to say something, to let my aunt know I was willing to talk to her about that, about *her* death, about anything. But I realized I was the child in the room, relatively speaking. I stood and moved close to my mother, whispering, "She wants to talk, let her talk." But my mother's quick wave of her arm, and stern expression, closed off any possible conversation.

I crossed the room and hugged my aunt, awkwardly, and gave her a pat her on the back, but then I walked away. I remember that moment, that nonconversation always, and tell myself that the next time anyone wants to talk about death, I'll listen. But I'm not sure that, when the time comes, I actually will do this.

I drive about two hours to a community college in southwestern New Jersey where one of my professors is giving a reading. She's the star attraction, and while a second, preliminary author is on stage reading from a humorous account of her attempt to camp in the Rockies, my cell phone buzzes in my purse.

In the hallway, I whisper hello and Gary wants to know where I am.

"I'm at a get-together with friends," I say. I anticipate he'd snicker if I said I was at a reading, because he's scoffed at my grad school plan. I suspect that he believes writers are either born or mysteriously inspired. He's sporadically writing a crime novel but doesn't talk to me about it.

"Why? What's going on?" I ask.

Loud, long sigh. Then he begins by telling me Dad has a broken hip. Doctors say it's an old injury, but they want to do a hip replacement. "What do you think?" he asks me.

What I think is my brother is uncharacteristically calling me on my cell phone and genuinely seems to want my opinion. I want to give it. But I also worry that if I do venture an opinion, and it's not one he agrees with, or if my opinion involves him asking ever more questions of medical professionals, it may spark an argument—or silence. Yet, he *did* call. He *is* asking.

"Well, what are the pros and cons?"

I'm surprised, then, that we have a calm and careful conversation. The operation will eliminate Dad's pain (the doctors say), and even though he may not walk again, of course we want him out of pain, to be comfortable in a wheelchair or bed. Yet, it's risky. And, he's a terribly noncompliant patient who probably won't do the physical therapy. I can't tell from Gary's tone if he wants me to advocate for or against surgery.

"Well, I guess we have to," I begin.

I'll remember this phone call for a long time because it is one of the only calls in which I feel we are talking to each other with respect and mutual interest in what the other has to say. Later, many calls will devolve on both sides into accusations, posturing, and occasionally hanging up on one another.

I want to get back inside the reading and hear another funny story about a clumsy camper who screams, "Bear!" when a tree branch brushes against her nylon tent. I want to laugh and forget and squirm out of the decisions, and at the same time, I want to oversee them. But I'm far away and want it to stay that way, too. I hope I will be able to think about this, but the doctors want an answer the next morning. I hedge.

"What do *you* think?" I ask.

"He's so weak. I don't know how long he's going to last, with or without it."

I let the line go silent for a bit. Then we each make guesses about how much longer our father may live—three months, six—but agree that we don't want him in pain for any of it, if that's possible. Neither of us talks about how Dad was complaining, since April, about terrible hip pain, about how we all presumed it was just another new arthritis site, just another complaint from a man who wouldn't follow advice about exercising his arthritic joints.

Finally, I say, "Do what you think is best." I know that means I will then have to refrain from criticizing his eventual decision. But I'm not good at that.

About eighteen months before the question of Dad's hip operation, there was another phone call I wanted to forget. I was at the sewing machine in my basement, working rather clumsily to take in some of my jeans after another weight loss. In the years since college—when I thought I was fat, but of course wasn't—I'd seesawed between a healthy, fit-but-not-skinny weight that looked okay in riding breeches, and periods of mild to moderate to severe overweight. I knew how to lose weight, in fact I was good at it, dropping 60, 80, 100 pounds on different occasions. Problem was, I was also good at putting the pounds back on via a combination of emotional and stress eating, restaurant meals, slacking off on exercise, binge eating, and inertia.

Mom is on the phone. "I can't take it anymore," she yells.

I have no idea what *it* means until she says, "He's half out of his head."

This isn't the first time I'm hearing about, or witnessing, my father's mental "slips." For my whole life (and maybe for his), he'd been legendarily forgetful, an "absentminded professor," we joked. But lately he'd made some worrisome statements and done and not done some slightly more concerning things. On my parents' last visit to New Jersey, he'd seemed confused when looking at a clock, unsure if it was morning or night (we told him he was jet-lagged, sleeping too late in the mornings, and in need of fresh air). He had trouble dialing a phone (I told him to just slow down, that the numbers on my phone were a lot smaller than on his at home).

Then, he'd dropped my mother at the hairdresser and had planned to visit his sister who lived about a mile from the salon. Instead, he got a cup of coffee from the deli next door and sat in his rental car reading the newspaper. When she found him there two hours later, dozing off, Mom asked, "How's Gina?," and he only stared back, not a flicker of understanding. Like everyone else, when she came home and told me the story that day, I rolled my eyes, rationalized that he was just being his usual forgetful self, maybe just getting more forgetful in his older age.

The phone call told me what I already knew.

I lay down my pins and asked my mother to calm down and tell me what *happened.* Nothing happened, exactly, she said. "He's just half out of his head." Either she could not think of a specific example because she was too upset, or the examples were now running together and there was only the blanket explanation.

They had only recently returned from a trip to Hawaii with their close friends Linda and Rick; the postcard was still on my refrigerator. It hadn't gone well. The Hawaii trip fiascos included my father one day refusing to leave the hotel grounds, even for a short half-block walk to an Italian restaurant; my father not remembering how to calculate a waiter's tip; my father not understanding that the island-hopping cruise wouldn't bring them back to Los Angeles; my father, who loved chewing the fat with his male friends while "the women" went off together, clinging to Mom's arm, begging her not to go off shopping with Linda and leave him alone with Rick.

This was, for me, a moment of stark clarity: this man who had for decades encouraged me to "eat where the locals eat," and "go exploring off the beaten path," and "avoid tourist traps" hadn't, I didn't think, lost his nerve but was losing his mind. Maybe there's something about a trip, strange environments, time zones, and boats that trip brain wiring.

"You have to get us out of Vegas," Mom continued. "I can't stay here with him like this and no help. Find us a condo or something so we can move back by you."

"Mom. You have to tell me exactly what's going on."

It tumbled out in a long string of short bursts. "Daddy is confused. He drove to the grocery store and didn't remember why. He put the new cold cuts in the garbage. He can't write out a check."

My first thoughts are selfish and accusatory because for a moment, all I can see are phone calls, a flight out there, stress. Not *oh dear poor Daddy*, not *my mother needs help*. But, *there goes my next month*. And, *why isn't my brother taking care of this?* "I need some help," she says.

I skip pointing out that she has a son living around the corner, and why isn't he helping her figure out this dilemma?

"Okay, Mom, if you want to move, you have to put your house on the market first. It's very expensive to live in New Jersey now. You'll need the money from selling your house to buy a nice two-bedroom condo here. Remember, you don't have a million bucks lying around anymore."

Twenty-five years of retirement eats into even a robust nest egg. As does the craps table. I also try to raise the logic of relocating someone whose mental lapses seemed to have been exacerbated by a recent shift in geography, and whether it would really benefit my father by moving him away from his son. I mention the harsh Jersey winters and how limited their mobility will be, her having not driven in the snow in decades.

She doesn't want to hear it. She insists the right thing is to find a place in New Jersey first, then sell the Vegas house, then buy the New Jersey condo—like putting a deposit on a winter coat in August and picking it up in November, but only if the weather turns cold enough and someone else hasn't claimed the coat. Finances aside, I picture the four walk-in and five oversized closets in the Vegas house crammed with stuff, the overfull oversized two-car garage, the heavy, expensive furniture, three breakfronts with china, Lalique, Lladró, and Hummels. Parting with any of it will be agony for her. But mostly I explain that even if they *could* buy something in New Jersey *without* selling the Vegas house, they can't afford upkeep on both. By the time I get through with the practicalities, she's calm, tells me, "Nevermind," and hangs up without ever revealing to me: what was the tipping point that made her call that particular day?

And I just let it go.

I don't call my sister and brother to brainstorm. I don't call back and try to initiate a fuller discussion. I don't even call my father and try to gauge for myself. I will remember that phone call in two years, in ten years, and my cowardice will sting fresh each time.

After that call, things went back to normal. I'd call, almost every day, exchange typical pleasantries with Dad, who hardly seemed even slightly muddled on the phone, but then again we didn't talk about anything much. He'd put my mother on the phone, she'd complain only the usual amount about the usual stuff—how he always wanted to go to the same old restaurants, wouldn't wear his hearing aid, read too many newspapers.

We hide, and lie, and deny for many more months.

———

When they visit me in New Jersey the winter before the stroke, I arrange for Laurie, now a real estate broker, to show them the elegant, spacious, newly built senior condo complex only a mile from my house. The buildings have elevators and no stairs, an indoor garage, and balconies. All those things are rare in the hilly older suburbs where I live, and my mother likes what she sees. My father says he wants to move back too, but to me his words are half-hearted. He seems impressed, but freezing on a mild day, and repeatedly wrings his hands.

Back at my house, we "work the numbers," something Dad used to enjoy doing whenever a family member was contemplating a sizable purchase or business plan. But he can't work out the math, adding up monthly maintenance fees and taxes. Nor can he acknowledge the reality that in order to buy this condo, he must sell his Las Vegas home, which he had custom built—not, I don't think, because he's stubborn or sentimental, but because it appears he has lost his grip on the idea of what buying and selling are all about.

On the same trip, though, he sits with my boys and names a long list of American presidents, first and last names, and plays a word game after dinner. I watch my parents stroll up and down my driveway holding hands, and I glimpse him cop a feel when they are making up the guest room bed. He tells stories about a Giants game from the sixties and about the time he flew to Europe a few weeks early to surprise Mom, Cathy, and me, who were on a seven-week trip.

And so, I decide it's not as bad as it seems. They leave, nothing decided. And again, I ignore—everything. But Cathy heads to Vegas and tries to get some answers.

That spring, I'm shopping, or really browsing—the thing I do to clear my head—when my phone rings. In Vegas, Cathy has visited and accompanied my parents to see a gerontologist who specializes in memory issues. Since she's flown home, there's been a follow-up visit. I've been trying to talk to the specialist myself, and now finally he's returning my call; I want to hear straight from the source.

I sit on a bench outside near the food court, smelling French fries, breathing exhaust on a humid afternoon. Cathy said this doctor had mentioned a list of possible treatments, medication options, hope. But what I hear now is resignation, that fake-kind-doctor tone that cloaks either the worst news or maybe a lack of creativity, a disinterest in certain patients or problems.

He begins by talking about dementia, about Alzheimer's. He suggests just one medication but doubts it will be effective. I don't catch the reasons why, but I do hear, "At this point, there isn't much else to do. I'm sorry. I wish I had more to offer."

I'm struck dumb because in between learning of the first visit to this doctor and today's call, I did what I always do. I did research. I do this because I know how, because as a trained journalist I can do it with a semblance of speed, because I will call anyone and ask any question, and because if I don't, I serve myself a large portion of guilt.

One of my calls was to the husband of a lifelong friend; he is a high-level research physician at a pharmaceutical giant, and though he doesn't practice daily medicine and barely knows my father, he's kind and curious and writes down what I tell him. He calls back after he's had some time to do his own research and explains that my father should be seeing a neurologist, not a gerontologist. He tells me that many illnesses or health crises in the elderly can mimic early dementia: silent stroke, clogged carotid artery, tumor, infection, sudden thyroid dysfunction, certain severe vitamin deficiencies, hematoma caused by a head injury (new or old).

I remind my sister that Dad, while getting out of his car the previous winter, had hit his head hard, twice, on a piece of shelving he'd jerry-rigged in the garage to hold Christmas decorations. He'd banged it just above the temple, and it had bled and grown an egg. But while Cathy thinks this could be interesting, she's in New England, and I'm in Jersey. Like most things I must tell my brother and hope he will explore—requiring yet more new doctor visits and more days off work—this was a hard sell, and I didn't sell it properly. And so this is one more time when I convince myself something has gone wrong in my father's care because I don't live where he lives, because I live where I was raised, because my brother won't do what I want.

Each time Dad sees a new doctor, whoever accompanies him has to remember to bring along a letter, signed by my father, granting the doctor permission to discuss his health with Cathy and me. I make both generic Dear Physician letters, and letters customized for individual physicians and email them to Gary, who doesn't like email, who has to download and print them and then get my father to sign them all.

Even with the painstakingly produced customized letters ready, I'm frequently hamstrung. One doctor's administrator tells me, "Dr. X doesn't talk to family members on the phone. You'll have to make an appointment to come in for a consultation," and even when I explain I am in New Jersey, she refuses to put me through or give him a message or arrange a future phone consultation, even when I say I will pay.

After my father dies, when I find several of the unused letters, his signature will seem both normal and not. In some places, there is a capital cursive *A* at the beginning of Anthony and an uppercase *C* at the beginning of Chipolone—something he never did. He always used a lower case *a* and *c*. The size of the signatures is different on each; two of them look stiff and angular, as if he was gripping the pen too tightly. The third resembles a schoolboy's early attempt at cursive, letters awkwardly joined, no relative uniformity.

When I talk to this gerontologist that day at the mall, he tells me a particular kind of CT scan might reveal more. (I don't bother him with the detail that my severely hunchbacked father can't lie flat for a CT scan, and I don't ask why this doctor can't see this for himself.)

The worst moment isn't hearing the doctor's dispassionate pronouncement. It is realizing with utter clarity that the person I need to talk to about this, the one who could normally help me figure out a next step, is my father.

5

No News Is Good News

IN OCTOBER, seven weeks after my father's stroke, I am at home in my white colonial house, about twelve miles west of New York City. It's late on a quiet Friday afternoon, a day when the autumn crispness winks, the kind of day I miss when only a few weeks later, winter announces itself.

I am at the table where we often eat, in what we all call "the porch," despite my efforts to get everyone to call it "the breakfast nook," and which is really a kind of mudroom tacked on to the kitchen by the house's previous owners. I've just made myself a cup of tea and have sat to tackle my weekly volunteer chore for Paul's elementary school fundraising committee—counting Box Tops for Education. An hour earlier, I'd collected bulging plastic bags from all the classrooms filled with a thousand or so small cardboard rectangles cut out from cereal boxes and other grocery items, the ones for which General Mills pays the school ten cents apiece. Not this day, but on previous days when I've been trimming, stacking and counting Box Tops, I've heard my father's voice in my head noting that it would be more efficient to persuade a few local companies to write donation checks.

Sean, who is in sixth grade, and Paul, in second, are in the basement adding on to their Lego city. I've opened the fifties-style crank windows to let in a little breeze, not enough to scatter my carefully stacked little piles of Box Top squares but enough that I feel it across the skin of my forearms. I take a sip of my tea.

My cell phone rings, and as I fish it out of my purse hanging on a nearby hook, I see on the display that it is my brother calling from his own cell phone, the cell phone he often says he hates using. I calculate that in Las Vegas, it is the time of afternoon when he is just beginning his shift, watching for suspicious activity on casino eye-in-the-sky cameras, and I recall that he is not permitted to use his own cell phone while on duty. I know it must be bad news.

My father's medical complications have multiplied in the last month. He's been to the hospital's rehab floor, back to ICU, had numerous tests and treatments, gone back to the rehab wing, and, finally, was settled into what I am assured is a top-flight, almost luxurious nursing home, where within days, he fell off the toilet, breaking his hip again, and has had a second surgery and another rehab unit stay. Now back in the nursing home, he was to have been moved to the hospice floor, with a somewhat murky prognosis of "three to six months."

We've talked a few times, Gary, and Cathy, and I—sometimes amicably, sometimes angrily, more often cautiously—about medical decisions, options, money. Cathy and I would research, talk to friends who are physicians or nurses, consult with others who'd dealt with aging parents, and then make suggestions. At the other end of the line, I often pictured Gary, smoking a cigarette, arms crossed—his usual demeanor when I tried to make a point. He'd often listen, but then explain that we didn't understand because we weren't there, that everything is done differently "in this town." Implied, always, was *if you don't like it, get on a plane.* He wasn't always wrong.

The fall breeze ruffles the Box Tops. My cell rings on. I hit the on button.

"Where are you at?" Gary asks, and I know immediately that my father is dead.

I suppose he wants to be sure I am not driving the boys home from school, or running a Cub Scout meeting, or in the checkout line at Shop Rite, pulling bags of frozen vegetables from the cart while the boys negotiate for gum. I know what he is going to say, but that does not make it easier.

"Daddy's gone. Dad's dead, sis."

When the news came on television that JFK was shot, I was playing with Tinker Toys on my living room floor. I heard about the Space Shuttle Challenger exploding on the radio in a taxi on my way to the World Trade Center, where I was meeting my cousin for resume tips. I know I was wearing green pants and a white flowered shirt when I found out I was pregnant for my first child. On September 11, 2001, I was doing a dinosaur puzzle on the family room floor with Paul when my friend Rita called to say, *turn on the TV!*

When I remember how I got the news that my father died, I will always see those pink-and-white inch-square Box Tops, heaped and spread across my table, the envelopes marked up with kids' handwriting, the yellow and crimson leaves falling like confetti in the backyard, the sound of my boys' animated voices from the basement. I was counting Box Tops by twos, the way my mother once taught me to count the pennies my father saved in a copper barrel on the floor of his bedroom closet.

I had once imagined what it might be like to get that phone call. I thought I might collapse onto the couch or clamp the arm of whoever was nearby, or maybe grab my stomach and keen. None of those things happen. Instead, Paul comes up from the basement, picking at a hangnail, nosing about for a snack, eying me warily. "It's PopPop," I mouth, pulling him close. "He's gone," I say, still listening to my brother.

Now it is a fact, a family event, and in another few seconds, I am also telling Sean, who has shot up from the basement, maybe pulled by a kind of silence or draft in the air. "Well, I guess it was his time," Sean says, and I want to hug him, and I also stifle an unseemly urge to yell, *Don't say that!,* because this is the first time I hear those awful well-meaning things kind people say when they are trying to comfort you after someone you love has died. I pull both of my boys to me and am startled that Sean is nearly tall enough to look me straight in the eye.

Gary is driving to the nursing home where our mother found her husband warm, but dead. I find myself saying some of the trite, pat, possibly untrue things I just shrunk from: that he did all he could, that Daddy was suffering, that it is for the best. I tell him to be careful, to drive safely. I say, "Don't call anyone else while you're driving." I say, "I'll do all of that." I say I will call Cathy and our New Jersey relatives and my parents' friends who still live here, who are still alive. I say, "Call me back later," and we hang up. There is no time to collapse. No keening, just the warmth of my sons, who by now are squirmy and leave my side to sit forlornly at the kitchen counter. Now my house phone is ringing, but it's just Frank's usual call on a Friday afternoon, asking if he should bring home a pizza or Chinese.

"My father died," I say without preamble, and immediately regret it, angry with myself for saying it out loud, for saying it at all.

I won't remember this for weeks: I don't ask Gary how my mother is, if the nursing home had called to summon her, what were the circumstances of Dad's death. I don't ask him anything, really. Something else I won't remember for a long time: earlier that day, the house was still and I was at my dining room table, drinking coffee and feeling melancholy, procrastinating over a freelance project I should have started the day before. I glanced out past the smudged window next to the patio, and slowly became conscious, fleetingly, of two thoughts—that it was my favorite season, vibrant-hued leaves piling up in corners of the driveway, and that the day reminded me of the early morning of 9/11, the blousy opalescent sky and drifting sparse clouds.

Wanting to shake the shifting sadness, I had gotten up and turned to the "All About My Family" photo collage Sean had once assembled for a school project. Was I searching for something in those photographs? The way my sister's hand rested on my forearm in the church vestibule before my wedding? That Paul really was still in diapers on that trip to the Maine beach? My finger came to rest over a picture of my father, standing upright and smiling on the patio of his own house, holding his grandson at age two. "PopPop and Paul," it says in wiggly red marker.

I was struck by how young they both were—a lifetime ago, or at least six years. I slid my forefinger back and forth across the matte glass, across my father's unpained face, stopping at the spot where the BAND-AID was visible on the center of his eyeglasses.

Without planning to, I said aloud, "Looks like you'll be going soon."

In my empty house, how very melodramatic I must have sounded, if anyone had been there to hear. I was alone, though at that moment, I felt as if I had company, almost as if someone was hugging me. I don't know why I said it; there was no sense of knowing. I suppose I simply needed to make a sound to quiet the noises of tumbling pillars in my head, where almost daily since I'd returned from Las Vegas, I'd been constructing possible end-game scenarios, all much more dramatic than a simple phone call on a lovely fall afternoon.

Frank says he'll be home right away. I hug my children again and send Sean to fetch the address book I keep in the drawer of the side table in the family room. The boys aren't crying, and neither am I. I know I have a job to do: make the calls. The boys are, I think, numb, in unfamiliar territory; our little family hasn't lost a close relative yet. I tell them to go back to their Legos if they want to, that their PopPop loved them very much, and that Daddy will be home soon. This seems to reassure them, and they're off.

I reach my sister's answering machine and don't leave a message, and I don't call her cell phone because she might be driving home after a day teaching high school math. I spend fifteen minutes locating the emergency phone numbers I had once insisted she leave me (in case I did not hear from her for days and feared she was passed out in her apartment where she lives alone 220 miles from me). The paper she'd written it on isn't in the address book, and I reason out in which logical other safe place I could have stored it. Finally, I reach her good friend Judy who lives in the same apartment complex, and it turns out she will see Cathy in a few minutes at a church function and agrees to tell her.

When Cathy calls me back, she says she will take the flight to Las Vegas she had already scheduled for Sunday morning, two days hence, because she had arranged a few days off to visit for Dad's eightieth birthday, the one we'd all assumed would be his last. At the moment, I don't think about Cathy's pain, how close she felt to Dad, how much he treasured her quiet understanding of his ways. I don't ponder what she must be feeling, to have missed the end of her father's life by just two days. I only think about this later, when I get to Vegas first and she's not there yet.

I start making calls to relatives and long-time friends of my parents, nearly all of whom still live in New Jersey. My father died four days before he would have turned eighty. Uncle Silvio mentions this when I call. My father died three days after the sixty-fourth anniversary of the day he first met my mother, something they celebrated, always. My sister mentions this. My father died the first day he was in hospice. My husband mentions this. I want to say to them all, *don't you think I know that?* But I don't. My father died on Friday the thirteenth. No one mentions this, but I sense that some are thinking it.

When I tell people that my father has died, I am mostly surprised at *their* surprise. I want to say: He had Alzheimer's, severe arthritis, emphysema. He was seventy-nine years old. He had a stroke, pneumonia, a broken hip, congestive heart failure. What did you think was going to happen? But I don't of course. I say, "thank you" and "yes, too young" and I'll "let you know about the arrangements." I'm not surprised. To me his death makes some sense in a way that I need something to make sense.

After talking to relatives and elderly friends of my parents', I begin to call my girlfriends. They are all so kind and sympathetic, offering to have Frank and the boys for dinner, have the boys all day any day while I'm in Vegas. When I hang up, I remember a girls' night out a few weeks before when Amanda joked that we were getting to an age when butts droop, chins double, there's less time between root touchups. Not joking, Margaret noted that we are at an age when our parents start to become our children. That we are at an age when we move closer to the front of the funeral car line.

Frank books me on a Saturday morning nonstop flight that will put me in Las Vegas by 11 a.m. local time. I decide to stay up all night, to be busy—packing, sending emails to cancel meetings and request deadline extensions, enlist my Mom-friends to shuttle and care for my kids. I gather newish photographs for the wake collages. I make lists and a color-coded calendar for my husband to navigate two weeks of the children's school, Scouts, sports, religious instruction. I charge my cell phone, pack the laptop, power cord, and work and grad school files, envisioning myself late at night in my parents' still house, getting work done, functioning, *going on*.

In fact, while I am in Las Vegas, I will do this. I will work, I will *keep up*. When I return home two weeks later, I will review everything I have produced and realize most of it is awful. I will read what I've written about my father, meant then for a possible grad school writing project, and I will not be able to judge if it's terrible. When I return home, I will be so sleep-deprived and unfocused I will need daily naps for weeks. When I return home, I will feel stupid for having spent that time in Las Vegas, when the house was quiet and I was alone and unable to sleep, *keeping up*, instead of resting, instead of grieving, instead of spending more time at my father's marble-top desk in his study, touching his clunky old adding machine, gazing at his handwriting on a four-month-old to-do list. I'll wonder why I didn't take more time paging through his scrapbooks, reconsidering the poems he wrote, which I had once high-handedly relegated as pap when I was an arrogant teenager too self-absorbed to notice—anything.

With the packing, organizing, and list making done, at around 5 a.m., I slide beneath the covers in our king-sized bed, mentally exhausted. Frank awakens immediately, rolls over, asks if I am okay.

I say only, "Make love to me?"

He does, slowly, gently.

After, we both doze fitfully, entwined, him holding me from behind, me clutching his forearm, for about an hour, then get up to shower and dress for the airport. On this Saturday morning even the highways in crowded Essex County are quiet, and in the scattering darkness, we are quiet too. I ask Frank to pull our minivan to the curb, not to bother parking and coming inside with our sleepy sons. The boys hug me from the back seat and Sean asks once again why they all can't come along too. In bed, in the morning, Frank and I had talked about this, if it made sense for the three of them to fly out once funeral arrangements are finalized. I said I'd rather they stay home, that it wouldn't be good for Sean especially who clings to routine—to disrupt the new school year. I also want to shield them from the fray I'm anticipating once my brother, his wife (often upset, perhaps understandably, about the demands my parents' dotage has made on her husband's time), Cathy, and I are all in the same place at the same time. Also, there's money. Each day my self-employed husband and my freelancer self don't work, there isn't any of it coming in.

Not long after I buckle into my airplane seat in first class (we used up all our credit card points for the upgrade, plus paid nearly $800 for the last minute, open-ended round-trip ticket), I pull out my notebook, the eulogy in mind. I don't yet know that while I am flying, Gary and Mom will have decided that the wake and memorial service will occur in forty-eight hours, on Monday, and not later in the week as Cathy and I anticipate. This makes it impossible for even just Frank to fly out: he can't arrange the childcare, work, and other logistics so quickly.

On the plane, however, I think I have the luxury of time, so I begin with a list, planning to pull it out into prose over the next few days. But I will be too busy the entire weekend with other death-related minutia:

selecting flowers and vases, ordering thank-you cards, driving back to the airport to pick up Cathy, and again for her daughter, Holly, who flies in from Atlanta, keeping my mother fed and moving forward.

When the time comes to eulogize my father, I have only my list, and I edit as I go, turning each listed item into an anecdote, realizing this is what my father did when he tried to teach me anything in life: storify it.

Those words were lost to the dry desert air, and only years later will I find my notes from the airplane, titled "A Few Things My Father Taught Me," which include *A love of reading and good writing. Independence. To do what I love—whether that meant riding horses, attending college in a freezing climate, going back to school at age forty-five. To be proud of doing any honest work for fair pay. To be serious about important things, but not too serious. To do the right thing, not the easy thing. To laugh at myself. To appreciate great food, good service, wonderful restaurants. To tip well.*

While making notes on the plane, I end with *Some lessons I learned well. Others I am still working on. So Dad, if I forget—tap me on the shoulder and remind me.*

But when the time comes, Gary speaks first, about all the things he learned from his father, as they worked side by side for forty years. He ends this way: "If I forget what you taught me, Dad, put your hand on my shoulder and I'll know it's you. Or give me a good swift kick in the butt!"

When it is my turn, I leave off my final planned lines.

6

At Sea in Las Vegas

AFTER I WALK past banks of jangling slot machines, Gary meets me in the baggage area at McCarran airport. In one of the few ways Las Vegas is simple and easy to navigate, it's just a forty-yard walk, across one wide crosswalk, to the covered parking garage, where my mother waits in the car angled into the closest handicapped-marked space. She is in black pants and a black blouse and seems much smaller than her five-foot, four-inch frame.

Before he even maneuvers the car into the traffic-choked roads outside the airport, my brother announces the Monday funeral plans. I know Dad wanted to be cremated and that he wasn't fond of funerals, so when I am told about the expedient arrangements, I assume it's because Dad left explicit instructions that it all be done that way. But he didn't. It's just, I'm told, how it's done "in this town."

Mom and Gary are both hungry, and Gary drives to a restaurant for lunch. This makes me angry, that we're not heading home right away so I can write the obituary and research the newspaper deadlines, and that they seem more concerned with food. Then I remember how my father was ruled by his stomach, always, first because of illness—ulcers, gallstones, diverticulitis—then by the lingering long-term effects of the bariatric gastric bypass surgery he had in the sixties when it was crudely used to solve all manner of otherwise unsolvable digestive problems and which made him always hungry, needing to eat every two hours to keep that resected stomach full. Once, he walked out of a restaurant at a mall—where he and my mother, my husband, and our sons were marking Mother's Day—because our food hadn't appeared on the table yet, and he was "starving, damn it." He found a Chinese takeout across the way, and came back to the restaurant table with his container of Chicken Lo Mein.

I decide maybe, after all, lunch *is* the most appropriate thing.

It is at lunch that I get the story, about how it happened, who was where, what they were told. It's a short story of Dad's surprisingly short stay in the hospice wing, and I'm glad of that; a longer story might suggest that I would have had time to get there.

But I can't shake the story. I keep needing to think of my father's last hours, and I keep getting it wrong, asking the wrong question. Even later, two years and even six years on, I will keep asking myself, *Why did it happen just then? That morning? Only three hours after entering the nursing home's hospice area?*

This is what I was told, and what my mother and brother told me they were told, and what I later piece together with my sister from the stories she was told. Perhaps it is all true, or maybe just what we, or I, choose to believe.

He was calm, settled, *serene* even, the hospice nurse noted, two hours before he stopped breathing in his sleep. For weeks before, when he'd been in hospital rehab and in the nursing home, he'd been agitated, restless, jittery. Unsettled. Rude, crude. Ungentlemanly, as he'd never been before Alzheimer's, though I remember seeing and hearing him that way even back in August when I felt the need to tell doctors, nurses, everyone, that he was normally so polite, so kind, so decent. The night before, my brother had found his once circumspect father drooling obscenities, dismissive, cranky. Gary had chuffed him on the shoulder and told him there was no need for that kind of language.

He was talkative, and lucid, *jovial* even, that morning when the nurse massaged him and stroked cream on his slack skin. When my mother had seen him, the day before, he'd been combative, sullen, depressed. Those last few weeks, even as she agreed to hospice and a do-not-resuscitate order, she still begged him, "I need you at home," and "Tony, don't give up—you have to get better."

In August, I recalled her making similar demands and being angry at her for not recognizing what I took to be a clear reality: he wasn't going to ever fully recover, and she wasn't going to ever bring him home, and it was unfair, cruel even, and not supportive and encouraging, to pepper him with urgent requests that he get better.

He was courtly, and *sweet,* when the hospice nurse asked what would make him comfortable that morning.

Dad said, *Thank you kindly,* when the hospice nurse shaved him, and he said he wanted to rest, and he asked, *Is that okay? Is it okay to rest?* and she'd told him yes, it was okay, it was okay to rest. This is what we were told happened at the elegant-looking nursing home I once mistook as the clubhouse of a luxury gated community.

She bathed him, shaved him, creamed his stiffened, arthritic, bedsored body. She slipped thick socks on his bony feet, smoothed his thin hair over the bumps on his head. She asked him questions, and maybe he called her *doll*. She massaged his atrophied muscles, placed warm compresses in places he might be hurting. She sang softly and prayed. She tucked him in, swathed an extra blanket. She laughed at his corny jokes. And she left.

Not long after, my mother arrived with her close friend Tessa, whom she'd met the first week she'd moved to Las Vegas twenty-five years before. Tessa went in the room first, so my mother could drop off chocolates for the nurses. When Tessa emerged moments later, my mother knew.

"He died alone," my mother lamented.

Of course he did. My father died alone because, I think, he needed to.

I like to think the hospice nurse somehow knew, and let *him* know, by touch and lack of need or demand in her voice and stance, or perhaps with words (*It's okay to rest if you need to*), that the only need in that room that mattered, was his.

She wanted nothing, needed nothing from him, unlike all of us who, in our ways, could not undo a lifetime of need, of asking. My mother, I believe, needed him to come home whole, to be the man he'd always been and not the sick, dying old man he was. Gary, I think, wanted or needed him to overcome, to continue to be the calm one, the wise one, as they'd been with one another for decades together in business. Perhaps I needed my father to be the lingering patient so that I could be the long-distance smart child.

A horse that eats everything you put in his feed bucket, that doesn't spread his manure too far around his stall, and has no vices (like chewing stall planks or pawing the stall floor) is known as an "easy keeper." I know my father would not have been one. That once he'd sunk completely into oblivion, he would not have become docile and sweet as some elderly vacant folks do, would not have compliantly taken his medication. I doubt that long-term, he would have been pleasantly demented. He'd have been a royal pain in the butt.

Still, even knowing this, the hospice nurse's report encourages me to doubt myself, to put aside our family's shared years of living with my father's stubborn insistence on his own way. Instead, it sounds as if (or I want it to sound as if) he was agreeable, and that soothes me.

Not that Saturday when my plane lands and we go to lunch before the obituary writing, when I order but can't eat a Caesar salad, not right then, but a few months later, I get the idea that I need to speak to that hospice nurse. I want to know the whole story, the rest of the story. But I tell myself it's unlikely she would remember a patient she tended for only one morning, and as the time stretches on and I keep this idea floating in my head for a year or more, her forgetting seems more and more likely, certain even. It's enough, eventually, to know (no, to imagine?) that he needed something perhaps none of his loved ones could provide, and that she did provide, and that's enough.

When I finally decide I will not track down the hospice nurse, I realize it's also because I do not want to find out I am wrong, that what I have pieced together, as accurately as I can, from what the nurses told my mother and brother, did not happen that way, or meant what I imagine it meant. I do not want to know if this nurse, this human being, whom I have, perhaps without merit, imbued with wonderfully empathic qualities, might turn out to be not so wonderful. Nor do I want to know that my father, in addition to being sweet and calm, also told her to go to hell or mistook her for the maid or a hooker.

I want only to remember that what I have come to believe happened was a good thing, a good ending, for him. For me.

———

After lunch, I write my father's obituary and have only forty minutes before it must be transmitted, over dial-up from Mom's house, to make the deadline for the *Las Vegas Sun* and the *Review-Journal*. I don't mind the job; it's keeping me in motion, fulfilling the point I suppose of early mourning and grief tasks, especially in a family not used to gathering very often and never for death: busy-ness in the face of incomprehensible loss. I meet the obituary deadline, but I forget to list my father's siblings, living or dead, and omit the names of all six grandchildren.

Before Holly and Cathy arrive, my mother and I fall into a kind of stupor, walking together from one end to the other of their large house, like silent little mice across the plush cream carpeting, from bedrooms to kitchen, family room to dining room, guest bedroom to guest bathroom. I have no idea what all the walking is about—making sure all is in order? For what? Whom? My mother is a meticulous housekeeper and the house already shines like an upscale bed-and-breakfast. I mostly move things, small things—a towel here, pillow there, a luggage rack, alarm clock, throw blanket, making a new order out of what was already in order. Surely we aren't just thinking of Cathy's and Holly's comfort; they will make themselves at home just fine. We just need to be in motion. We avoid my father's den, though in a week, I will find myself in there almost every night, around 1 or 2 a.m., when the house falls even more silent and I can be alone with him.

After Cathy arrives—also distressed but reconciled about the speedy arrangements—we all visit the florist, a bright little square place with lots of windows and, I suspect, a ventilation system that pulls much of the heavy floral scents out; otherwise, I would not be able to stay there for more than a few minutes, and we stay there for many, many minutes.

So many decisions. Beautiful glass vases in unusual shapes so Mom can keep them afterward? (Yes, especially a three-foot-high, slim fluted clear glass one to hold a precious and pricey single orchid—and which is placed afterward in the marble entry of my parents' house and which I will knock over two years hence, shattering it and a certain part of my heart.) Do we pay separately, and choose colors, flowers, sizes, and arrangements that reflect our individual tastes and budgets? Or do we pool funds and choose only what we all unanimously like? Should there be individual small arrangements from each set of grandchildren, with the appropriate signifying ribbons, or would one large heart from all six of them be the right choice?

I want to scream about the inanity of it all, the expense, the fact that my father, of all people, likely could not have cared any less about flowers in a funeral home. But we make choices, pick flowers, and in the end my mother decides to pay for it all, as of course all three of her children knew she would, and that's a good thing because the bill is somewhere north of $800.

At the funeral homes I went to when I was a kid (and kids in large extended Italian Catholic families in our area of New Jersey in the 1960s went to a lot of them), there was always a basement room, a lounge they called it, where I was sent along with all of my young cousins. Going to funeral homes was never scary for me then, because I knew I'd get to play in the lounge, unsupervised by adults, except for those who strode through occasionally on their way to the restrooms or to smoke a cigarette. On both my mother's and father's side of the family, it was necessary to attend the wakes of everyone who died, however distantly related and even if they were not related.

In those days, none of the adults considered that funeral homes might not be a good environment for young children. We went along because we always went along.

For a long time after I reached an age when I could decide to stay at home instead of going to funeral homes, one reason I gave was that I hated the smell of funeral homes, the smell of death. It wasn't until I was in college and our sorority house was filled with floral arrangements for a dance that I knew it's the smell of *flowers* that I detest, that I associate with death. Even when I become a rather good gardener and grow flowers in my front yard in vibrant hues, I spend a long time at the nursery choosing every new plant, leaning over to smell it, and feeling satisfied only when I can't smell anything other than earth. When my husband brings me flowers, or a client sends thank-you flowers, or when my once-tiny kids so sweetly picked flowers for me, I'd smile and put them in water but put the vase in a far corner or out on the patio.

In the family in which I was raised, no one was ever heard to say to another family member, *I'm upset and need to talk* or *I want to talk to you about what you did (or said)* or *I'm sad/mad/confused,* or even, *help me.* We didn't do that. What we did was to sulk, to go stone silent, to walk out of the room, to cry in secret, to ignore someone (or everyone), to pretend nothing was wrong, to get moody, to brood, to watch too much TV, to read, to take it out upon ourselves, often with loads of junk food. I joke sometimes that it's a good thing none of us like to drink, or we'd have all found solace in the bottom of a bottle.

In the family that I made with my husband, we are often heard to say to another family member, "I'm upset and need to talk," or "I want to talk to you about what you said (or did)," or "Help me," or "I'm sad / mad / confused." That is what we do. We may all, occasionally, still sulk, grow quiet, walk away, hide tears, try to ignore someone, act as if we're not as hurt as we are, flick on the TV, go back to our books, play too many games on one screen or another, or go in search of the cookies. The difference is, when we are done with that, we all always wind up at the kitchen counter or on the family room couch, talking about what's wrong. Crying. Yelling, and then hugging, talking some more.

And so, living like that for eighteen years, living with a husband I can talk to, and with two children we're raising to understand it is okay to say what we feel, what we think, what we're pissed off or sad or worried about, I am unprepared for what happens on the second night that I am in my parents' house—now only my mother's house—the night before my father's wake.

In their capacious ranch house, there is a wide and long counter that separates the oversized tiled kitchen from the enormous Cathedral-ceilinged family room. Along the counter are four chairs, facing the kitchen, and this is where my parents mostly ate, where my father read the newspaper, where my mother folds the clean laundry, where any casual guest is seated for a cup of coffee or a glass of iced tea.

My mother is standing in the kitchen, leaning on the counter, and across from where I sit, with Cathy, who is still jet-lagged, and her twenty-seven-year-old daughter, Holly, who called her grandfather Popsicle and has left her new husband in Atlanta to fly in for the wake. Cathy is at one end of the counter, and I am at the other end, Holly between us, the three of us making a kind of a lopsided triangle with my mother. Cathy has been in oldest-sibling, all-business mode since she arrived. Holly is quiet and subdued except when she's quoting scripture (something that makes my Catholic mother wince and roll her eyes). My mother seems so worn out, not just from the grief and stress of the last three days but also from the months of daily trips to the hospital, rehab, and nursing home. Cathy and I keep asking her to please sit down or, even better, to lie down on the family room couch. She won't. Staying upright seems to give her some strength. For the first time since I've arrived, I have nothing that must be done, or at least nothing that can be done late on a Sunday.

That's when, so to speak, finally, *it all hits me.*

His life, their life together—it's all over.

My life with two parents is over.

My father is dead.

My father, whom I never knew well, is gone, and now it's too late to know him.

For the first time since touching down in Vegas the morning before, I cry, quietly, my head angled down. I study my tea. The tissue box is within arm's reach, and I take one, dab at my eyes. At first, the three of them continue talking and don't notice my tears, or at least, don't say anything. But soon, Cathy reaches over and strokes my feet, which are propped across Holly's lap. Holly starts massaging my calves. By then, I'm slobbering.

That's when my mother says, "What are *you* crying about."

It is not a question. Her thin, hard lips form a quivering straight line. I cannot quite discern the meaning at first of what seems like sarcasm or accusation. Why wouldn't I be crying? My father's dead. Tomorrow is his wake. Am I not allowed to cry because he wasn't my favorite parent? Because decades ago when I was a snotty teenager, I wasn't nice to him? Because I didn't find some miraculous way to get him, or both of them, moved to New Jersey? That makes no sense. But then I start to understand what she does *not* say.

This is my serving of guilt for not having flown out between August and now, as she'd more or less begged me on the phone every week in September, in October. I'd tried to explain about paychecks, a son who didn't tolerate change well, and being in graduate school. I knew of course, I could have arranged it, accepted the stress and difficulty of doing so, quit things or deferred things or asked for a loan. But I didn't, and now is not the time for explanations. I know she will, eventually, regret (but not say she's sorry for) the barb, that she'll be compassionate later, as is her way, that now she's just wounded, striking out.

I stop crying about my father, but cry on, thinking about all the times she's struck out at my father similarly, only I hadn't seen it as that, then, but only as old-married-couple-bickering. What did I owe him then, or now? My sister increases the pressure of her hand on my calf, tosses me an expression that says, *let it go.* I decide that grief's insidious grip on my mother, on anyone, is both unpredictable and sharp, unrelenting and apt to sweep an angry path past any other untethered emotion. I let it go, like in the old days when I grew up in a house of throbbing silences. I wish I were back home, my home, where it would have been all right to cry at the kitchen counter, where someone would hand me tissues and cry with me.

Las Vegas, it turns out, is a curious place to carry out death rituals—or maybe it's just the Las Vegas I experience that week. We're booked for what I am told are standard wake visiting hours at the nondenominational funeral home nearest my parents' house: from 1 p.m. to 8 p.m. *Seven hours, straight?* Yes, I'm told, because those who work any of the three round-the-clock shifts in hotels or casinos are likely to have some time off during that time period. I don't really buy it, but I have no choice. Used to Italian Catholic funeral homes in New Jersey that have afternoon visiting hours of 2 to 4 p.m., a break for dinner, then resuming with evening hours from 7 to 9 p.m., I'm flummoxed, and I'm worried how my mother will find the stamina for that long of a stretch.

No worries, I'm told, there's a family break room where we can order in dinner and rest, and it has full-size windowed walls to the viewing room and the lobby, so if new visitors stop in, we can dart out to greet them. And so, the next day, we are on display in our glass box, eating deli sub sandwiches for dinner, feeling awkward and doubly sad.

Very early on Monday morning (who can sleep, after all?), my mother decides that nothing in her vast walk-in closet (larger than one of my sons' bedroom), will be appropriate for the wake. Incredulous, I pull a half-dozen black dresses from the clothing bar. They're nixed, and we're off to a store, open very early, like everything in this unusual city.

Inside, we pass the men's department.

"I'm going to miss shopping for him. I guess I can't buy men's clothes anymore," she says in a voice thin and weary.

Of all the ways in which I had imagined her missing my father, this was not one I had even remotely considered, but which makes sense. I thought about all the perfectly pressed pants hanging in my parents' room-sized closet, the seersucker shirts on the right side, the long-sleeve velour pullovers for the mild Las Vegas winters on the left. I thought of dress shoes, loafers, and summertime whites, paired and evenly aligned on racks below. I thought about his armoire, stacked with cardigans and v-neck sweater vests in blues, gray, browns, and cream. I thought of dozens of cufflink pairs in boxes from stores that no longer exist, in the top left-hand drawer of the triple dresser. I thought about unopened packages of blue striped boxer shorts and sleeveless ribbed undershirts my mother stockpiled, and when my father complained that all of his had holes in them, how happy she had been to retrieve them, and how ridiculous I had always thought her for taking pride in what seemed to me a subservient deed. It was all something, which I—with a husband who buys all his own clothes at the warehouse club—always failed to appreciate.

I see what she was up to now, every time she had stepped into a men's clothing store, into the closet, up to the ironing board. My mother had loved being in charge of my father's wardrobe, knowing which colors he should wear, when sports jackets needed elbow patches. She decided which ties went with what suits, when to take out the summer-weight suits, how to store away the Mohair overcoats. It was a currency, an offering.

"I guess I can shop for the rest of the men in the family," she says vaguely, and I think about her moving through Macy's or Dillard's, picking out shirts, PJs, belts, sweaters, for her son, son-in-law, grandsons, and great-grandson. I know that she will do this, and I know that the garments she selects will all be the right size and color and style because that is one of her gifts. But I am heartsick that while these things may travel home with her as usual, in crisp shopping bags, they won't then be emptied with pride, my father watching, occasionally fingering a shirt, smoothing the nap of a pant leg. He'd always know, and announce, the type of fabric, the weave, and its relative merits. *Beautiful worsted wool. Gorgeous jacquard. Nice poly cotton blend.*

Back home, she pairs her new black sweater with an elegant but rarely worn black skirt she already had, black shoes, a black belt, and black purse. Cathy and I both tell her that, in 2006, it is not necessary, especially in still-hot October, for a woman in the American Southwest to dress like an old-school, mid-century Italian widow. She waves her arms at us.

On the way from her house to the funeral home for the wake, my mother insists we stop at the dry cleaners, where my father had been a regular for twenty-five years, always walking in smiling, teasing the counter girls, asking after everyone's health, kidding that the prices were too high, leaving a tip. Nina, the shop owner, is silent, shakes her head, and reaches across the counter to squeeze my mother's black-clad arm.

The next day, Mom says she wants to sort some new clothing my father had never worn. From his armoire, she pulls pullovers, pajamas, and shirts, and we make piles on the king-sized bed. One pile to Goodwill, the other to the church clothing drive; these for the Mexican day laborers who help the landscaper on Thursdays.

In the closet, I recognize the suit my father wore to his grandson's wedding four years before, back when he could still stand up straight and dance with my mother, the suit he wore to Holly's wedding eighteen months before, when he could still understand most of what was happening. There are the straight-leg Levi's I bought him fifteen years ago which he never wore, folded neatly over a wooden hanger; and the flannel-lined, comfort-waist, relaxed-fit, brushed-denim ones I sent from L.L.Bean last winter when he said his legs were always cold, and which my mother tells me were his newest favorites.

I linger with my right arm up the left sleeve of one of his tweed sports jackets, the one with the suede elbows patches he wore so often. We teased him for impersonating a college professor. I think he liked that, maybe (who knows) secretly yearned for an academic life he never had any opportunity to even dream about. We often called him a frustrated philosopher, but it was not a joke, not really. All of his adult life, people he knew, in business or over the luncheonette counter, would remark, "That Tony is such a smart man" or "Your father is very wise."

We don't get very far on the clothing-sorting project, just the armoire and the first few inches of the closet rack. It's too much, Mom says, too much. I let it go. It can wait, I decide, and it does; it is all waiting for me four years later, when my mother is in the hospital and she asks me to handle disposing of his clothing while she's not there in the house to watch.

Then, I will find the two-dozen sports jackets, twice as many suits, and dozens more pants and dress shirts, all still neatly hung. I will go through pockets and find nothing. I will make tidy stacks in the roomy trunk of his old Grand Marquis and drive it all over to the Salvation

Army, where I'm told everything must be stuffed into tied black plastic trash bags, and an attendant thrusts a dozen in my hand. I will stand in the parking lot there, crushing and shoving all of my father's spotless clothing, so meticulously cared for, twist the plastic ties and hoist the bags into dirty canvas hoppers. Years later I will wonder why I didn't keep at least one suit, never mind that it would not have fit my husband, would have been too big for either son, and out of style too. I will mean to stop in the Salvation Army office for a donation receipt (I can hear my father: "It's a tax write-off!"), but I will forget. I will remember driving away, turning off the air conditioning, opening all the windows, letting the dry broiling heat and sand in, helping me feel grounded somehow, as if what I'd just done was good or real.

My father wore a burnished gold ring with a domed oval sapphire stone for thirty years, its star glinting from the smooth blue surface, flashing when he turned the pages of the newspaper. Other than his wedding band, which was plain gold, and a topaz ring he wore on occasion, this is the only jewelry I regularly saw him wear, and he stopped wearing it when arthritis claimed his metacarpal knuckles. The morning after the wake, I see it, in a vintage leather ring box on top of his dresser. My mother cannot decide whether to give it to her son, or to one of her four grandsons, or to her only great-grandson.

I tell her Gary should have it, and though it won't fit his finger, maybe he'll get it made bigger. All the while I'm thinking, it would slide easily on Sean's slim hand, but he is too young for that kind of ring, that family weight. I seem to remember a story of how Dad bought it on a Cuban gambling trip in the late fifties or early sixties. I will always remember my father's hand with that ring in place, dinking against the tabletop when he moved an ashtray into position, tapping against his wedding band when he applauded at the theater or when I won a sixth-place green ribbon at a horse show, or clapping at my boys in their infant seats, their wet mouths curving into smiles.

When my father visits me, after he's dead, I notice the ring on his finger.

7

What Happens in Vegas

WE TALK.

We talk, my dead father and I.

I know, even at the moment of our first *conversation*, that the idea is ridiculous. Surely I am talking to myself, to some wishful memory. Yet, there he is, at his marble-top desk at 1:15 a.m. in his Las Vegas house. No, I am the one sitting at his desk. Well, nothing makes sense. I won't even remember this until later, at least a month later, this first encounter, the feeling. I don't connect these talks (is that what they are?) to my wish to not go anywhere (like a cemetery) to visit my dead father. I don't see the logical way I've made it easy for him to instead "visit" me. But, we talk.

Not about anything important. Not yet. Chitchat. Small talk.

He asks me what I'm doing up so late. I remind him that's my way. I ask him why he's here—at all. He says he's just checking in on me.

On those silent nocturnal treks from my bedroom at one end of his airy barbell-shaped house, to his den at the other, across the quiet carpeting, I pass by the family room bar crowded with flowers, and hold my nose the way I did when I was a kid passing by the viewing room at funeral homes on the way to the basement lounge.

My father spent a good portion of the time he was at any funeral home on the sidewalk out front, ostensibly to smoke cigarettes. I began to notice—I don't know when, maybe when I thought I had gotten too old for the kids' lounge and took a seat in the back of the viewing room— that my father would make one perfunctory walk past the casket, quickly kiss the grieving widow or adult female children, slap the widower or adult male children on the back, then make for one of the arched doorways, where he stood, arms crossed in front of him, until one or another of the men in the gaggle suggested a smoke.

As a young adult, I began to see that my father also avoided visiting relatives or friends in the hospital who might be in serious condition, that he did not once go to a nursing home until his own father took up residence there, and then only for twenty minutes at a time. He never talked about the inevitability of his own death, except to say a couple of times that he wished to be cremated, and this only came up in the context of some other discussion about, say, the usurious costs of the American funeral industry.

I'm a bit surprised to learn that my father has not purchased a burial plot or mausoleum space either for himself or my mother, either in Las Vegas or back in New Jersey. There is no file in the drawer of his much-loved desk in the den. This circumspect and well-organized man hasn't—like the fathers of many of my friends—marked an easy-to-find file, "When I die," or "Important—Final Requests." He's left nothing in a place where we can find it. This puzzles me; he had always been such a practical, methodical person, who took care of everything. Was it that he hadn't done so until the Alzheimer's took hold, and then if he had done it after that, well, he could just as easily, after dotting *i*'s and crossing *t*'s, have tossed it in the trash barrel in the garage? Without instructions, last wishes, a list of hymns, we know nothing. We wing it.

I lay awake on Sunday night and realize that for all his practical and deliberate and capable qualities, my father was not fearless. I believe my father feared death; he feared a lot of things, it seemed, things that were unlikely to happen but of course sometimes did, justifying the galloping caution he was known for. He'd run with firefighter swiftness to the side of anyone choking, or a knife slipping across an index finger, to the sound of a fall, the sniff of something burning, a minor car accident—things he could do something about.

Maybe his lack of final preparations is simply an unwillingness to take an interest in something he could do nothing about, though for a man who had shielded his wife for fifty-nine years from the mundanity of even paying the water bill, I do wonder how he justified his lack of foresight on her behalf. Then I remember, of course: he knew she would be passed along, in a way, to his son, who would assume the running of her financial life.

When my father's widowed mother, age ninety-three, was dying at his sister's house in Florida, Dad only reluctantly flew there from Las Vegas, and brought only casual clothes. Later that week, my mother packed up a suitcase with three dark suits and pale shirts and calm ties and sober dress shoes, and my brother put it on an airplane to Fort Lauderdale, in the days when you were still allowed to send an unattended piece of luggage.

My mother recalls her husband being relatively unconcerned with the details of his own parents' wakes and funerals, leaving most of it to his siblings. Suddenly, the *Papa's Dead Conversation* seems more logical. When his mother's remaining household goods were being tug-of-warred by his sisters and their children—furniture, appliances, everything he likely paid for—he stayed out of the house and out of the disbursements. He never gave a eulogy.

When my Noni, my mother's mother, was dying the year I was eight, my mother came home from the hospital one night to tell my father, "She keeps asking for you. Anytime she wants something, she keeps saying, 'Get Tony for me. Tony will take care of it.' Maybe you can come with me tomorrow? She's begging for you."

He was the favorite son-in-law.

My father paid many of his mother-in-law's bills, let her live with us for a month after her leg was amputated while she got used to the wooden leg, made sure an illiterate woman with a long-gone bigamist husband wasn't taken advantage of.

But he didn't go to the hospital.

This strikes me odd because it seemed to me my father valued showing up. He may have shown up and stayed silent, been awkward and seemingly disengaged at a moment when he should have been effusive, but he showed up, in person, by telephone, by letter, by his good wishes. Except sometimes it seems, when it involved the approach of death.

Yet, he often told us, "If you take a man's money, you have taken only his money. But when you take a man's time, you take a piece of his life." My father gave out pieces of his life all the time. As a governor of the Clifton Moose Lodge, he worked to raise funds for handicapped and orphaned children. But he did not only persuade his business colleagues to write checks, he made trips to the orphanages and camps and other places Moose funds supported, often traveling to the Midwest by train in the sixties. He wanted to see those funds in action; he wanted to be sure that his time, and everyone's money, was being wisely spent.

But he didn't go to the hospital to see my Noni.

Whenever someone my father knew opened a new business—a restaurant, a shoe store, an accounting office—he was a frequent and loyal patron, often bringing along others, recommending and touting the ventures of his friends and colleagues as if they were all the top of the line. He spent a piece of his life there.

But he didn't spend a piece of it at the hospital visiting his wife's mother.

This seemed, even to me at eight years old, out of character; probably then I would have just said, mean. There were other clues as the years unfolded, that he held a deep-seated fear of mortality. As I write about his death and what comes after, the thing I'd like to tell him, if I could, is this: something does come after. In this world you were so afraid to leave, you're still here, in a way you could never be while shuffling around in your bedroom slippers, nose buried in the newspaper.

Once, during a holiday meal, when talking about—oh I can't even remember what—my father said, "If I should ever die . . ." Gary and I both laughed and simultaneously said, "If?," which brought a quick, humorous end to the discussion.

I sometimes wonder what he had planned to say.

⸻

Occasionally, I'd find my mother crying for her dead mother 20 years, 30 years, and 40 years later, on the anniversary day, which is also the date her first granddaughter was born (though this timing does nothing to mitigate the flow of tears). She cries, too, each time she hears a certain few Italian songs, especially those in a scratchy black-and-white movie she has on videotape. She cries on March 19, St. Joseph's Day, because her mother's first name was Josephine, and each year she sends me $20 so I can put flowers on her mother's grave, which I never visit, not because I didn't love my Noni and not because I don't miss her, but because I prefer to *think about* those who have died instead of "visiting" them.

I always say okay, that I will buy the potted flowers and plant them, or buy the palm cross and pound the short stake into the ground, or lay a plastic evergreen grave blanket in mid-December, and sometimes I do.

I even have photographs of the times I did this, with one or the other of my sons in a stroller nearby or wielding a small child's garden spade. But there are other times that I say okay, but I put the money in my wallet and instead use it toward new eyeglasses for one of my sons, or the basketball league sign-up fee for the other. Once, I used the twenty to buy graham crackers, bananas, and packages of vanilla and chocolate pudding so I could make an icebox cake, such as the kind Noni and Aunt Mary had waiting on Sundays when my mother and I visited while my father sat outside in the car. I never tell my mother that I didn't plant the flowers. I say, "Yes I took care of it" because in my own way I did take care of it—I remembered my Noni. In my own way. But of course, in my own way too, I was lying.

As we're getting dressed for the wake, my mother tells me that two of my father's four surviving sisters—Aunt Carmela, who is married to an Italian and has lived in southern Italy for forty-five years; and Aunt Connie, ninety-one and living in Florida have both asked for pictures of my father in his coffin. I don't think Mom chooses me for this act because she's noticed that death rituals interest me (I certainly never would have discussed it with her, someone who has trouble uttering the word *cancer* out loud). Maybe it's because I am detail oriented, not squeamish, and that, like Cathy, I'm sometimes more understanding than Mom of her own Italian culture. But later I will remember that it was my father, not my mother, who noticed those sorts of things about me. Maybe I'm assigned the photography task because I am the one handy when she remembers the request.

Later, I get curious and do some reading and learn that this reluctance to confront death in photographs is a particular quirk mainly of modern-day Americans, one that foregrounds our reluctance to face so many supposedly unpleasant and natural things. In other societies, in countries below our borders and across oceans, photos of the dead are still commonplace, and until the early twentieth century, both Europeans and Americans regarded such photos as a natural extension of photographing the person throughout his or her life, as is still the custom among some African American cultures. The shocked response when anyone takes postmortem photos now, and especially if the media publish photos of the dead, puzzles me. If we can look at photos of blood-streaked screaming newborns on a hospital scale, veins visible through papery blue skin, testicles engorged, why can we not bear its opposite, the likeness of a dearly loved family member at the end of his or her natural life?

While photo and video tributes now play a significant role in American wakes, memorial services, and funeral masses, and a continuously running DVD loop of photos of the dead person's *life* is okay (talk about a life flashing before our eyes), then why are photos of the dead so taboo? For that matter, why do those collages so rarely include a photo of the dead person near the *end* of life? Wasn't that part of life too?

My husband tells me I'm morbid, this interest in how we handle death, and by extension, how I hope to die. He says that when it's his time, he wants to die in his sleep, while I want to know when death is near; I want to plan and talk about what's coming, make lists, and say goodbye. I want someone to take pictures.

I take my father's casket photos, and Cathy asks that when the photos are developed the next day, I keep them in the envelope in my suitcase so Mom won't see them. Gary says he never wants to see them. When I see the photos the next day, I think my father looks very much like himself. I find my mother's address book, and two heavy-stock note cards, and I slide two photos inside each, and seal and address the envelopes to Avellino and Boca Raton, along with the obituary clipping and short notes about some of the things said by those who came to the wake.

The rest I take home and for a long while, they disappear in my house. I will find them three years later, while clearing clutter from a cabinet in my family room, tucked in apparently without much care, with pictures of my kids' school functions and swimming pool antics and other innocuous events. When I look at them, then, except for the huge nose my father was teased for his entire life, I don't recognize this brown-suited man, this body in a coffin. Did he really look that bad, that much *unlike* himself? Had he really lost that much weight? Was his face really that drained of the intelligence, the compassion I used to think resided so clearly right on its skin? And did I really take those pictures and not see at the time how truly awful they were? Did I really tell friends and relatives, on the phone from Las Vegas, that the funeral home "did a pretty good job"?

Years later, my friend Laraine Herring, who has written about dead fathers and has researched death rituals tells me, "It is well documented that the way we see a corpse of someone we love doesn't yet look like the corpse looks to a detached bystander. We still see who used to live there."

His hands, folded one atop the other in the coffin, *did* appear very much like his hands in life—a bit flaccid but strong and purposeful, wide and pasty. They did, didn't they? I wasn't seeing them as I wished, was I? I might know if I had taken a picture of those hands I so loved and will find myself writing about. But I didn't take that picture.

Mostly, though, when I find the death photos, I will smile and remember how little my father might have cared. I'm glad that those photos exist, though even now they are again lost, perhaps accidentally, perhaps with intention, among the detritus of busy lives, somewhere in the lovely clutter of a house where a family lives, still intact.

Two days after the Vegas service, I notice it is morning in the same instant that I begin to acknowledge what I believe, for me, is true about my father's death: It was preventable. I believe that we should have sued the nursing home where the attendants left my father alone in the bathroom. I believe they, or someone, is accountable. I believe his care was mismanaged from the first day he was admitted to the hospital. I believe the MRI should have been repeated, that the CT scan should have been done *with contrast*. I believe his body should have been autopsied. I believe the cause of death written on the death certificate, *dementia*, is not accurate or at least not complete. I believe it is listed that way, instead of *pneumonia* or *complications from surgery* or *congestive heart failure*, because any of those might imply something might have been done, a treatment attempted, a medication tried.

Or, perhaps his body just gave out.

In my semiawake stupor, I reason only for a second, then I am back to backward thinking. I believe that my father's complaints, at first at home and then later in the hospital and the nursing home, were brushed off because he made so many of them and so often. He was a high-maintenance patient, probably the kind a nurse friend once told me she used to indicate in notes to the next shift with the shorthand PITA (pain in the ass). And so I start to think that someone, someone tired of the endless complaints, a relative, a doctor, nurse, therapist, hospital discharge coordinator—it could even have been me—missed it, ignored the one important and authentic complaint, that, had it been handled differently, could have changed the outcome.

On the other hand, I am relieved that that someone technically could not have been me, because I was tucked away in far off New Jersey. I am also scared that that someone *should* have been me, the only one distant enough to point out what my mother and brother, so close to the daily decisions and drowning under a wave of unfamiliar medical information, could not. The only one who, because she'd once worked for two medical research organizations, knew the language, how to talk to doctors so they would listen and to listen to them and then translate their dense and offhand pronouncements into information, options, tools. But I was physically absent, and often, emotionally walled off by a belief—true or not—that my opinions weren't taken seriously.

I decide I can never say any of these things I am thinking to my mother, about what was done wrong, or not done, and so when I find her at the dining room table that morning, slicing open envelopes containing sympathy cards, I only lean over her from behind, cross my arms over her chest and say, "Oh Mommy."

But I cannot really let it go, and so I go to the place I always go when I need to work something out, the place and activity that help me discover what I am thinking: I go to my notebook. I make another of the lists that take me through life, making order of everything that's chaotic or important, esoteric or trivial.

The title of this one is *The List of Alternative Theories*.

1. What is the nursing home protocol for leaving patients in his condition alone in the bathroom?
2. Maybe 48 years of smoking two or three packs of cigarettes a day took its toll?
3. Did someone made a mistake with a medication?
4. The stroke, the kyphosis, the emphysema, the Alzheimer's.

5. Was Dad's excellent supplemental health insurance coverage a factor when scheduling the second hip operation? More a factor than the unlikelihood he would never get out of bed again?

6. The osteoporosis, the congestive heart failure, the severe arthritis.

7. We can't sue anyone because his body was embalmed before I arrived. (Las Vegas is a fast town.)

8. The myasthenia gravis, the pneumonia, the multiple vitamin deficiencies.

9. Doesn't Alzheimer's take many years to kill? When did it really start?

10. We won't ever really know.

I want to witness my father's coffin enter the crematorium chamber. I don't understand why everyone around me thinks this is strange, macabre, or ridiculous, and according to at least one person, selfish. I simply want to witness this act, the finality of my father's earthly material existence. I suppose you could say I don't want him to be alone, although I unwaveringly believe *that's* the ridiculous part because I understand without equivocation that his soul, his individual personhood, is already gone, or at least is separate from his body. I know this because it makes sense, and also because I've talked to him and I know *he* is not in that coffin. It's complicated.

The crematory director feeds me a line about liability waivers and local health ordinances; when I persist, he proposes he could work it out but that there will be a $400 observation fee. I know I could argue and perhaps prevail, maybe investigate and find this is illegal on his part, but I give up because of my mother's forlorn face and my sister's feverish, anguished pleading to "let it be." Still, I find it hugely disturbing that on a Thursday morning in October, two days after his eightieth birthday, while his two daughters and his wife are trying to busy themselves with minor household chores, and his son has gone back to work, six miles away my father—no, my father's body—is lowered (or slid?—I'm told there is a conveyer belt of sorts involved) into flames.

That morning, in the enormous home he financed and helped design and so loved, we are moving about the spacious rooms trying not to bump into one another. A year later, I will read Kate Braestrup's memoir *Here if You Need Me,* about her early widowhood, and she tells of how she insisted on being the one to bathe and dress her husband before he was placed in the coffin. She insists, despite vigorous objections, because she knows the laws of her state, knows she is allowed to do so, and so she does. When I read this, I will chastise myself for not knowing if the line about local health ordinances was true or what Nevada law says about being present at cremations.

But on that morning, when I know what is happening across town, I feel profoundly that I have disappointed my father. I wanted to prove to him that I was strong and able to do the hard stuff, the kind of person I always imagined he'd wanted me to be.

Betrayal is the word that keeps going round in my brain. Betrayal and, *witness.* No one he loved is there to witness the end of his corporeal body. (I also inexplicably can't get out of my mind a scene at the end of the original 1960 *Ocean's 11* movie. In a Las Vegas funeral home, the thieves sit vigil, having hidden the stolen millions in the one fallen thief's casket, which suddenly, unexpectedly travels from chapel to incinerator via a curtained door in the wall.) I try to unpack the emotion, the guilt, and the feeling that I'm missing out on something interesting about death and realize that perhaps I feel this way because no one was there either to witness the end of his physical life, when he died alone in his sleep. I remember something I heard in a movie once: "Make no mistake. We all die alone."

That night, I thrash under the comforter, rewinding in my brain yet once again, the tape that begins with my father complaining of pain in his right leg, then hip, months before the stroke. For at least ten years, he had been extremely arthritic, and so everyone, even his rheumatologist, all attributed the new leg and hip pain to the disease staking new territory. It had happened before, when his spine became involved, when his left hand was suddenly always cold, when he could no longer lie on his right shoulder in bed. It made sense. But it may have meant something else.

I begin to ask questions (of no one, of myself, of the air): Should the rheumatologist have recommended an orthopedic consult way back in June? Should we have intuited that this new pain was different?

Was it a stroke or something else, even then? Or a stroke *and* something else?

I get up, open my notebook, make yet another new list, this one a backward-chronological timeline, vaguely noting approximate dates and physical events. I fill two pages with single-spaced notes, littered with question marks, capital letters, underlines, and arrows. When the arrows at the bottom of page 2 point back to the top of page 1, I hear my father. "It's over," he says. "That's enough." I throw the pen on the floor and smack the book closed.

People say, "You cannot go back," but you can, in your head. Problem is, it only leads back to the present, where the dead are still gone. I recognize that this is circular, downward-spiraling thinking, fast and furious and of little use. I get back in bed, no longer thrashing, but I do not sleep either, though I seem to "wake up" some time later. There is a particularly deceptive form of rest, I discover in the two weeks in Las Vegas, that masquerades as sleep: one's eyes are closed, sounds recede, breathing slows, but all the time, you are aware of not sleeping, or of sleeping but not resting, and of moving and repositioning and being slightly awake yet also dreaming, of seeing events and feeling emotions and hoping these are dreams but being just alert enough to know they are not. Instead of waking from this type of sleep, I simply get up and begin to move through the day, only upright and with my eyes open.

For the next couple of days, while Cathy and I are both still in Las Vegas, I remind myself that all these questions, the speculation, the anger and guilt and frustration about his care and demise, and especially the lists, will not help Mom. She believes doctors always know the answer. She wants to know it was out of everyone's hands, that things happened the way they were going to happen, no matter what. The questions can wait. I'm the only one who wants to ask them. So I ask only myself, and provide myself with half answers, built out of nothing, out of hope, regret.

Enough.

Craving distraction, I partially unload the cabinet where my mother keeps new DVDs she and my father had not yet watched. Not that he'd had ever had the idea of unwrapping a new DVD and watching it together; that was his wife's territory. He didn't even know how to work the DVD player, or before that, the VHS player, and everyone often teased him for his bumbling attempts to work any kind of gadget, electronic or otherwise. Funny, though, how he once understood how to operate metal balers and automated fabric double-folding machines, and how the reverse osmosis water filter system in the house worked. As I'm sorting, I compare his ability to understand complex abstract concepts like supply-side economics or global monetary markets, against his comical shaking of his head and waving of his hands at the VCR and his pronouncement that he "can't figure that damn thing out." We all always thought he was being lazy, or unimaginative, or just rude, that this may have provided just the right exit strategy, so he could hibernate yet another evening in his den with *Money Watch* while my mother watched old black-and-white movies in the cavernous family room alone. But now I consider that something else may have been at work, some neurological short circuit that stymied him more than us, and I'm sorry for every time I made fun of his frustrated aborted attempts at technology.

At first my idea is merely to organize the DVDs, to give myself something to do so I won't have to attend to some additional death task my mother thinks is essential but I think is nonsense. We *all* need something to do, so I root around for something Mom, Cathy, and I can watch together in relatively companionable silence or at least something to provide background to our sometimes strained chitchat.

Most are classic motion pictures from decades past, and I am not in the mood for frivolity or westerns or comedy. There are some documentaries too, and because the cover photographs on one of them reminds us of our parents as they were in photos from early in their marriage, Cathy and I decide on *The Greatest Generation,* Tom Brokaw's paean to the men and women of World War II.

Early in the film, I can see it making my mother noticeably uncomfortable, especially when I casually ask if certain of my uncles were in the service. I already know that my father was called but then exempted from service because of a chronic stomach ulcer and other ailments. Still, he was patriotic and circumspect about duty, like most men of his generation, and I wonder if we chose this film because my sister and I just want to be in their company. We switch it off halfway through, Cathy perhaps exaggerating that she's exhausted and Mom quickly agreeing, getting up off the sofa with more energy than I've seen all week. I slide the disc from the player, place it back in its case, and linger a bit at the photo collage of proud once-young men on the back cover.

Over the next week in Vegas, I pause to watch every gray-haired, neatly dressed, shuffling old gentleman I see in the grocery store, at the airport, bank, bookstore. There seem to be so many who remind me of my father. In church on Sunday, I study an elderly, kind-faced man, wearing the exact immaculate pale yellow cotton zip jacket my father favored in fall, as he takes a half step back to allow his wife to precede him in the communion line.

Surely, around the next corner, or the next, my father will appear.

When flipping TV channels in the coming couple of years, I will pay more than the usual amount of attention to certain famous older men I remember my father liked, or who share some particular characteristic with him; men who remind me of him, like Paul Newman, Kirk Douglas, Larry King, Eli Wallach, Tony Bennett, Dick Van Dyke, Yogi Berra (who lives two miles from me, and from whom we all suspect Dad took punditry lessons). As long as they are around, I know there's a chance I can surreptitiously catch a glimpse of my father.

When Paul Newman dies in the fall of 2008, I reel a little. There goes another eighty-something-year-old gentle man, humble and humbled by his own success, with a vulnerability that is somehow a strength, another man whose hand gestures were poetry. In 1983, I was part of the public relations staff for the National Horse Show in New York City. One of my assignments was to escort to the press room the parents of the winner of the Maclay national equitation finals, and to make contact with them in advance to go over logistics. The parents in this case could have been Paul Newman and Joanne Woodward, whose daughter Clea, in a field of more than two hundred, was favored to win. After a frustrating search, I finally found them, seated not in the VIP section but alone in an otherwise empty upper tier of Madison Square Garden.

"Excuse me, Mr. Newman, I'll be right over here. If she wins..."

He smiled at me, kindly. "Oh, darling, if she wins, we'll be long gone."

When I told this story to my father the next day, he said, "Of course that's what he'd do. That's class."

As each one of these old men dies or fades from public life, I designate others to take their place, men slightly older than my father was at his death, older than he ever got to be.

Anthony and Domenica Chipolone dancing at their wedding, Clifton, New Jersey, 1947.

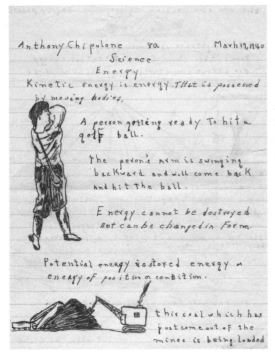

A page from fourteen-year-old Tony's eighth-grade school notebook, 1940.

Tony in his early twenties.
Courtesy of Cathy Chipolone-Collins.

Tony and wife, Mickey, flanked by his parents, Frank and Louise Chipolone, early 1950s.

Tony holding one-year-old Lisa, 1960.

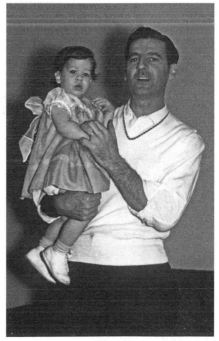

The author, about age four, with siblings, Cathy and
Gary, and mother, Mickey, around 1963.

Lisa, about seven, with parents at a showroom, probably Las Vegas
or Miami Beach.

Hike

Dr. Gerace said a decision has not been made which grade would be part-time. But, he indicated the fifth grade was receiving strong consideration.

Residents questioned him on new programs instituted in the high school. One of these cited was the data processing class.

Recalling last year's $100,000 budget cut, they asked Dr. Gerace how it was possible to add new programs under such conditions.

Dr. Gerace said: "Of course this budget can also be reduced. But I think you're lowering your sights when you do."

Last year's budget was trimmed to $2,031,601 after two defeats.

Bloomingdale Cuts $54,000 From Budget

BLOOMINGDALE — The Board of Education caucused for 1½ hours late last night and came up with a decision to cut $54,000 from the school budget.

Instead of $38,000 being taken out of surplus funds for capital expenditures, $60,000 will be transferred from that account.

Instructional salaries will be cut $20,000 and transportation $12,000, to reduce the amount to be raised by taxes by $54,000.

The board went into the closed session after the public budget hearing at which more than 75 persons heard the board refuse to take a stand on double sessions, saying that was a matter to be decided after the Feb. 13 election.

Board President Arthur Vandervoort said the increase in students left three alternatives, bigger classes, eliminating kindergarten or split sessions. The portable classrooms installed this year were temporary and could not be added to, he said.

Councilmen Walter Price, Albert Pacifico, and Howard Smith all spoke out against the board's insistence on maintaining what they consider too large a surplus. Smith pointed out the budget lists a surplus of $110,327 of which only $38,000 is allocated. Estimating an additional surplus of approximately $55,000, Smith said next year it would total more than $127,000.

—Staff Photo by Dan Oliver

Anthony Chipolone surveys burned-out building.

Big Clifton Blaze Blamed On Burglars

CLIFTON — Yesterday morning's $100,000 blaze in a factory building at 310 Colfax Avenue was almost certainly touched off by burglars, authorities believe.

A quantity of copper was found to be missing from Athenia Metal and Waste Co., which shares the building with Cath-Gar Textiles, a fabric salvage operation. The textile company was nearly destroyed and the roof of the 2-year-old building fell in.

After 25 firemen brought the blaze under control around 2.90 a.m., investigators found that a hole had been chopped in the cinder block wall at the rear and the metal reinforcement in the concrete snipped.

"The overhead door at the rear was also partly open," reported Fire Chief Stephen J. Lendl Jr., "so that it is possible the intruders had to leave in a hurry, perhaps because the fire started, and used the door."

Opening the door touched off a burglar alarm, and the patrolmen answering that turned in the fire alarm.

The local newspaper account of the 1968 overnight fire that destroyed a portion of Cath-Gar Textiles.

Lisa, twelve, with Uncle "Silvio" and racehorse Chester Devil, after a win at Pocono Downs. Gary and wife, Susan, are at far right.

Tony with his first grandchild, Anthony Wyman, 1977.

Lisa (*left*) and friend Laurie, with Tony and Mickey at the Las Vegas Hilton, around 1975.

Lisa competing with Cool Shoes in a hunter class in Ocala, during the Florida horse show circuit, 1983. Courtesy of Pennington Galleries.

Lisa dancing with Dad at her wedding, 1988.

The author's sons, Sean and Paul, loved to crawl into bed with their PopPop when he stayed at their New Jersey home. Circa 2000.

At a charity event in Las Vegas, Gary and Tony, posed with legendary UNLV basketball coach Jerry Tarkanian.

Tony at his granddaughter Holly's graduation from Wheaton College in Massachusetts, 2000.

Tony got a kick out of meeting another "Chip" at Disney-land, 1997.

Tony laughed at himself when the family gave him rolls of duct tape, on Christmas at Lisa's house, 1990.

Lisa's two favorite men: husband, Frank, and her father, at Dad's seventy-fifth birthday party.

Tony and his firstborn, Cathy, dancing at her daughter's wedding in Atlanta, 2005.

Courtesy of Cathy Chipolone-Collins.

Tony in his final years, with wife, Mickey, on an outing to the Strip.

Even on his last visit to Lisa's home in New Jersey, Tony made sure to pick up a fresh loaf of Italian bread every day.

Frank, Lisa, Sean, and Paul, April 2016.

Tony with author's son Paul, 1999. This is the photo the author was looking at the morning her father died.

Original family at Gary's wedding, 1972.

8

Leaving Las Vegas

SURELY, WE COULD HAVE handled it through the mail. Or, online. I know this. But my mother wants to go to the Social Security office in person, doesn't want to wonder if the mail got to the right person, at the right time. Doesn't want the first of the next month to come and go without a check in the correct, proper, legal amount. So we make the easy five-mile drive to the modern low-slung office building on a busy road in a mixed residential and business neighborhood.

We are here to report my father's death, which will increase the amount of my mother's social security check, but will stop the larger monthly check in my father's name. Another loss. There is a computer terminal immediately inside the door, and we are required to punch through several screens to specify the reason for our visit. "Other" seems the only appropriate choice. I have the death certificate, my father's birth certificate, driver's license, and Social Security card in a manila envelope. Like at a deli counter, we are issued a stub with a number on it, and the screen tells us to be seated.

When it is our turn, a tactful clerk with a musical Spanish accent guides us through the procedure of reporting a death. My father died mid-month, but we learn that we must return the entire amount of the Social Security check that arrived on October 1, and because my mother has naturally already deposited this check, we are in the awkward position of having to write a check *to* Social Security. Next month, he explains gently, in addition to a check in her new amount, Mom will also receive another in the amount of $253, a one-time "death benefit." I want to quip, *Who exactly does his death benefit?* But I don't. I stay quiet. I listen.

Her new monthly check will be about $250 more each month than she was currently receiving, but this will be around $975 less than the two of them were receiving combined. I'm thinking that, except for Dad's medical bills, newspaper subscriptions, and some food and incidentals, her expenses will be about the same, living in the same house, paying the property same taxes. This is not good news.

My father's Social Security check usually went to pay household expenses, and hers was the one they cashed and used for restaurant meals, travel, gifts, and other miscellany. Of course there is other money, stashed in long-term savings accounts, CDs, checking accounts, and money markets, the profits from polyester. But without a pension or life insurance pay-outs, she may need to use as little of that as possible, a hedge against any possible nursing home or other elder care costs. My mother finds it extremely difficult to accept a less expensive brand of toilet paper when she is a visitor in my house, so I wonder how a drastic shift in how she will have to apportion her funds might play out. In one of my many selfish acts in the two weeks that I spend with her in Vegas, I decide that this will be my brother's problem, not mine.

Already, in the months before he died, when it became apparent that my father would either never come home, or at least certainly never again deal with the checkbook, my mother had asked her son to assume control of their finances. Although for decades she's competently handled a personal checking account for her department store charge accounts and mail order gifts, she is convinced that she cannot be in command of the ongoing, nonfrivolous demands of the household checkbook, or read and file the few statements that arrive about their now-slimmed investments. I try to talk my mother into staying involved, and taking an interest in the day-to-day expenses, but perhaps true to her generation, she insists a man must do that. I don't agree, but if she won't do it herself, then after all it's likely what Dad had foreseen, and why Gary already knows everything about their finances.

At the Social Security office, there are new citizens proudly showing the papers that qualify them for Social Security numbers. There are young women there to adopt their new husbands' last names. The man who is helping us says he is sorry for my mother's loss. He tells us we did not have to come in person.

He had a way, my father, a very slow and deliberate way, of moving through a room—any room—and touching things in his path, often when someone else was trying to talk to him. Adjusting the stack of mail, toying with bric-a-brac, neatening coffee table magazines, repositioning kitchen canisters, straightening things on a shelf. He would move each item a fraction of an inch maybe, lining them up neatly, straightening objects into a more symmetrical fashion. Dad never said, "Why is this here?" or "Let me straighten up," the way my mother always did; he just silently manipulated the environment, ever so slightly.

I used to think he was fiddling around because he found what I was saying to be unimportant. But when I learned that some people with Asperger's Syndrome find it hard to meet others' eyes during conversation, and that they like to line up physical objects, I wondered. Yet, I also chose to see what he was doing all that time as symbolic of what he was doing in life: trying to make everything pleasing, to make things right, because that's what he did: he fixed things.

Then again, maybe it was just a nervous tic.

He did something similar in conversations, particularly with his adult children, weighing in on something that he needn't worry about, or that he couldn't do anything about anyway: trying to impose order, or fix things for others. He'd pester me to call the airlines and "reconfirm" my flight (though I explained many times that it's all done online now and that travelers have not been reconfirming flights for a decade). But he also had an unusual mantra for someone who worried so much: "No news is good news." This was his way to explain why a traveling family member had not yet called home. I tried not to call too often with bad news.

He'd ask how much I was paid for a magazine article, then pronounce, "Pah! Those publishers are scoundrels." I thought he was obtuse, refusing to change with the times. That he was stubbornly exaggerating, refusing to face the reality of my mediocre talent.

Once in my early twenties my four-wheel drive vehicle (paid for by him, of course) conked out, and I needed to get from one horse show to another, a packed schedule leaving no time to car shop. He immediately offered me the use of his Lincoln for a few weeks, the largest, most luxurious model, and I'd reacted as if he wanted to hold my hand at a job interview.

In the days after the wake, however, I rethink it all. I wonder if, like his habits and quirks, his opinions and beliefs, like his Listerine breath and Vitalis hair, the bad jokes and overcautious bromides, these tiny movements and pecking reminders, were only the packaging, some-thing I could have looked past, if I had had the right mix of curiosity and compassion, then.

Instead, I had loved, and cringed at, most everything about him. I secretly admired his outdated chivalric stance, despised his overprotec-tive inquisitiveness. Only at the end—no, past the end—do I really see that it all was just his way, and not judgment, not passive-aggressive reproof. I imagine him even now, wandering into the bedroom in his house, the one everyone always called "Lisa's room" (though I'd only lived there part time for six months after college), finding me at the desk, fingers on keyboard, and asking me what I'm working on, saying, "Humph," and on his way out, arranging the spilled contents of my travel toiletries bag in a pleasing order.

The day after the cremation, the funeral director enters her office carry-ing a cardboard box that could be mistaken for a parcel UPS might have just dropped off, and perhaps did. On it is pasted a paper label that reads,

This box contains the cremated remains
of Anthony L. Chipolone

The box is sealed with packing tape, and when first Gary then the funeral director try to yank any side open, the packing tape holds fast and leaves little space for a finger. For a brief moment, I think about all the boxes my father wrapped and sealed and shipped me over the years—college care packages, gifts for my sons, birthday presents my mother had wrapped first with floral paper—and how it was a standing family joke that if Dad taped up a box, you can forget about prying it open with anything less than the huge ungainly pair of fabric shears we each have in our houses and which used to live in his polyester factory. I push the thought away, because it reminds me that his boxes were like him—hard to penetrate, reliably filled with both predictable and sur-prising contents, and always represented security—but not before Gary jokes, "Of course we can't get it open! It's one of Dad's boxes."

There is a short fruitless search for a scissor or letter opener before Gary finally pulls one side open to discover two interlocking polysty-rene packing pieces. When pried apart, they reveal the box my mother has chosen—of dark gleaming wood, with a carved mountain scene on the front, very like a jewelry box, and about the shape and size of a four-slice toaster.

The funeral director hands my mother a small plastic bag containing my father's wedding band, the Moose pin from his lapel, and the serviceable, inexpensive leather wristwatch he favored for decades though he could have long afforded something flashier. Where are his eyeglasses, we all want to know? They were on his face in the casket during the wake (we'd insisted, against the funeral director's advice; he just wouldn't look like himself without them), and the director had calmly assured us that they would be taken off and placed with his other personal items before he was sent for cremation. I watched the casket closure but can't remember if they were still on his face or not. What had I been looking at? Think. But the glasses are nowhere, they are gone, burnt probably, or would they melt? My mother is shaky, her mouth twitches. I comment that Dad never could keep track of his glasses anyway, which is universally true (we were always phoning restaurants and stores to see if they were found), but this does little to smooth the moment. Loss follows loss.

Because he was cremated, we have no need for discussions about whether to bury him in the Nevada desert or in the New Jersey ground from which he sprung. We place "DAD" on the family room bar that was rarely used to serve alcoholic drinks, though a sign proclaiming, "Tony's Bar" hangs over the sink, just above the mounted barracuda caught on a Florida fishing trip in the seventies. We flank his wooden box with flowers that have been arriving at the house for days, and with large framed photos—my parents' wedding photo, my father and Gary on his wedding day, and a color photo of my father, at age thirty-five, lean and attractive, holding me, as a two-year-old. I had gotten it restored and enlarged and presented it to him on his seventieth birthday because I could not think of one thing he needed.

I cook a simple dinner of pasta and semihomemade tomato sauce, and when we sit I complain that it was tacky of the funeral director to hand a widow a cardboard box. Couldn't she at least have opened it before we arrived at the appointed time, taken the wooden "urn" out, wiped off the flecks of stray polystyrene, then place it on her glass desk?

My brother reminds me that it is part of authentication, to assure the family that the contents inside the sealed box were not tampered with since being swept from the crematory chamber into a plastic bag that lies, unseen, inside the box. This makes no sense to me; after all, out of our sight, which is where those details were handled, anything could have occurred, anyone's remains could be in there, or nothing at all, or just a couple of heavy books.

Once placed on the bar, the cremains box could be any decorative object, a cutlery chest, or a humidor, any attractive object built to hold stuff, picked up perhaps on one of my parents' trips to Hawaii, Sedona, the Bahamas. We talk about the box needing an engraved plate. Back in New Jersey, at the same cramped trophy shop where I order Boy Scout plaques, the one that smells of plastic, I order one, and the clerk tells me my father's gleaming plaque will be ready "in a jiffy."

Later, Mom will move the polished wooden box from the family room, to where she wants it, atop my father's side of the triple dresser in their bedroom. I think of it, of him, there with her again. It doesn't occur to me for at least five more years that there was never any discussion among Mom and the siblings about divvying up the ashes. Later, I'd hear about friends doing this, having parts of their parents in pretty ceramic boxes.

The cremains remain on his side of the bureau, except for a few days during an unfortunate episode two years later. I learn of it when I arrive to care for my mother after a heart attack (swapping roles with Cathy, who had just done a three-week stint), and I ask Mom if everything went okay.

"She put him on the shelf in the closet in his den," my mother says.

"Him?"

"Your father."

"Why?"

"Who the hell knows? Some bullshit about how I might feel better if I didn't have a visual reminder every day. As if need a reminder that my husband's dead!"

I think of the kindness and well-intentioned compassion that runs so naturally through my sister's veins, and I know both that I'm not getting the whole story and that sometimes her well-meaning attempts to help others feel better backfire because in this family of our origin no one especially wants to address feelings.

The future fate of the cremains box is decided four years after my father dies, when I am told to purchase for my mother (in advance this time), a $7,000 mausoleum drawer at a cemetery five miles from my house; it is the only nearby cemetery to allow cremains to be placed inside a spouse's coffin.

I will also have the choice, then, to purchase a mausoleum drawer with or without a permanent copper flower vase affixed on the front. I choose one without.

The night after the cremains box arrives at the house—while Mom, Cathy, and Holly debate what to do about dinner—I go in search of my father's copy of Kahlil Gibran's *The Prophet,* one of his favorite books. It is, secretly, one of mine too, though I always hope that if one of my literary friends asks me to name a favorite book that I remember to say *Middlemarch.*

My father's original 1923 edition has a cloth cover, turned-down page corners, passages underlined in pencil, a bound-in bookmark ribbon. Fingering the pages and skimming the text ignite a memory from when I was a teenager of my father reading the book one winter night alone in his den while the rest of the family was watching something on HBO. This dispatches a tremor in my hand and a shiver down the back of my neck. Although the idea feels foolish and maudlin, it is as if I can hear the music of my father's soul, writ there. He passed on to me this love for the power of words, powerfully arranged, for poetry and the music inside prose too. The book flaps opens on its own to Gibran's section "On Children," where my father has underscored, "Your children are not your children. . . their souls dwell in the house of tomorrow, which you cannot visit. . ."

The words seem familiar not only because I have read them before, but because I so clearly remember my father once paraphrasing it, telling one of his contemporaries who had been complaining about the choices of his adult children: "Your children are only loaned to you." I had once discounted this remark as my father's nicely worded excuse for being a distant parent, uninvolved in my adult decisions.

I put his copy back on his bookshelf, knowing my mother's taste in books will let it rest there, undisturbed, and hoping that maybe one day it will travel back home with me. I cannot take it now, though I can't explain to myself why I feel it must stay here, and when I do get back to New Jersey, it is the one thing I regret not pilfering. Back home, I do have my own copy, a more modern printing tagged with yellow sticky notes along the page "On Marriage," which I consulted when choosing readings for my wedding.

Later, when I pick up Chinese food, I hear one of my father's favorite songs, "What a Wonderful World," on the car radio, his car radio, and Louis Armstrong's deeply rich and sad slow voice slices into my heart, and I have to pull over and catch my breath. I tell my mother about it when I get home, a little bit excited that the song has found me, and she twists her mouth and says that it was never one of his favorites. I wonder if all these years I thought it was his song only because it's a song sometimes heard in the trailing hour of Italian-American weddings when, like I once did, daughters take a second dance with their fathers.

My mother tells me about her manicurist, Darna, whose father emigrated to Las Vegas from the Philippines in the 1980s. He had not been back to his country until last winter, when, already ill, he asked Darna and her brother to take him "home." There he died in the armchair of a relative's house the second morning of his trip.

"Do you think he knew he was going to die that day?" Mom asks, which I take to be her way of asking if I think my father knew that *he* was going to die on October 13.

In the hospital, as Dad's dementia was worsening (or the drugs were slowing down his mind), and he had pleaded, *Take me home. When can I go home?*, Mom answered with some variation of: "When you get better you can come home." But even when it seemed he might be stabilizing, she confided that she could not envision coping with him back at the house with what would have necessarily been round-the-clock nursing care. (*We can't have strangers in the house. He'll be calling out for me all day and night, I won't be able to stand it. What if the nurse doesn't show up?*)

My father, a lifelong traveler had, in his 70s, become a nester, and claimed to love nothing more than staying in his beautiful, comfortable house, relaxing on the patio, curling up in his den, walking the perimeter of his backyard, past the Japanese water garden he'd designed and had built. It was something my parents fought about, her still wanting to go out for dinner, to a show, on vacation, him wanting to be still, in familiar surroundings, quiet.

Did he know, before anyone else caught on, that Alzheimer's was working its way around his brain? That the increased forgetfulness, the fondness for home, the spiked worry when not home, was not him becoming an old fart, but him needing to stay safe?

If she is asking me now if I thought my father knew he was going to die that day, I don't know. But *soon*? Then my answer is yes. Can I say that? I believe that in the end, if he knew that he would forever live in a bed in a nursing home, that he would never again stand up or sit straight, that despite being urged to get better, getting better wouldn't get him out of there, then he may have seen death as the *safer* alternative, though not the better one. I believe when he could think about it clearly (if he could think about it clearly), he longed for the couch in his den, his chair on the patio, the tinkling of the small waterfall in the backyard—and knew that was all already lost.

Even as we have this conversation, I blame her for not bringing him home, and I also forgive her, and I know that it's presumptuous of me to think she needs my forgiveness or understanding. I know that I do not understand any of it, that I have no idea really what I might have done had I been her, walking about that big house deciding where to put the hospital bed.

Now, she walks to where his wooden box sits, two pink carnations crossed on top. She places a hand on each side of the box and says, "I guess he knew this was the only way he could come home."

I say only, "Maybe."

Two days after our father is cremated, Cathy flies home to Massachusetts, where I hope her teaching and church routine, and distance, might provide balance in the tenuous equation of grief and going on. A day later, Holly flies back to her husband, to their missionary acceptance letters and an international move. Flowers stop arriving, neighbors no longer drop by, the pool maintenance man and the gardener and the mailman no longer ring the bell first and shake my mother's hand before performing their duties.

After breakfast on the third morning when we are alone, I tell Mom we need to get out of the house. When you need to get out of the house in Las Vegas, you do not go to the mall, the park, or the movies.

You go to The Strip.

My mother, in the usual way she has of wanting to show off her adopted city when anyone visits, wants to show me the new Wynn Las Vegas Hotel, a 50-story resort slicing the Las Vegas landscape, interrupting the view of the mountains in shimmering gold and concrete. Inside, bright carpets and hundreds of flowering plants open onto colors, music, strolling vacationers. Here are people who are not grieving, in a place not aching and empty because one person is no longer there. Here is a place wide with the thrum of activity that does not involve opening sympathy cards or making photocopies of a death certificate. We need this, this distraction, gaudy and bright, overly done and precisely, exquisitely, without charm.

We have an early lunch in a self-consciously decorated "café" the size of a bowling alley. "Six bucks for a tomato juice," I say, but we eat and wave our arms and say, "C'est la vie."

Mom wants to stay in the casino a while, to play. In the twenty-five years my parents have lived in Las Vegas, except for a few random slot machine pulls, I have willingly gambled only a handful of times. The last was when Frank wanted to try craps the first year we were married. My mother, who for many years stuck to nickel slot machines, now slides a twenty-dollar bill into an automated quarter poker machine, then punches buttons marked bet, deal, draw, stand. On each deal, she bets just one notch above the minimum, 50 cents, and tells me that Gary always good-naturedly, though seriously, reprimands her because if she has a winning hand, she will only get a minimal payout and she may one day be sorry she did not bet the maximum six quarters on each hand to win the largest possible jackpot.

A half-hour goes by, forty-five minutes. As Mom plays, she seems to soften, to animate. I am reminded of a teenage boy at the controls of a video game and understand immediately the self-medicating attraction. Mom says it is my turn, so I stab at the buttons, mistakenly tossing away a hand containing a pair of jacks. My mother tells me about the last time she and Daddy played here, him playing three hands at a time, betting the max, $1.50 each on each, running through twenties like handfuls of Tic-Tacs. They won a little, then of course lost, laughed and left. I want to bet the maximum six credits, to appropriate my father's risk-taking role, but I also want to honor my mother's conservative system, because she is after all, sitting right here.

I am dealt a hand with four spades: King, Jack, Ten, Queen, and a two of diamonds. I discard the two of diamonds, and the Ace of spades appears. I know this is good, but I am not sure exactly how good. My mother claps her hand over my forearm.

"You hit the Royal Flush!"

We have won $135. She insists we split it down the middle, as I stifle a clumsy urge to insist in return that she keep it all. I do not want to make her play the frugal widow, putting aside found money.

We agree not to tell my brother, who would only remind us that we could have won $1,500. My mother and I decide it will be our secret, along with how, the day before, when she was talking to Tessa about her dead husband and suddenly her face changed and she signaled for her purse, and I fumbled, spilling tears all over the soft leather, because I couldn't find her nitroglycerin tablets, and instead pulled three baby aspirin from my own purse and told her to swallow them. This found money secret is different, and better, than the sad shared secret of what it is like, in these days after my father died, when it is just the two of us.

One afternoon, while Mom is resting, I gaze out the window of the spacious family room where I'm trying to work and notice the oleanders, more than a dozen tall tree-like shrubs which line the cement wall bordering the back edge of my parents' thoughtfully designed rear yard. They must each be twelve feet high, flowering in red, pink, white, and fuchsia, directly across from the covered patio where Dad sat each afternoon sipping lemonade, often eating a pear or peach, or munching on peanuts, or prosciutto on a slab of Italian bread, and reading the *Wall Street Journal*. They're swaying ever so slightly in a soft breeze and I whisper into the silence to ask my father if he misses his backyard. *I see it all the time,* he whispers back. *I see you too.*

When my father was alive, he instructed the landscaper, Pedro, to prune off the tops of the oleander bushes as soon as they skipped over ten feet, which nearly always coincided with the sprouting of new growth and budding blooms. No words from Pedro, no outraged cries from visiting friends, citing the universal gardening edict that pruning occurs *after* the bloom has died, would persuade him otherwise. He didn't want sloppily drooping foliage, no matter how pretty, tipping over into the back neighbor's yard. I wonder if, while my father was in the hospital and nursing home, Pedro had finally had his way or if this is recent new growth I'm seeing now. I know that I am casting about, hoping to attach meaning to randomness, and attributing symbolism to the flora that sways green and colorful and vibrant, straight in the strong desert breezes. Is it corny, I ask myself, to want to see new bloom here, now? To want to know that new life is happening, something maybe Mom can appreciate?

That night, a friend sends me an email, a quote from Elizabeth Gilbert's memoir, *Eat, Pray, Love:* "It's time for something that was beautiful to turn into something else that is beautiful. Now, let go."

The quote does not say how to do that.

One night when I can't sleep, I go rifling through drawers stuffed with newspaper clippings and photos, and I find, in the back, letters and receipts and other papers that tell me new things, but not whole things.

There's something there, a line in an old letter, about a woman named Viola in Chicago, a story I've heard a fragment of once, but nothing in the letter explains anything.

I find an old something—diary page? letter?—that gives me more information about a partial story I heard once, about how one of my father's sisters was once engaged to a Jewish man and just before the wedding, both sets of parents prevailed upon them to call it off. The house the couple had already bought, it turns out, is the house I grew up in—the one Mom always hated and begged Dad to sell—because there would have been shame and dishonor involved in backing out of the real estate deal. Dad gave his word to his parents before telling his wife.

I find the note on which is detailed how Dad had once taken a diamond ring as collateral for a loan, and the loan wasn't repaid, even after several second chances. I realize this is the ring he once gave to Cathy, who at twenty-two, didn't want to wear what looked like an engagement ring, and so had the diamond set into a necklace.

There was another diamond ring, the one we all called "the rock," a big yellow diamond set atop two rows of baguettes, the ring my mother repeatedly promised to me to help pay college tuition for my sons. The ring that had to be sold, six years after Dad died, to help pay her caregiver costs.

My Dad passed away last week. My father died, and I'm still in Las Vegas. These words come out of my mouth or appear on my computer screen or phone, without any real sense of my having planned them, without my consent. I utter or type or thumb these words, then mentally disown them. I write them in emails explaining my absence from my regular life. They begin to enter my journal. Words are how I interpret the world, the way I come to understand anything. I once had a writing teacher say, mashing up Nora Ephron's advice from her dying mother with a Joan Didion edict: "Take notes: nothing bad ever happens to a writer. It is all copy someday."

I take notes, trying to figure out on the page what I think, especially in the quiet moments when nothing at all is happening, but I feel the air changing. When I feel my father hanging about.

While still at my mother's house, I am reading Didion's *The Year of Magical Thinking*, which traces her grief journey following her husband's sudden death, a book I have been assigned. Before she left, Cathy was a bit startled to find it on my bed stand, but the book and its words comfort me. Didion says that she writes in order to understand what she thinks and that the words she writes are who she is. I write: "I am a daughter who did not know her dead father well enough, and who is struggling now, when it's surely too late, to figure out why, to get to know him." I write that I need to know this man, and that I am not yet sure why this feels so urgent now, and I write that it is not because I feel guilty but because I don't.

Of the other books I have with me, I keep returning to Paul Auster's *The Invention of Solitude*, in which he describes a recently deceased father he didn't understand well enough in life either, a father whose behaviors, quirks, rigidness, and separateness I instantly recognize.

Auster's father, in his inability to connect with his son, feels familiar, sadly so.

"It was not that I felt he disliked me. It was just that he seemed distracted," Auster writes.

I read that and experience a quickening of recognition. My father too, though he may have liked you, may have loved you, seemed, so often, *distracted*—by the news, newspapers, the stock numbers in his head, food, business, his parents, the world.

When studying photographs of his late father, Auster has a moment of clarity and writes that studying those photos give him "the sensation that I was meeting him for the first time, that a part of him was only just beginning to exist."

I will read and reread Auster's book, carrying it around for the next few years, caught by the photo on the book's cover, of his dad, handsome and sort of vague looking, playing cards with four other versions of himself.

Each night after my mother goes to bed, I open my computer, plug it into the phone jack, and wait while the dial-up service connects. My email inbox is my first stop. Before she left, Cathy complained about sympathy notes arriving electronically, about all the pixels that say, *sorry* and *let me know if there is anything I can do* and *you are in my thoughts and prayers*. But I study, and mostly savor, every empathetic email I receive, even though I greatly dislike and do not appreciate much of the actual wording or sentiments. I do know people are trying, trying to be kind. I consider each missive, and make up sarcastic imaginary replies.

He'll always be with you in your heart. Duh.

He lived a good life. He did. He was still living it; he wasn't done, he had good days. That's life too.

He was a good man. Yeah, but if he weren't, what might you say? That I'm best rid of him?

It was his time. How the hell do you know? Wouldn't a better time to depart have been *before* the pain, the surgeries, the Alzheimer's? Wouldn't that have been a better time?

He wouldn't have wanted to live that way. Who can say? Despite everything I know about his final day (which is to say, everything I hope I know), and his being sad about not coming home, I also think that if he'd been able to be comfortable, watch TV, grumble a little, he may have voted to stay.

It was God's plan. Don't get me started.

Let me know if there's anything I can do. There is a lot you can do, but I can't let you know. I can't think straight, figure out whom or what to ask, and risk a no. Just do it, please, anything that might help.

You are in my thoughts and prayers. Great. Now, when I get home, talk to me, let me talk. Don't be shocked.

I don't reply this way to anyone, of course.

Yet, even with their cloying or empty-seeming phraseology, their well-intentioned and often trite ideas, the emails are all, to me, a soothing backdrop, a quiet background against which I can be excused for not responding. I like having time to think before speaking; I've long understood that this is part of why I write, why I deflect in-person debate or confrontation. On my feet, in the moment, I go dry, blank. But in the silence, and the glow of the screen, alone, or on the smooth possibility of the empty notebook page, I can try to formulate my words, delete them, try again, and again. (In a few years, this will create huge problems and scathing insults, when Gary and I need to discuss my mother's care, and he insists we talk by phone, and I, in a different time zone, and with the need to think through my responses, will insist on email.)

When I turn on my computer deep in the night at my mother's house, to carry on and keep up, I read the new condolences messages, and for a moment there is an undemanding shoulder, there is pause, there is time to think.

When I get home, it will be different. People will say to me, in person, in the bank, at the grocery story, the PTA meeting, the basketball game, that they are sorry and I will have to respond immediately. I will say thank you, when what I really want to say is something like, *Sorry is the heavy wooden box in which my father's burned bones lie, sorry is the empty old gardening shoes by the patio door, sorry is the newspaper still folded on his hall table.*

When I wake up on the thirteenth morning in Las Vegas, I long for home. I feel suffocated and confused here where little makes sense and what does burrows under the sensitive patches of my skin. My father is both here and not here. He's not humming in his bathroom, whistling on the patio, strumming his fingers on the kitchen counter during breakfast. The lemonade still sits in the refrigerator, the newspaper still thuds each morning onto the front walk. My mother is shuffling about in her thin bathrobe, eyes round and wet, like someone who forgot her bifocal sunglasses on an August day. All the new normal, sadness and silence.

That morning, Mom asks me to cancel my father's newspaper subscriptions.

"Don't you want to just keep one local paper?" I ask.

"No, I don't read it," she says. I know this is true, but still I want her to have it. But, I call. I cancel.

My mother finds me crying into the phone that afternoon, and her eyes register fear. For a moment I realize she thinks the tears are about some kind of bad news, something happening in New Jersey. I shake my head, cover the receiver. "It's okay. It's Frank. I just miss my kids. I want to go home. I'm sorry, but I do." She says that's normal, that of course I miss my kids, I am supposed to miss them, and that I should go home.

Two weeks in Vegas is enough.

I nod, and ask Frank to call the airlines for me. Although I have been making my own airline reservations since I was fifteen, a new wave of grief is lapping at me and it's got me paralyzed: I fear leaving my father's house of my own will. I fear that when I leave, I will no longer be able to feel close to him, that I will be unable to so deeply miss him, that he will, in fact, be not only out of sight, but out of mind, for good, that I might not be able to so easily conjure him anywhere else. I worry that he won't visit me in New Jersey. Will his den, his patio chair, his car be the only places possible to find him? I'll be nearly three thousand miles from those places. I experience this as another betrayal of my father; I want so much to go back to my own home and kids and husband, and yet I want to stay here, in his home, in his presence, in the place that maybe, if I were to even believe in such things, he might... haunt.

I do not know yet what I will learn in the months and couple of years to come: that there will be no place, no location, no house or home or hotel where his absent presence will not visit and from which I will simultaneously want to flee, and to cling.

While my father was in the hospital, then the rehabilitation center, then back in the hospital, then in the nursing home, my mother had purposeful, wifely duties to perform, a role. She made twice-daily ten-mile drives on roads that at age seventy-eight she had never before navigated alone. In the unbroken tedium of bedside visits, in the telephone calls from doctors she only half-comprehended, my mother had been lost but knew exactly where she stood. Her husband was ill, maybe dying, and she had work to do, a place to go every day, someone to be: she was The Wife.

Now she is The Widow, and in the first week, as she moves from task to task, her children and grandchildren, her few local friends, all populate her house, drive her car, mind her meals, keep her busy with the business of death. Then, most of that stops. Gary has had to return to work and his own domestic duties, cooking and cleaning and all the errands his disabled wife cannot manage. Her two adult grandchildren who live locally are busy building their twenty-something lives. Cathy and Holly have left. Finally, it is only me, missing my own home, heartsick for my own children.

I wonder about what else I can do, what I should do, before leaving Las Vegas.

I decide to visit the Roman Catholic church Mom attends a few times a year. I'm groping for something. Because she opted to have Dad's service at the mortuary and not in church, I can't rely on their even knowing she's a recently widowed parishioner. But I head there anyway, only a few miles away, on roads my mother is comfortable driving, and find the office, a bright and busy, but welcoming room, and I inquire after a bereavement support group. I'm given a brochure and shown the room where the group meets, and I ask if my mother can simply show up or does she have to call ahead. Anyone is welcome, anytime, I'm told, Catholic or not, regular church-goer or not.

At home, I hand Mom the brochure with the two different meeting times underlined. She takes it from me without much apparent interest, lays it on the kitchen counter near her grocery list. One of the two weekly meeting times is the same morning she always stays home so she can talk with the two women who have been cleaning her house for a decade, who have each lost their own husbands. The other is the same day and time of the week when, except for the past three months, she'd had her hair done at the same beauty shop for twenty-five years.

These old routines, abandoned for months now so she could be The Wife, I suspect will for The Widow, be both salve and salt, reminders of life returning to normal and, too, some new normal she doesn't want and may or may not embrace.

As it turns out, she will go to a few meetings of the bereavement group. She calls me after the first one: "Nice people. It felt good." But then she abruptly stops attending: "Who needs to hear all those sad stories?"

I am leaving Las Vegas in a day and half, leaving my father's house, leaving my mother. She asks me to drop her off at the hairdresser, where everyone puts down their scissors and blow-dryers and brushes dripping with cream hair dye and gives her a quiet and gentle hug. They invite me to stay, but I retreat to Starbucks, to coffee, to a familiar and neutral noise.

I order, sit at a small table, and open my laptop. I try to concentrate on what is overdue; even though I've gotten extensions on both work and school projects, I know it will not be enough time. I wonder if I will ever be able to concentrate again, though I know I will one day, it just doesn't seem likely now. I am distracted by the barista's trilling out the first names of each customer and what they ordered ". . . Andrea—venti latte skim; Jose—grande vanilla decaf; Tara—tall double mocha espresso; Tony—short coffee regular." A minute ticks by. "Tony, please pick up your coffee."

Tony never appears.

I am trying not to listen, to hear, to look. I don't want this reminder right now that Tony is (was?) my father's name, that regular is (was?) how he takes (took?) his coffee, or at least that is how he always asked for it, and I am trying not to picture how he'd then tear open five or six packets of sugar and spill half the grains on the counter. I don't want to concentrate on the truth that in our family, only my father and I truly loved a cup of coffee, a few times a day, but while I could substitute tea or root beer or cranberry juice, he was caffeine-addicted and it used to upset us all that at any activity—a daughter's graduation, a grandson's baseball game—he would excuse himself to find a lunch

counter, doughnut shop, any likely coffee purveyor, and that sometimes he would not excuse himself but simply arise, in the middle of
the speech or inning, and miss what he was there to see.

I am stuck now, in my head, and stuck in my seat at Starbucks, and
the barista keeps calling for him, calling for the owner of the unclaimed
Tony, coffee regular, and though I felt steady when I walked in, now I
wonder if in my panic over the overdue work and the regular grief about
a parent's death, and the anxiety that I may be doing everything wrong
about helping my mother, and the guilt that I am leaving Las Vegas
too soon—I consider that I may have mistakenly asked for coffee in
my father's name.

I am relieved when the barista calls out, "Lisa—tall decaf," and I
collect my correct brew. As I'm picking up the cup, she yells out again,
very close to my ear, for Tony, and I am undone and I tell her I will
give the coffee to Tony, and I take the *coffee regular* cup to my table and
place it next to my laptop and for the next hour no one approaches the
counter to say his name is Tony and he did not get his coffee.

I will strain, wanting to tell this story to someone, maybe even
a stranger in the coffee shop or the stylists at the hair salon. I want
to write it in an email to a friend, or tell my husband on the phone.
But I don't tell it to anyone. I tell it to no one because I am not able to
locate the right tone that must exist somewhere between skepticism
and serendipity and intelligent dismissal.

I am leaving Las Vegas soon, and I cannot tell anyone there how
my father came to visit me in a Starbucks two weeks after he died. I say
nothing because I am afraid my mother will think it's nonsense. I am
worried that my spiritually inclined sister will say it is a sign of some
sort, but not what the sign means. I am terrified that my brother will
either shake his head, or that he will cry. And I am afraid I will tell the
story badly.

When I leave Las Vegas, I tuck the story away.

On the plane trip back home, a film plays, *Click,* which from the pre-
views sounds like a comedy and it is, at least for the first half, when
the main character, hungry for career advancement, money, and pres-
tige, fast-forwards his life with the help of a magical remote control
device. Click, raises and promotions and bonuses pile up. Click, there's

a splashy new house, a hotter wife, better clothing. Darkness ensues, however, when he learns too late that it is not possible to go back again, and he finds himself rich and successful but also older, divorced, adrift. He's been too busy to notice, among other things, the death of his own father. Distraught, he is allowed to watch a replay of the life events he's missed, and he confronts an image of his father as an old man, hunched, thick-waisted, slow, and slow-witted. He clicks on a frame, and a glitch allows him to enter the past and embrace and kiss his elderly father, but just for a second. I know of course that it's an overly simplistic circle-of-life coda, choreographed for maximum cinematic effect. But I like the tone, the reminder of how easily one can miss noticing your father's life unfolding to its finale.

Later, he asks his own grown son, "What happened to Grandpa?" and the son replies, "Nothing happened, Dad. He just died."

I'm tossed back to another flight, a late-night airplane trip home from Las Vegas, around 1994, winging through the inky dark over the Rockies, Frank and I handing a sleepy irritable infant Sean back and forth like a relay baton. We both were bone tired, but neither wanted to duck out of doing baby duty on board. Playing on the cabin screen that night was an extended music video, or maybe a documentary, carefully edited photo montages of the late singer Nat King Cole and his daughter Natalie Cole, their deep and sad voices, singing "Unforgettable," together and separately, a duet across two worlds. They are joined, nearly three decades after his death (when his daughter was a teenager), joined in a way they could never be in life, by technology but, more urgently, by something more. This was long before my father died, three years before Paul was born, long before I even consider becoming a daughter who could have a dead father. Although I recall Dad liking the elder Cole, there's really no connection for him, for me, with that song. But it is that song I will so often hear in my mind, years later, those two voices, so mournful, so joyful, when I'll try to explain to myself, the here-ness and gone-ness of my dead father.

Before the *buckle seatbelt* sign blinks, I sense the airplane descending, so slowly it is only fractionally detectable. I try to recall how I learned this feeling, this minute internal shift in cabin and body pressure. Then

I remember: it was something my father taught me, on a flight to Florida, decades ago, when he held up his hand and moved it like a descending airplane, down, down, but just a fraction of an inch at a time. It happened when I was young, and he was younger then than I am now.

That night, back in my own bed, Frank snoring beside me, my bedroom door, slightly ajar, pushes open and I awake to see what I think is a man looming over me, though it is only my son Sean. Maybe it is my supine position, or maybe it is that I have been away for two weeks, or that I am dreaming about my father, but when I look up I see both my son *and* my father standing there, one behind the other, both of them with their hands against their flat stomachs, slipped in the waistband of their pajamas.

This is my first hint, and so I begin to quip, that *my father has followed me home to New Jersey, and he's decided to stay for a while.* I say that the father who visits me, beginning late that October, is not my imagination, not wishful thinking, not a figment, that somehow, in some other-worldly way, he's "real."

I will have no idea, then or now, if that's the truth, only that it feels true.

Startled in my bed, I'm also comforted. It's time now, and Dad seems to agree, for me to burrow back into the love of my own little family.

9

Conversations We Can and Cannot Have

But first, I am a bitch to my husband.

I become fixated on my father-in-law. He has a pacemaker that acts up. He has high blood pressure, an enlarged prostate, and congestive heart failure. He and my mother-in-law, at eighty-four and eight-six, still work and still drive, and together they put in twenty-seven tomato plants last June. I decide that my husband does not understand how precious this all is, having his father still, doesn't see how dear it is that his father isn't half out of his head, that they have time.

I tell Frank that he should—now while he has the chance—talk to his father about what may happen, about their shoe supplies business, how the old man feels about life support. My husband waves me off. He thinks there will be time to talk about all of that. Let's not and say we did.

We go on.

For months, through the "first" holidays and the gray winter skies and snow, I ashamedly nurse a seething, petty anger at my own father for leaving, at Frank for having a father who is here. When my husband, who always got along well with my father, says anything about him, anything at all, even something neutral or funny—like how Dad could never understand the rules of any board game (which he couldn't)— I think, *Shut up. My father is dead and yours is alive.*

I detach and watch myself. You bitch, I chastise myself, silently. How could you so selfishly, impetuously, think you hate your husband because his father is still alive, and living in the same town? Still, I want to scream, *My father died and yours did not and god damn it, that's not fair.* This is a terrible thing to want to say to the man you have loved since you first saw him in a high school play when he was sixteen and you were twelve—even if you know you will never say it out loud. You want to, but don't say, *You have no idea of the pain that is in your future. I don't want you to feel it.* But really you *do* want him to feel it. Because the hurt is also about the love, it is a—what are the words for it?—an exquisite pain?

My mind jumps around, grasping for something that might make me feel better, or worse.

My father was younger than yours. As if that mattered.

My father was intelligent, polite, impulsively and steadily generous. Yours is often curmudgeonly, sometimes rude, negative, famously miserly. Your father is also funny, sentimental (at least since that ministroke), helpful, and peaceful. But I'm not interested in that just now, in balance and being fair, in what you have still. I'm only seeing what I'm missing.

My father liked you, treated you with respect, laughed with you. Not long after we married, your father thought I should sign something so that if we divorced, like you did once before, I wouldn't get a small slice of his small business. Your father snaps at me when I say anything contrary, or too liberal.

My father offered you business advice, wanted to see us invest well.

For years, your father refused to give you a raise, a piece of the business.

I conveniently forget that they *each* paid for sizable chunks of our wedding, that your father gave us a piece of the down payment for our house, that *my* father once said that if I married you I'd have to work my whole life, as if that were a problem.

Your father takes his pills, keeps his doctor appointments, goes to physical therapy, practices the preferred swallowing method, plays word games to keep his brain from turning to mush. My father never finished a bottle of antibiotics, doubted most doctors, cancelled appointments or just didn't show up, was always too tired for physical therapy.

My father wanted homegrown vegetables, knew all about nutrition, but delegated the garden chores to paid gardeners, watched from the patio, and went to restaurants. Your father has been coaxing prodigious buckets of produce from the ground for sixty-three seasons, loves every moment in his garden, knows every summer meal pivots on what he sows.

My stupid plusses and minuses add up to nothing, in every direction they add up to love and loss.

Your father lives, and mine is dead, and your father is your best friend, and so for your sake, of course I want him to live forever.

My father is dead and yours is alive, two miles down the road, calling every other night: something is supposedly broken, but I think he just wants to see you. You go; you fix it. You have a glass of iced tea with him, listen to him complain, laugh about something trivial.

Someday you won't have anywhere to go. You'll see. Something will be truly broken, and you won't be able to fix a thing. And maybe you will then ask me, "How did you stand it?"

I will say nothing, just hold you.

I don't say any of these cruel and insensitive things out loud, except for the one night when I do say, "Don't try to understand. You have *no* idea what it's like to lose a parent."

The next morning, when I take my first sip of hot coffee, my eyes find my father leaning against a bookcase in my office. "Don't ever say that to Frank again. He's a good man. So is his father."

The hot liquid swirls in my mouth, and by the time I swallow and think of something to say in return, he's gone. I was going to say that I know Frank's a good man, that of course he is, that I married a man who reminded me of my father in the important ways.

Finally, I will realize that one reason I am so hard on my husband in the wake of my mourning, is that buried deep—planted I think by my mother and aunts and other women of that generation—was the nagging idea that with my father gone, I'd lost the guarantor of a male protector. That seems a strange idea for someone so independent, who tries not to depend on her husband in traditional ways. Although I had chosen a man like my father—someone who also worked with, and then took over a gritty business from his own father, someone funny and deceptively mild who also seemed to avoid conflict—but someone who, *unlike* my father, wouldn't tell his wife what she could or could not do. Yet, in the wake of my father's death, I yearned, in some primal way, for Frank to become more like him in a traditional sense. It wasn't about money exactly, more about cushioning, being a bulwark against any harshness life had yet to deal me. That vague, stodgy old notion suggested that Frank was now the only man standing between me and disaster, between me and nothingness. And, God forgive me, I worried that my husband—who had recently passed his old minivan to me, broken heater and all, when mine died, while buying himself a new one—wasn't up to the job.

I don't say that.

We go on.

Back at home, I dig back into my children's routines, see for myself that while they hurt a little, they aren't floundering. They are busy and maybe they even learned something in the two weeks I was away, that Mom can leave for a while and they will be okay.

Then I turn my attention to my paid work, letting clients know I'm back and ready to work and reassure them, "I'm okay." In other words, I lie. Then I turn to my own writing. When he heard of my father's death, one of my professors emailed me to say, "Life first, writing second." While I took the advice and attended to life (and death), I want to try now to recapture some of the momentum that had, for reasons I don't yet understand, begun building before Dad died. I had been getting some recognition—low-dose, small-scale to be sure, but alluring. Acceptances were arriving, I'd won a writing contest, been invited to read at a conference, asked to write for a national magazine. When I flew west, everyone was understanding, but the pieces had not fallen back into place so easily. That sweet and slippery momentum had dissolved in the mist of airplanes, obituaries, condolence notes, flowers, grief, family nitpicking, and a slicing sense of creeping ennui.

As part of an editorial project for *O The Oprah Magazine,* I was to write—from the perspective of someone who had, several times, lost and gained major amounts of weight—about the experience of interacting daily with Martha Beck, a life coach, who was trying to help me recognize and understand the connections between food, eating, behavior, and weight gain—or as she called it: "the mood, food, brood cycle." In fact, three days before my father died, I was in a Manhattan photo studio, prepped and primped by the magazine's photographers.

While I am in Las Vegas, Martha writes in an email that she's not surprised to hear that so many stressful events, and also so many wonderful things, are happening for me all at the same time, that significant events tend to cluster in this way. So my father's dead and the writing is alive, and that conundrum worries me. Can I be this happy and this sad all at once? *I can't think about work right now, my father just died. I can't think about my father's death now, my work is exploding.*

Just before the *O Magazine* shoot, an essay about my years as a horse show competitor was chosen for a prize that included presenting it at a conference. I made a hotel reservation, but the conference fell in the middle of the two weeks I spent in Las Vegas. So instead of reading aloud about how the horses—bought and trained with my father's polyester money—had shaped me, I prevail on a friend at the conference to read in my place, even though she is afraid of horses and I need to tutor her on the pronunciation and meaning of various equestrian terms via telephone the same afternoon my mother argues with me about who should write the thank-you cards to those who attended the wake.

At home, trying to pick up again, I am sad and angry and defeated that the sense of building toward something has seemingly derailed, even though Martha assures me I'll find my way and that I could try to view these experiences with curiosity. I will, for the most part, fail at the curiosity part, until much later.

Eventually, I try to think about my school schedule. I'm behind in writing and reading, and don't know where or how to begin again. Once my new faculty mentor heard about my father, she told me only to take care of my mother and myself, to not even contact her again for a minimum of three weeks, that I'd need at least that much time before I could consider diving back in. She knows; she lost each parent while in the middle of writing books. Right on cue, at the three-and-a-half week mark, I'm ready. We map out a plan. She invites me to her home for a restorative writing retreat, but I cannot come to grips with another airplane flight, another disruption. I tell her I want to write about my father, and I do. Momentum winks at me.

Too soon, though, all my time is taken up with making arrangements for a wake visiting day we'll hold at my local funeral home, and the New Jersey memorial mass. If there's even a modicum of satisfaction—dare I say pleasure?—in supervising the New Jersey wake and mass, it's that I alone get to make many key decisions. And so I do. To augment the photos I brought home from Las Vegas, I choose photographs from my personal archive, order them the way I like, and deliver them to the funeral manager who will make a DVD that will run on a large-screen TV. I choose background music, and I make two collages with yet more photos. When she gets here, Cathy and I choose church music that compromises my desire for something that doesn't feel too church-y ("Morning Has Broken"), and her and my mother's more traditional bent ("Amazing Grace").

I communicate the importance—when going through airport security with my father's cremains in its lovely wooden box—that Mom have with her not only the death certificate, but also a special "remains transport" document that must be signed by the Vegas funeral home director.

I decide with Bill, my local funeral home owner—and the father of twins who were once on my own sons' pre-K soccer team—how to set up the room (there are more options when there's no coffin). I ask Bill to place a small marble-topped side table along the wall about six feet from Dad's cremains container. The morning of the wake, I slip off to the bread shop where my father, whenever he was visiting me, went each morning for a cup of coffee, and brought home a loaf or two of Italian bread. At the funeral home, I place on the table a cup of take-out coffee, a broken-open loaf of their best semolina, and a folded-back copy of that morning's *Wall Street Journal*. I tell no one I'm doing this, and I'm worried that someone, or everyone, will think it's hokey and contrived or wildly inappropriate, but instead almost everyone tells me it's a wonderful, funny, quirky, and entirely perfect tribute to a man who couldn't go more than a few hours without any of those things. It's only my mother who I can see is not amused when she sees the table, though she doesn't say so.

Downstairs in the funeral home lounge (no ashtrays, no wild children), I linger for a minute after I exit the ladies' room, and there's my father, smiling a little.

"Well, I guess if you had to do something, this is pretty good," he says, then takes a deep drag on his cigarette. "It's nice, kiddo."

"How did you like the newspaper, bread, and coffee?"

"Tony—coffee regular!" he trills, raising an imaginary cup, cracking me up.

I glance up the stairs to be sure I'm alone. And when I look back, I am alone.

Early that evening, in the three-hour break between the afternoon and evening viewing times, we gather at my house for a meal of Chicken Milanese, salad, and pasta, which Laurie, still my father's "third daughter," prepared and arranged on my kitchen counter in advance. About ten people are gathered tightly around my dining room table, and others are eating on trays in the family room or around the kitchen counter. The group includes relatives who traveled from North Carolina, Massachusetts, and Las Vegas, and from across the town and state. It includes my husband, my mother and sister, and my brother and his wife; three of the six grandchildren, two nieces and their husbands, and Laurie and her sister and mother—a widow herself who, with her late husband, Dino, made up one of my parents' dearest couple friends.

As everyone eats, and talks, and even laughs, I announce: "I know it's for a lousy reason, and this may seem strange to say, but I'm so glad you're all here." Except it's not really for a lousy reason, but for the best reason: you all loved him, you love us, or at least want to comfort us. From grief, we're making a new, good memory.

We reminisce about a vacation to Mexico City with Laurie and her family. Dad emerged one afternoon from the hotel suite bathroom to announce, "The toilet bowl was shaking." Dino teased, "Whatever you're drinking, Tony, I'll have a double!" Dad smiled and shook his head. "No really, it *was* shaking." Two days later, back in New Jersey, the radio news announced that Mexico has had one of its worst earthquakes.

In church the next morning, Father James, a cantankerous, intellectually lively, and liberal Franciscan priest I like to squabble with, who has never met my father, delivers a homily so moving and specific, everyone asks if he and Dad were friends. When he'd met with Cathy and me two days before, he'd asked probing questions and seemed engaged, but now he appears to have intuited so much else about our father, even we are shocked at the precision of his words.

After he speaks, he invites the immediate family to the altar to join hands in a circle of prayer and remembrance. I'm positioned across from Paul, my sentimental little boy, and all I can see are silent tears sliding down his apple cheeks, and how he doesn't break the circle to take his hand away from his brother's hand and his cousin's hand to wipe the tears.

My sons called their grandfather PopPop, and for the six weeks each year (three in the winter, three in spring or fall) when my parents stayed at our house, my boys followed him like ducklings. I have pictures of them, at ages two and six, crawling on top of my father like lapdogs, just after he'd awoken on the sleeper couch in our family room; and at six and ten, sprawled on lawn chairs beside him; and at eight and twelve, sitting all together on the family room floor at night, getting a bedtime story. PopPop fake-crying and proffering a $5 bill as the boys point to the Swear Jar. Those pictures tell me I did not just imagine it: my sons loved their PopPop. This is important to me, that my father meant something to the generation of males in our family who may come of age at a time when no grandfathers are likely to be around.

I write, and then I read, a much longer, more formal eulogy, Cathy standing next to me for a time, holding my elbow. I make sure to find each of my boys' eyes.

I want them to know that their PopPop had given time to others. (*How I wish I had taken more of my father's time, given him more of mine.*) I want them to hear that the most important lesson he taught me was about giving your word. If my father told *anyone* that he would do *anything,* even if he later came to realize that doing so was perhaps not such a wise move, he would not renege. "I gave my word," he would say, and that was that.

I also want to acknowledge that he had flaws, that we aren't eulogizing a saint, but a man. He was stubborn, sometimes sexist, often easily irritated by others' lack of discipline or shoddy service. When he did not know something, he made up an answer, and while it was sometimes funny, it could also be infuriating.

I trace a bit of his work life, emphasizing that he had recognized and ridden the wave of several innovative business trends before many others saw their potential: "secondary fibers," the precursor of the recycling business in the sixties; polyester fabrics in the early seventies; Las Vegas sprawl in the early eighties. He ran a vertically integrated business probably before business schools began teaching the concept, and he likely did not even know the term. But he did know that if you owned or controlled the trucks, the yarn, the double-folding machines, the sales force, and at least one retail outlet, then you could have some control over your business destiny.

One reason he wanted control was so that he could hire as he wished. He gave a lot of people employment, who in the sixties and early seventies, might have had a hard time finding not only a full-time job with benefits, but a welcoming atmosphere. He treated his employees well, and at a time when he legally could have done otherwise, he hired people of all races and religions; he hired the physically handicapped and the mentally challenged; he hired women and immigrants and ex-cons and people technically old enough to retire who needed income. He had jobs for the teenage children of friends and relatives, and even for the adult children who were having troubling launching themselves into the world. He did these things, and he never talked about *equality, race relations, tolerance,* never knew the term *diversity.*

Laurie eulogizes her "second father," and recalls when he let the two of us work for him one summer when we were about fourteen. "I was excited to think that I would be doing some office work. This was not what he had in mind for us. What he had in mind, was the factory. Lisa and I stood up all day cutting and folding remnant fabrics." Thus, we learned the value of hard work, and she got to observe my father interacting with his employees. "Mr. Chip had the ability to make everyone feel important. When he walked into that factory, he fussed over each and every one of those ladies and made each one feel important. He recognized that the heavy lifting was done by the workers."

I want people to know all of this, and though I suppose those in the church, who knew him over the decades already *do* know this, repeating it, having my sons hear me and others speak it aloud, is important to me.

Before the New Jersey service, my mother's plane landed in Newark on November 13, an exact month after Dad's death date. For the three weeks that Mom's here, no one mentions the significance of the date of travel, or even the date of Dad's death, though I guess some think about it. I wonder what my father—who always playfully reminded us why hotels never have a thirteenth floor—would have made of the date of his own death. Poor timing all around, and if you believe that people have a say in the day of their death, then it's a surprising choice for a man who, in life, had usually known how to time everything—when to buy, sell, and hold stocks, when to hit or hold in blackjack, just when to approach a business prospect.

In my own typically complicated and esoteric way of trying to understand meaning, I think the date has symmetry to it, four days short of his birthday, almost eighty years exactly. My mother, however, attaches morbid significance to the date. The thirteenth was bad all by itself. But Friday? Friday made it especially dark. Her husband's favorite number—which paid off on many a keno ticket and roulette wheel spin—was 17, which was also his birthday, and we all wonder why he couldn't have waited three more days. Next October, when Cathy and I also have birthdays, what has always been a happy—or at least a busy—month in our family might be something to dread.

On December 13, my mother, by then back home in Las Vegas, reports that she went to mass that morning and lit a candle, which I reason must be cathartic and purposeful, entirely appropriate. She sounds surprised on the phone that I didn't do the same.

My father and I are discussing something important when the guy in the car behind us at the green light taps his horn. In the passenger seat, my father, always polite, does not flinch, just glances in the rearview mirror and says, "Hold your horses, buddy. Life is short." I want to say something to my father, but when I turn my gaze back again, he is gone.

I think back thirteen years to when I was newly pregnant with Sean. It was a high-risk pregnancy, my doctor wanted me resting most of the day, my progesterone levels were so low my husband was giving me daily morning injections, and my blood hormone levels needed to be taken every morning at a lab six miles from home at precisely 8 a.m. My parents were visiting at the time, and for a week, my father drove me back and forth in his luxury rental car, so I could lie in the back seat, my legs propped up by three bed pillows. We hardly spoke, as usual, but there was no ill will in the air, just each of us thinking, maybe worrying—present, but quiet.

When he pops back in the passenger seat a few minutes later, at another red light, I ask my father if he remembers driving me around that week.

"Did I?" he says, and then, "Look at those hydrangea, that's a pretty color."

My father and I did not have any telephone conversations between the time I visited him in the hospital in August, and when he died seven weeks later. I told myself it would be better not to call. Since I could not visit in person, I did not want to confuse him on the telephone with my voice. If my voice meant nothing to him, he might be confused or upset—or, more likely, I would be. Or he might have asked me to come see him. I did not want to have to remind him that I was, in fact, back at my own home in New Jersey and not still in Las Vegas, taking care of my mother the way I had promised. I had, after all, given him my word.

"Take care of your mother," he had said. *"And the house, and the garden, and the pool."* It had been a shock to hear my father ask me, ask a *girl,* to do these things. He was half out of his head by then, I knew. But I had liked the sound of it, his asking, his asking *me.* He had gestured with his good, unstroked right arm, pointing to his arthritic knees and atrophied hip. "You'll have to take care of everything now." I didn't ask why he hadn't charged Gary with any of this, nor suggest it, and anyway maybe he already had had this same conversation with his son. I just lied and said I would, that I would stay with Mommy, that I would make sure everything was all right. But I didn't. I flew home a few days later.

The truth is, I did not call him because it was easier for me not to. It was easier if I remembered our last conversation at the hospital, the one where he reminded me to always lock my doors and always tip generously, as *the* last conversation, though it wasn't.

The conversations, it turn out, go on.

I work at my desk in my well-equipped home office while my sons are at school. I have worked mostly at home for sixteen years, and in our older, drafty house with original fifties windows, it is a struggle to stay warm in winter. I'm too stubborn and frugal to crank the heat up on the entire second floor when it's just me home, but I also don't like the feel of thick, constricting layers of clothing.

The first winter after Dad dies is especially cold. Nearly every day, I wear one of my father's sweaters that my mother managed to pack up and send, meaning them I'm sure for my husband and, eventually, my sons. But Frank says he already has too many sweaters (pilled, stained, a bit outgrown, I remind him, but to no avail), and I know my sons will both balk at wearing their dead grandfather's old man sweaters. So I do. I wear them. A cable-stitched cotton v-neck in blue, and the same one in gray; an itchy-scratchy wool crewneck in brown and again in black; and one that becomes my favorite—a zip-front tan cashmere cardigan so soft and warm it sometimes makes me groggy. Wearing his clothes is a bit maudlin, I know, but it makes me happy, in a sad way, and for a few months, I'll take happy any way.

The sweaters—all hanging in my closet on padded hangers I remember my mother swiping from a hotel when I was a kid—are a conundrum. My father was a slim man and a sharp dresser, and I don't recall him ever wearing baggy sweaters, so why do these fit me without pulling across my bust or my hips? I am a large woman, fat. So what's happening here? Maybe he did not in fact wear them much, or at all, now that I think about it, though they didn't come with price tags. Maybe they were gifts and too big to begin with, or my mother judged wrong in the store, which on its face I know is impossible. His armoire was always stacked with new and carefully cared-for clothes. I can't puzzle it out. And while the sweaters are not attractive on me, they feel wonderful, soft and welcoming. When I walk past the hall mirror on the way to the bathroom, I startle myself.

Before I start work each morning that winter, I reach for one of his sweaters. Sometimes I do remember a time when he was wearing one of them (or maybe one like it), the blue v-neck with the white stripe, yes, I think I remember him wearing it when visiting us here in New Jersey, about a year before he died. It was another chill winter day, and I was telling him that I had decided to change some things, to change my life.

"I'm going back to school, Dad." I was forty-five and needed a change, a midlife reboot.

"Good for you," he'd said. Then, almost as an afterthought, "Hey, that's going to cost a pretty penny."

"Not so bad," I lied, and waited to see if he'd offer one of his low- or no-interest loans, like the mortgage he'd extended us fourteen years before, or the ones he'd given his other kids for a new car and a child's wedding. But by then the Alzheimer's was staking its early hold and he demanded, "Wait. You went to college already. Remember?"

I remember.

Two years after he dies, on the day I walk across the stage in my black graduation gown and blue, yellow, and white graduate degree regalia, I chat with my father. We're alone in the bathroom at my hotel room; I'm annoyed that even my sleeveless black-and-white print dress will not keep me cool enough under the scratchy nylon robe. It's an unusually hot and humid night in Freeport, near where the MFA program at the University of Southern Maine convenes.

"Why am I always so friggin' hot!" I whine out loud, to no one.

"Stop fussing. You look fine. More important, look at what you've accomplished," my father says. He's sitting on the edge of the tub, his knees crossed, and he's wearing the soft beige zip-sweater.

"So you know? That I finished grad school?"

He waves his hand in a reassuring gesture. "You did good, kid."

I spin back to the mirror to put a barrette in my hair, and in the reflection, I see only the back wall of the shower.

Except for him, I don't see dead people. Yet if I had my druthers, half the people I'd like to talk to these days are dead people. My aunt Mary, my husband's aunt Mary, my Noni, all the old ladies of my past who gathered around dining room tables and patios and living rooms talking about infuriating men and good food and wayward children and secrets. None of them come to call. Only my father.

Parents die. Parents die, and their children continue their lives, sometimes it seems with one singular regret: that their gone parent did not live long enough to see the better version of the child. Even as I complete my degree, I still want my father to see me as I know I will be one day, maybe soon: the improved, actualized, fully realized, brighter, shinier me. Surely at some point, in the near future, this is who I will be, when I am "done." All my efforts to improve, enhance, are still in progress; I want to make him proud, and for him to witness my best accomplishments, certainly still ahead.

And yet, I do know that he was proud of me in life, inordinately so at times. "My daughter is a top public relations executive in New York City," he once said, when I was twenty-four and working an entry-level position in a mid-range agency. When I became a parent of course,

I understood—that it was his role to be my cheerleader, my crazed fan, the one person to always see me as the cleverest and the most talented, with the best ideas for whatever project or job or harebrained scheme. I missed that guy who would always say, "That's a great idea." "You ought to get paid double." "That client doesn't know how lucky he is!"

A few days after my graduation, I dream that my father and I are walking beside a wall covered with photographs showing the key moments of an entire life—not his life, but mine. I am jawing about how sorry I am that he will not be around to see all the things I am going to change, all the ways I'm planning to improve my mind, mothering, work, writing, the way I save money, invest, look, behave. He turns to me and says, "Take it easy, kid." Then he waves his hand toward all the photos, "Would you take a look at that?"

I write and publish an essay about no longer being interested in improving a single thing about myself. Good enough is enough. I half-believe it.

In the mornings the first two winters I am father-less, I open my laptop with one hand, and I hug my father's sweater to my torso with the other.

My father was not a hugger. He was not a *satisfying* hugger. He hugged almost everyone with just one arm. We all gave up trying to puzzle out why. Sometimes I figured it was because he often had a lit cigarette in one hand, or because the other hand was slipped into his waistband. Once, my sister speculated the one-armed hugging was a passive-aggressive gesture—that he didn't want to be lashed to us, that he was too smart and worldly and needed a wider life. My mother just shrugged and said, "He's hugged that way since we were both sixteen."

I think about other male arms, male hugs. When Paul hugs me, I think I may choke. It's a never-let-me-go clutch around the neck, his one hand grabbing his own opposite upper arm just behind the nape of my neck. It hurts and it feels wonderful. He punctuates each hug with, "I love you so much, Mom."

Sean, who has low muscle tone and is just now learning to grasp social cues and isn't always sure about when his own affectionate gestures are appropriate, hugs me with his arms at his sides, elbows bent, his hands either resting on my hips or my lower back, or cupping my shoulders. He is so thin I don't dare hug him back too tightly, and when

I do I can feel his heart throbbing. If he says anything, it's "How you doing Mom?"

Frank hugs hard and long, rubbing his big hands up and down my back, my upper arms—a bear hug. It feels like protection and sanctuary when it doesn't feel like a demand for something more, an invitation and entreaty—even twenty years on—for more contact and less clothing.

I hug my brother at my father's first wake; he's tree-trunk solid, and just as when I was five and he was fourteen, his hugs feel as though they are about making a fortress.

My father's half-hearted hugging did not stop him from being my protector, though I rarely admitted needing protection. I was a wiseass, know-it-all child, a fourteen-going-on-twenty-two sort of teenager who, for a few years, treated her father badly, mocking and alienating him with her petulant attitude and snotty rejoinders.

I find myself apologizing to him for this in a conversation we have in those first few months after his death, when he appears next to my desk while I am shredding another draft of a too-predictable essay.

"Forget it kiddo," he says quietly, cuffing my shoulder. I could almost feel it through the soft thickness of his sweater.

"Easy for you to say. You don't have to write it again, send it off and get it back with all kinds of red notes."

"You're going to do just fine," he says.

"You're just saying that because you're my father and you love me."

"At least you know that now," he says, and chuckles a little.

I am not overcome with sadness at most of the firsts—first Thanksgiving or Christmas, or first Father's Day without him. I attribute this to having lived a continent apart for so long. What slams me, though, are the missing loud phone conversations he often had with Frank after a New York Giants game, cursing the defense, usually. I do sob for a minute in early April, when I realize that the tiny palm crosses that arrived faithfully, annually, inside a flowery Easter card, displayed every year in my dining room breakfront—even in the final two years when his memory was shot—won't show up. My husband, on my first father-less Palm Sunday, fashions me a crude one while we are still in the pews at church.

My father is gone, and I have trouble thinking in the past tense. No, that isn't it exactly. I have trouble thinking about the entire year that has just passed—illness, resignation, all of it. I notice my hand getting tingly, or falling asleep whenever I am writing in longhand, which I love to do, despite my appreciation for my computer and the delights of the delete key and the wonders of electronic cut and paste. I make a mental note to ask my father if that is how his arthritis started. Then I wonder: Whom or what would I be asking? I want to ask the father who lived in this world, who rubbed his gnarled hands at the dinner table and massaged his knees in the car, not the dead father who comes to visit and is mostly upbeat and positive and who is probably only in my mind or at least probably only says what I want him to say. Even when he isn't in a lovely mood, and he says something a bit harsh, or something I don't especially want to hear, I know, and yet I don't know, that he's someone *I* conjured up. And I want the real thing.

I circle an item in *The New Yorker* about a new book I think my father might like. I even scribble in the margin, "Birthday for Dad?" and before even lifting my pen, I feel idiotic. On the internet, I see a report of a merger of two multinational corporations and wonder if my father, the uber biznews consumer, has heard about it yet. Then a wash of stupidity and anger swamps me. He's dead, you silly, silly girl. And when he was alive, you'd do these things—mention an interesting book, remark on some corporate news—only in passing, not in real conversation.

When he was alive, my father and I butted our stubborn heads, yelled across holiday dinner tables, and it seemed to me, regarded each other as if the other were not only wrong but also stupid. But if you had asked me, in those months when his death was fresh, what sorts of important issues we once saw differently, I could not think of one thing. I know that this is sentimental of me, and maybe smacks of revisionist history. I know that I am protecting myself as well as the dead we should always speak well of. I can't help it. He's here, and here, and something about his being gone keeps him present.

10

The Brotherhood

My father's eighty-four-year-old brother Silvio gets married for the second time, less than two months after my father dies. Some people used to mistake Silvio, usually called Silv or Silvie, for my father. I couldn't see it before. My father, who went by Tony, was tall, elegant; he had 1940s movie-star features and a 1920s gentility. Silvio was shorter, shifty, unpolished, a little crude. And he swore. (My father swore too, but usually in private, or only when he was with a roomful of men.) Yet as they aged, my father's humped back made him appear shorter, and they both had full heads of bright gray hair. Widowed at eighty, Silvio had called his brother every week, sometimes every day. My father sent him money, folds of cash in plain white envelopes.

When the invitation comes for the wedding, my mother tells me she's ripped hers up, and I can tell in her tone she doesn't want me to go either. She hasn't spoken to Silvio in a year, unless you count the terse "I'm sorry Mickey," and "Thank you" they exchanged at the New Jersey memorial, where Mom had hissed, "I can't believe he brought *her.*" I couldn't understand the remark: his wife and his mistress were both dead, surely all of us expected that he'd have a new *companion.* Later, I'd realize she'd decided that the cash my father had sent his brother for the past couple of years had financed his latest courtship—though Silvio's daughter tells me that except for an occasional drive to Atlantic City, they mostly ate in diners. I tell Mom I'm going to the wedding. I live nearby, I say; I have no excuse not to go. Secretly, I go because I see it as a healing opportunity. Weddings and funerals and all that.

The church, in a down-at-the-heels section of a small nearby city, is a denomination I'm not even slightly familiar with, and the theater-in-the-round seating leaves me cold. I go seeking comfort and intimacy, but this feels like performance. I cannot keep my eyes on the altar, and yet I can hardly pull them away. From my seat, halfway up the incline, it seems as if my father is standing down there, marrying a stooped old woman with dull reddish hair. I should be happy for my uncle, whom I've always liked despite his foibles, and who has never been anything but nice to me, making me laugh dozens of times.

When, at age fourteen, I'd finally convinced Dad to buy me a horse, it was Uncle Silvio who took me shopping for one, because he knew a guy at the track who knew a guy in northwestern Jersey who sold pleasure horses. It had been Silvio's mistress, my "Aunt Marion," who'd arranged my riding lessons a few years before that, and it was Silvio who negotiated a lower price for the horse, though he also never questioned whether a novice rider should start out with a two-year-old, barely trained horse, good breeding aside.

Before I had that first horse, Silvio and my father were partners, investing for a few years in mediocre harness racing horses that ran at tracks within a few hours of home. For reasons I never unraveled, it was always Silv's name on the racing form, and the one time when I saw one of their horses win, it was Silvio who pulled me into the winner's circle photo (where my braces caught the night track lights) while Dad stood off camera.

At the small wedding dinner reception, I have a hard time hugging my uncle with both arms. I grow still when he takes my freezing hands into his and he tries to tell me how much he misses my father and how he wishes his brother could be there. A nasty loop starts in my head: *So, if you loved him so much, why didn't you fly out there to see him, one last time? All that money he gave you, and you couldn't buy a damned airline ticket?*

As Frank and I slice into our filet mignons, I understand I came to the wedding because I had the notion that Silvio was the closest I could get here on earth to my father. Yes, Dad and I were talking, he was visiting me, but those conversations, while often warm and lovely and reassuring, mostly had me off kilter, confused. Those first couple of months, I mused that I would give anything to have my father back. After the wedding, I stop saying it, because it's a ridiculous notion, a stupid expression. I wouldn't give *anything;* I would only give something. I half-jokingly think: *I'd give Silvio.* But I wouldn't give my good husband, I wouldn't give my children, and it's while I'm watching Silvio eat with one hand resting on his new wife's arm, that I understand he isn't the closest I can get to my father on earth.

My children are. I am.

That night at about 2 a.m., a hot flash pulls me awake, and when I go to the bathroom to soak a wash cloth in cool water, Dad's waiting, but he doesn't want to talk about Silvio or weddings, or anything much.

"Feeling okay, Dad?" I ask.

"Very funny, kid." He laughs.

My father was part of the last generation for whom it may have been possible to become the classic "self-made man." He did it mostly by way of a kind of continuing education program he'd fashioned for himself as an adult: reading. He read his entire life, and he passed on to me this great love of words and books and story when I was so young I can't even remember.

When I was a small child, he made up bedtime stories several nights a week, frequently with one bully child or mean animal, and one or more kind, good kids or wise, helpful animals.

I knew he wrote too because occasionally he'd show us one of his short stories. In my teenage intellectual superiority, I rejected them all as so much pap: the underdog naturally prevailed; justice and order was always restored; the dejected doubter always in the end engaged joyfully with life. When he was gone, I thought of them differently, as stories that reconfirmed for himself the goodness of his quest to do the right thing.

He was a son of Italian immigrants who needed his wage-earning hustle, not his cerebral muscle, to help feed seven siblings. He did the right thing, worked long hours, and instituted profit-sharing at his company early on, so that all the relatives he employed were left in good stead when he retired early in 1981. I fantasized once that he might have found more time to write, but it appeared the only intercourse during retirement with the written word was that he seemed to read more— biographies of politicians and European statesmen, poetry, the occasional thriller, American history and geography.

A year after he dies, I find a half dozen stories I've never seen, in his slanted printing on the top shelf of a closet in his den. Some are on the stationery of hotels in cities he had traveled to for business, years, even decades before. There is so much I don't know, will never know, and maybe shouldn't know. Should I even be reading what he's so clearly, carefully hidden away? Or are they not really hidden, but just neatly stored, like his paints and easel?

There are also awful, lovesick poems dating back to meeting my mother in 1942; nimble, light verse about each of us kids; and singsong Valentine's Day dribble. But there, too, I discover one artful prose poem about fatherhood and time, a sophisticated short story about searchers and sinners, both with equivocal endings. Reading them, I shudder and say, "shit" through my tears, as every cruel thing I had ever said to him comes back to me, along with every encouraging, exaggerated piece of praise he had ever heaped upon even my worst high school newspaper drivel.

"Dad, how come you never showed me any of this?" I ask him a few weeks later, as he lounges on my living room couch. "I never knew you were a real writer," I say and immediately regret the tone, my indecorous literary guise. He simply smiles.

When I was in journalism school, I had occasion to tell my father that George Elliot was actually a woman. "No kidding?" he said.

"Yes. Women often had to change their names back then to get published," I said. "But don't worry, I won't change my name." But I did, the day I got married. In every byline he saw after that, I wondered if he missed seeing his name linked anymore to mine.

I am in the shower one day after a seven-hour drive, when my husband barrels into the bathroom telling me an editor from the *New York Times* just called and wants me to call her right back. On the message pad where Frank has written down her name, title, and phone number, the handwriting is how my father used to write, a distinctive mix of slanted upper- and lowercase letters, some printed and others in cursive. I know this is not how my husband writes.

"Hey, how come you wrote it this way?" I ask Frank, showing him the pad.

"I was in a hurry, who knows," he says.

I want to know.

When my essay is published, on Mother's Day as it happens, my father sits on my patio on a balmy New Jersey day, the *Times* folded back just so, a glass of lemonade at hand.

I begin to say something, but he places his finger on his lips. "I'm reading."

My dead father and I begin to have longer, fatty conversations, devoid of the angling and defensiveness that once drove my mother crazy when he was alive. There isn't time for all that. I never know when these unplanned, haphazard meet-ups will end. I know, it reads like a sappy cable TV movie: grief-stricken daughter talks to her dead father. But that is all right, that is allowed, even for smart, supposedly sophisticated daughters who agreed philosophically that cremation was sensible, but then sobbed like a sick sow when her father's eyeglasses were accidentally incinerated.

Usually, I have a question that needs answering. One day, I want to know why, in his big house with a large den of his own, he kept his easel, paints, pastels, and paper—everything he asked for as retirement gifts—deep inside the closet? "Why didn't you make some art, Daddy?" Then I remember a scrap of an argument I overhead one day soon after my parents had moved into their dream house: my mother telling him he had better put the easel and paints and pastels away after he'd finished using them, each time. "It was because Mom didn't want you to make a mess, right?"

He wrinkles his lined forehead and averts his gaze, nods slowly, as if it pains him to confirm this. "Well, why didn't you—" I begin. But then he holds up his arthritic hands. I remember the arthritis grew surprisingly, incomprehensibly worse soon after they'd moved from the frigid, humid Northeast to the dry, warm Southwest. He didn't have to curl his hand around the handle of a snow shovel anymore, but then he began to find it painful to grasp a pen, a paintbrush.

When I return to Las Vegas, I rediscover in his den a cache of other gifts still in boxes, lined up in rows along two deep lower closet shelves, given to him by me, by my sister and brother, over decades of birthdays, Christmases, Father's Days. I'd noticed it on occasion in the past, and took it as another example of my father's possibly undiagnosed, never-discussed OCD, like the way he always had to stack up old newspapers so neatly, line up condiments on the picnic table, pile up the spare coins on his side of the dresser, quadruple check the locks or that the garage door was closed, confirm and double-check and reconfirm reservations.

The day I find the unused gifts—a business card holder, a smooth leather planner, a folding travel clock, a boxed silver pen set—he's watching me from his favorite spot on the small couch across from the small TV.

"Dad, why didn't you ever take all these things out of boxes and use them? Didn't you like any of these gifts?" I ask.

"Oh, I appreciated all of it honey. But there was so much stuff. I gave some to the Mexican gardeners—they have nothing."

Sometimes when my father shows up, I'm busy doing something and I can't think of any questions. But he always has questions for me, questions he might have asked in life and which I would have heard then as criticism, as judgment.

"What are you going to do about your lack of retirement savings?" my father wants to know one dreary February day. I tell my husband that my father asked me this in a dream, and suddenly it is something the two of us can talk about without my screaming Frank's not a better provider or his yelling that I'm too controlling. I tell my husband I saw my father in a dream because who knows, maybe it was a dream—and anyway, if I said that my father and I were talking on Tuesday afternoon while I was waiting for the kids in the school pick-up line, well, that might sound absurd and then we'd have to talk about how I'm coping with my grief instead of about the retirement account (though since we are both self-employed with no company pensions, there isn't really a "retirement" account, only an "old age/nursing home" account).

When my father was alive, I often talked around him, lived around him: it was my mother I mostly talked to, across the breakfast table, at lunch in the middle of all-day shopping trips, on the phone. This made sense, but in time I came to see that it wasn't, as I'd always thought, because my mother and I were more alike, but because she never asked any difficult questions, didn't challenge me on anything more troubling than what I might wear to a holiday dinner. The time she and I spent together

kept me, in many ways, from getting to know my father better, especially when I was an adult and our visits were brief. Then, I was more
likely to agree to my mother's plan to walk the malls than to sit on the
patio with my father; even when I had children, I'd leave them with
Frank and my father and go off with Mom.

Once he's gone, I see more clearly: it was my father I took after—
why hadn't I ever noticed before? The books, writing, the appreciation
for creative pursuits. The entrepreneurial bent, quiet observation, serious attitude. Could it be that I was the child who must have reminded
him most of himself? The one who, during his lifetime, acted as if we
couldn't possibly have anything in common? I wonder how that must
have felt.

I don't ever ask him.

My friend Dee, who believes death is not an end, tells me that my
father's visits make sense. "You have unfinished business. Pay attention," she says.

So, I pay attention, but sometimes I can't tease out what unfinished business we could be completing when we sit silently on the patio
together watching my sons shoot baskets in the driveway. Or when we
gesture at the TV and huff about "damned politicians" while watching
CNN. But I pay attention. Maybe that's the point. Maybe, I decide one
day, the point—the message from my father who refuses to reside in
any part of my consciousness that holds dead people—if there is any
message at all, is this: pay attention. Period.

And I do. When my sons come in from school, I notice how much
darker the hairs lining my older son's upper lip have gotten, and I register that I can rest my head on the top of my younger son's head, and I
listen to their rambling explanations of what happened in school or at
basketball practice, and I pay attention.

For all his engagement with the world, my father wore an enigmatic
separateness. He enjoyed his colleagues—but never accepted their invi-
tations to spend a few days at their Jersey Shore vacation houses. He
took care of his aging parents—but made it clear they would never
live with us. He loved us all, I know—but kept us all a little bit at one
arm's length. He showed up (mostly) at family and friends' events, a

child's special something, a neighbor's party, and he would do and say the right things, but then he might fade, pull back, slip off for a smoke, walk, coffee, solitude.

To me, in that solitude, he seemed a little detached and world weary. My father supported others with the big gesture that was not always matched with everyday curiosity. So often he said, "I'll take care of it" and wrote checks and rented apartments for struggling relatives, underwrote school fundraisers and mayoral campaigns, cosigned loans and dispatched hired hands, called in favors for jobs or theater tickets. Later, when I try to understand what made this man generous and yet distant, I'll think that the money, connections, and logistical help may have stood in for deep connection and conversation.

He took his own "jobs," of giving others a leg up, seriously, maybe as seriously as he took the roles of provider and good son. He wasn't, however, a *Father Knows Best* or *Leave it to Beaver* dad, having meaningful spur-of-the-moment heart-to-hearts with his kids, concerned over whether or not they felt good emotionally. I wanted *that* dad and probably punished the one I did have for years because he wasn't Jim or Ward.

Once, I left college for a semester after a brutal break-up with my first serious boyfriend and was working my way slowly, painfully back to my former confident self via therapy and medication. My parents and I were at our neighborhood Italian restaurant when my father said something, and I teared up. He rolled his eyes at the ceiling and sarcastically grumbled, "Oh, I'm sorry if I hurt your *feelings*!"

Many years later, long after my dead father stops talking to me, I will spend a few months on a *Law and Order* binge watch, and not at first know why, only that I can't look away from the screen. I think back to Dad's line at the restaurant, and hear it delivered by Detective Lenny Briscoe, played by the consummate actor Jerry Orbach with a quiet integrity coupled with a judgmental and not always polite demeanor. He holds himself separate. I rewatch the film *Dirty Dancing,* in which Orbach plays a caring but taciturn doctor-father, who immediately grabs his medical bag to attend to a young woman who he will soon discover has used money he lent his daughter for an illegal, and botched, abortion. The duty, and complicated unspoken love for his daughter, that flits across Orbach's face haunts me, and I see that same expression again on my father after he dies and we talk in the night.

"I gave my word," my father explained when I questioned him once, when I was in college, about why he was paying part of a relative's college tuition. *Yes,* I wanted to say, *but you gave that word ten years ago, when the parents couldn't pay the phone bill. He shrugged.* Since my own tuition at Syracuse University was paid in advance every semester, and the account holding the money for my horse's monthly board, training, and horse show fees was always full, I couldn't think of a reasonable way to argue. He said he had once promised that he would help put that kid through college and now he was doing it. Period. When my father died, that kid did not take the morning off work to come to the wake or the funeral, or to the repast lunch, and did not call or send a card.

My father and I discuss this one icy winter day. "Can you imagine not showing up?" Of course, I must script his answer, but not out of nothing.

"Your cousin does important work," my father says. This is true.

"But after all you did!"

"Forget it, kid. There's no time for that."

———

All that first year after his death, and into the second, I am not naive. I understand that, perhaps to stave off the more typical grief response of wanting to determine just where a deceased loved one has gone, I am instead conjuring him so that I know where he is: right here. And when he's not, he'll be back.

I know too that once a parent is dead, our memory gets to slough off the legitimate, grating flaws that once accompanied that parent's earthly form. So I make a point to remember: my father was also often rigid and frustratingly contradictory. Before I married, he did not think it disrespectful to ask a new boyfriend how much he earned and to tell him, through word or gesture, it wasn't enough. But when I became engaged to Frank, who knew how to turn an uncomfortable inquiry into a joke without insulting the questioner, Dad backed down. When my father delivered reasons why something was right or wrong, he dared you with a sharp stare to argue. If he didn't know an answer, he made it up, and despite his winks, sometimes it wasn't so funny.

(Although later, when my sons learn this trick, we all declare, "You pulled a PopPop!" and it *is* funny.) It took months, sometimes years, to convince him of the merits of something he naturally was suspicious of adopting. Only after three years, and only because I stopped trying and Frank finally had a stab at it, did Dad admit that it was a good idea to switch his Visa card to one that awarded miles for the airline they always flew to New Jersey.

Once, years ago, when Dad called me to be sure Frank would be picking him and my mother up at the airport when their red-eye landed, I said I would be there instead. My father rattled off alternatives— a car service, taxi, Uncle Silv. Finally, I yelled into the phone, "Dad, believe it or not, I can pick you up at the airport even though I don't have a penis!"

He must have blushed, deeply. I knew his chivalric nerve would sustain damage, which is why I aimed for it. I was in my thirties, old enough to know better, young enough to still want to land that arrow deep enough to be noticed, not so deep to draw blood.

Over time, our postmortem conversations grow more one sided, and I worry that they will fade entirely until it's just me yapping into the ether. The more I get to know this father, the more I'm glad for the precious time. This is a man I don't want to push aside to get to my mother, even if he is also—or maybe not—the same man who kept himself to himself in life and frequently registered as aloof and impenetrable. We're both a little different now.

Neither of us is exactly who we were when he died, or even who we were in the hospital a few months before that, talking at cross-purposes about dying fathers and tipping and who could or should take care of what. I notice that each time he shows up, we are not even, anymore, who we were the last time we talked, or maybe I should say the last time I imagined we talked. I must remember this, that this father I talk to who is dead is also someone *other*.

I know that, for reasons I don't completely understand yet and maybe never will, I've constructed this father to fill in for the one I could not talk to before. Emily Dickenson wrote, "*Absence is condensed presence.*"

I know that this is not even the same father who, decades ago, handed me lit sparklers on the Fourth of July and stayed close by with a pitcher of water, or the one whose trusted hands held me in the hashing ocean of Miami Beach when I was scared that a riptide or a jellyfish or one of my cousins would hurt me.

This new father lives not in the real world, and likely never did, but in my imagination, dwelling in the interstitial byways between memory and hope, standing beneath the connecting gambrels of grief and gratitude. This father is gone, never was, and he is sitting right next to me.

I'm not always happy to see him, however, and I especially don't like it when he says something that reminds me: he could be a complete pain in the ass, could drive everyone who loved him crazy.

"Let's go. Get a move on," he'd say, jingling coins in his pocket, while waiting for others to get ready. Bound by ritual, afraid of being late, he got us to airports two hours ahead—decades before security check-ins. Sometimes, we purposely dallied, teased him, and he'd pace and tsk-tsk.

No meal could begin unless someone had gone out and returned with a loaf of fresh Italian bread. He always knew better than professional service-providers. He could be disdainful of others' goals. He didn't like it if you set a table with plastic cutlery or paper plates. Every household repair he undertook ended with swearing and duct tape. He whistled too loud, made clucking and other nonsense sounds at inappropriate times. He wasn't careful about modulating his own voice if others were working, sleeping, having conversations in the area; he had hearing loss, but denied it for decades. We teased him about it, cursed him about it, ignored him around it.

When Sean was three, and Frank and I were learning a new vocabulary surrounding developmental delays and sensory integration and processing disorders, I began to reconsider my father's "pain in the ass" behaviors we all loved to complain about. Suddenly, because I had words to describe my son's quirky behaviors, I also had words that may have explained things about Dad. Maybe my father had Asperger's Syndrome? Sensory Integration Dysfunction? An auditory processing delay? Cathy found this interesting; I don't remember if I mentioned it to Gary. Mom wasn't convinced. In any event, I purposely forgot about it for a few years, once I understood how hard my little boy had to work to overcome his tendencies, how long it took each one to sub-side, how much mental energy was required to extinguish the tics that nettled him. Once my father was in the nursing home, demented, bed-ridden, what did it matter what had made *him* tick?

"I was a real pain in the ass, huh?" my father asks the summer after he dies.

I smile, nod yes, and say, "Forget it."

"But I was," he says.

He liked to have the last word.

One fall night, I awake around 4 a.m., sweating, broiling from inside my chest, pushing the covers aside. I'm only forty-eight, but I've had symptoms of perimenopause for years. When my feet hit the cold floor, I start to gather up my nightgown, but before I get it over my head, I detect a shadow in the hallway, where I find my father. We exchange a few words, and then I cast about for my notebook and write down frag-ments of our already fading conversation.

"What?" Dad calls, his voice hoarse and creaky. He's scratching his head.

"Nothing. Go back to sleep," I say. "Don't worry."

He's in his suit, leaning on the stair rail. He seems to want to go down, but I say, "Stay."

"Don't worry," he says. Then, "I'll be back."

I go in the bathroom to fling off my nightgown, and sponge off the sticky fret of midlife.

11

Memento Mori

IN THE FIRST few years after Dad is gone, I travel back to Las Vegas several times, and on one of those visits, I return to haunting my father's den. It's taking my mother a long time to begin sorting any of his things, and this room especially has barely been touched, though Gary has staked out a place, arranging things differently. The checking account statements, the water and sewer and auto registration bills are waiting, along with notices about health insurance premiums. My father paid every bill within hours of its arrival, but Gary's system is to visit the desk once a week, usually on the same day and approximately at the same time. There's an ashtray with spent butts in it, something my mother would never have allowed to accumulate unemptied when my father was alive.

I decide to go through the desk drawers, what's left of the files in the two-drawer cabinet, and one small shelf in the closet that holds piles of papers. The only way I find I can do this, without feeling as if I am invading my father's privacy, is to talk to him as I move along, to narrate. I notice that when I do, I'm not only in the den in Las Vegas, but in New Jersey, in my youth, in my head, in this year and then that year, in history and in some kind of present infused with the past. I idly wonder if this is what it's like in the early stages of Alzheimer's, but of course I am going on these mental and emotional excursions willingly.

I am going through your things Dad, and there is the black-and-white Kodak picture with the curly edges, me on Thunder, just a Sunday morning. Oh Daddy please take me for a pony ride, please Daddy wake up it's Sunday morning, let's go you promised to take me to the pony rides. No I want to ride the big, fast horse. Daddy can I please have riding lessons, Aunt Marion said she'd take me when she takes Angie, it's only once a week okay Daddy? I got straight As again Dad, so that's $5 each right? Dad look at these cool new shoes I got at the store on the ship Mommy and Cathy and

I took to France. Hey Dad, can we go to a Broadway play for my birthday this year, thanks Dad, and can I bring four of my friends too, thanks. Dad, will you get tickets for me and AnnaMarie to the David Bowie concert, the Elton John concert, Beach Boys, Chicago, Frampton, Three Dog Night, the Steve Miller Band?

When I was a child, and even through most of my teenage and young adult years, my father seemed to be able to buy or procure anything, get anything done, arrange anything, fix anything: tickets to any event. The son of a friend out of a parking ticket. A nephew out of jail. A new toy every store was sold out of. Broken stuff fixed, in the house, car, factory. In touch with someone important, maybe even famous. The backstory. The back way to get somewhere. The right thing to say. How to convince someone to do, or make, or arrange something that person did not want to do or make or arrange. Reservations, when every seat or room or table or flight was booked, had been booked for months. The right amount to tip. Which person to tip, and the way to fold the bill and when to offer it and how.

I am going through your things Dad, and here is the canceled check I mounted and gave you with a big THANKYOU written across it, the one you wrote for my first horse, for Poco. Remember? Dad can we take Laurie on the trip to Florida so I'll have someone to hang out with, oh thanks Dad. Can Laurie come to Bermuda, St. Thomas, Puerto Rico, Las Vegas, everywhere? That's great Dad. Dad I'm going to need a better horse, my trainer says so, so how about it, I want to go to the better horse shows. Oh, about six thousand dollars I think. Dad can I go to drama camp, take acting lessons in New York City on Saturdays, go to modeling school, get a summer job at your friend's newspaper? Hey Dad it's time for another horse, I'm getting better my trainer says. Around eight thousand dollars.

I recall having a sense that no matter what terrible thing might happen, or threaten to happen, it was okay, because my father would be able to fix it, smooth things over, make it right. He knew, it seemed at the time, everyone. Important, influential people. Or he knew how to get to them. Anything, everything, could be worked out. I was in awe of this ability, and of course, I abused it. Tickets to events I was not even that interested in going to, but I knew that being able to get tickets at the last moment would make me, at least momentarily, a certain kind of popular.

I'm going through your things Dad, and here is the letter I wrote you from college. This is the college for me Dad, one of the best for what I want to do. Dad I'm going to need a new car to drive around in the snow up there. Can my horse come too, there's a stable not far from campus. I want to live in the apartments junior year Dad, please it's not that much more. Hey Dad thanks for the necklace, the Giants tickets, the Amex card. I'm doing great in the horse shows Dad, and my trainer thinks it's time for the next-level horse. Maybe twelve grand or so.

In 1975, when I was editor of the newspaper in high school, and a football fan, dreaming of becoming a sportswriter for the New York Times, I pressed my father to arrange an in-person interview for me with Roger Staubach, superstar quarterback of the Dallas Cowboys, when the team was in New York City to play against the Giants. Because my father and Staubach were both briefly on the board together of the same Dallas-based charity, and because one of my father's Texas polyester buddies knew Staubach socially, the favor was arranged, and with tape recorder in tow, I met Staubach in a conference room of a Manhattan hotel for an hour. He patiently and politely answered my questions (hatched with my brother's help the night before), signed an autograph, and kissed me on the cheek.

It was not until about eight years later that I wondered how many return favors or concessions on a future fabric deal this may have cost my father. It was not until I was working in public relations and had occasion to schedule Olympic athletes and NFL players for media interviews in connection with sponsorship and charity appearances, that I understood the imposition this had to have been on Staubach's time on the day before an important game with a tough rival. It was not until I had my own children that I recognized that that day had been made possible through equal parts childish entitlement, parental love, and gentlemanly good manners. I am not sure if I ever said thank-you.

I'm going through your things Dad, and here is the program from that big

horse show with Cool Shoes' name in it. Dad, after college I want to com-
pete on the horse show circuit and do freelance writing for a few years. But
I need to do it with a different trainer, a better trainer, in Southern Califor-
nia okay? I'll just get a small apartment near the beach, if you'll help. To do
this right I'll need a second horse. I think about sixteen thousand. The East
Coast winter horse show circuit is better so now I need to go back, to West
Palm Beach, Tampa, Jacksonville, Ocala. I'll pay for gas and food if you take
care of the trainer, hotels, entry fees, transportation, farrier, vet. I'm writ-
ing for the equestrian magazines, Dad, it doesn't pay much but I've got lots
of clips. Dad I'm going to sell that second horse. Do you want the money, or
can I put it toward expenses? I'm moving back East Dad, got a job in New
York City, but apartments are so expensive in New Jersey now, can you help
with the rent? I'll need about $150 extra a month okay? Daddy we're get-
ting married. Would I rather have $25,000 instead of a big wedding—ha!
Very funny! No, we want a wedding, thanks Dad. I found the gown of my
dreams, Rolls Royce limousines, the house of our dreams. The bank wants
nine percent interest on the mortgage Dad. You would, for five percent? Oh
Dad, that would be great, yes we will, a check every month just like we were
paying a bank.

I did not see the limits of my father's street smarts, skillful network-
ing, and his ease with the art of subtle manipulation, until he was in
his late sixties, and I noticed that it wasn't nearly as easy for him to put
together the Las Vegas financing and development deals he and Gary
were counting on. About ten years before, he had purchased a large
parcel of empty land on an outlying feeder highway ten miles from the
Las Vegas strip, hoping to one day develop it into a small hotel-casino.
He'd foreseen the inevitability of gaming properties sprawling to the
edges of the city and spilling over into the once-empty desert. Alas,
unlike his prescient hunch about polyester, this time he was about ten
years too soon, making attracting investors the hardest sell of his life.

Stymied by crushing costs of predevelopment, working in a city
where his influence cast a much shorter shadow than back in northern New Jersey, and operating in an arena far removed from the hand-
shake world of textiles, he very nearly floundered. Yet finally, they'd
secured a financing deal, gained the variances, and had booked seats
on a flight to Chicago to finalize the paperwork, when suddenly, in a

confounding confluence of events, the local zoning board rescinded its gaming approval, and the same day the relevant interest rate zoomed up about 12 percent. Finally, they sold up, certainly making a profit on the land, but I often wondered if the checks that arrived each month (my father had acted as mortgagor), had been a too-frequent reminder of a certain kind of failure. Pragmatic on the surface, always, he said he was glad to be out from under the property tax burden and the never-ending development drama. When the business pages reported, a half-dozen years after he'd sold the land, that the most valuable development properties in Clark County were now those lying on the perimeter, along the gateway highways, I used to think I saw in his eyes something close to vindication, something closer to regret, some sadness, a loss of something.

I am going through your things Dad, and along the way I'm finding crisp twenties and folded hundreds, in books and drawers, and papers, so many papers with numbers on them. And oh, what's this, file folders swelled with clippings, everything I ever wrote, edges brittled and yellow, and my dean's list certificates, pictures of me and my horses in horse magazines. Here are the poetry books with their uncracked spines, which I will take back to my home, where I write essays about what it was like to be a rich kid, to be privileged and ignorant and carefree and entitled, and to understand too late what it was to be cherished and to be yours.

I find a poem that tugs at me, because it is about a family I will join one day but can never know, the family before me, of two parents and one girl and one boy. He wrote this poem about a seven-year-old Cathy, and a three-year-old Gary. It is untitled and not brilliant, but I love it because it was written by a father I could never know, even in life, the one who existed before he became *my* father.

I slip it into my suitcase.

––––––

A pattern emerges, of Mom going to church on the thirteenth of every month, not just for the first year, but for a few years. Cathy, Gary, and my mother's friend Peg, who had lost her husband eighteen years before, all will think, eventually, that my mother is being a bit overly dramatic. Each month, usually on the 12th or the 14th, but never on the

13th itself, she will phone one of us or all of us and remind us that she was planning to, or did, go to church on the 13th.

"Oh that's nice," I will often say, and she will habitually respond with some variation of "You know why, don't you?"

"Yes of course I do, Mom. I think of him too, you know."

In the silence over the phone line, what I hear is *What good is thinking about him if you don't do anything?* The oddest part is that, for years, except for the days around the thirteenth of the month, my mother will not mention my father at all in any conversation except in connection with leftover death-related paperwork or not knowing what to do about certain chores or activities he had always handled and were now flummoxing her.

In the first year after he dies, when I try to talk to my mother about my father, she offers one- or two-word replies. If we're together, she finds something else to busy herself with, and if we're on the phone, she goes silent. This disturbs me, her intractable avoidance. At home, over coffee, I talk to Laurie about my dead father and about Dino, her dead father; they were next-door neighbors, fast friends for decades. We fling their stories into the air between us, catch them for one another, laugh, cry, and for a few minutes, those two fathers are there, at my cramped kitchen counter, at her spacious kitchen table.

I want to do the same with my mother and can't understand why the one person who is central to our connection, is a subject we can no longer discuss. Although she's often said, like so many Italians, "Don't speak ill of the dead," I want to know why we can't speak of him *at all.* She just never mentions him. Not in love, not in anger. Just, not. Not to me, anyway. Perhaps she talks about him with other widows, like her cleaning women who now mop the tiled kitchen floor, an activity her husband used to reserve for his Saturday morning exercise.

I know that part of what bothers me about all the ritual and the silence is that I think my father would have found it quite silly, or at least maudlin. I recall how easily and often he talked about his own father, joking about the old geezer's "selective hearing loss," his stingy ways, and also his ability to keep finding new sources of income for his family of ten. More than a few times, I heard Dad refer to many of his late mother's religious rituals as *rigmarole.* Then again, there were the small palm-frond crosses in the mail after Palm Sunday.

Once, at about the six-month mark, I challenge Mom: "Why can't we talk about Daddy anymore? Why don't you ever talk about him, except on the thirteenth of the month? And why do you have to go through all this rigmarole every month?"

"Because it gives me something to do," she says, and I regret belittling the social actions that for her symbolize the deep devotion they had for one another.

One early evening while I'm making tomato sauce, the kids playing outside in the snow and Frank not yet home, Dad is hanging around the kitchen island. I ask my father about the business of the thirteenth of the month.

He waves his hand and smirks, the way he sometimes did when one of his relatives was bragging, or embellishing some story. "People do what they have to do," he says mildly.

"But the histrionics, such theater——"

Dad reaches over and breaks off a hunk of Italian bread from the new loaf, and dips it into the almost boiling sauce. I do the same, but reach too far, and burn my fingers, so I turn to the sink and run them under cool water, and I know before I turn around again that he's gone.

I decide from then on to simply admire my mother's diligence in going to the church every month on the thirteenth, no matter what else is happening, if she feels well or ill. Until I learn that although there is a Mass each morning at 9:30, and that she usually arrives at 9:15, she only lights a candle in the entry foyer, then leaves and drives the few miles back home.

"If you're not going to stay for the Mass, then why don't you just light candles at home?" I suggest one day. "Just put a candle next to his wooden box. You can say a prayer as you do it."

"No, it's not the same. I told you, going to the church gives me something to do."

I still don't get it. I know I may never get it, but now I understand that there's little use, and no honor, in questioning how any other person grieves. What, I wonder, would people say if I told them that *my* way of grief—though I haven't yet come to understand that it *is* grief talking—is to talk to my dead father, to watch him move through my house, to think that we're getting better acquainted?

On a shivery day the first anniversary of his death, the sky is ach-
ingly blue with twizzles of clouds, sun streaking between branches, a
pile of yellow leaves swirling to a corner of my patio. For lunch, alone,
I am eating my father's standard sandwich of Genoa salami, provolone
cheese, and tomatoes, on crusty Italian bread. This is the sandwich he
often made himself to eat at night while watching TV, or in the afternoon to tide himself over for dinner.

This is my way of lighting a candle. I search for Dad, but he's got
other lunch plans that day, it seems.

Five years later, after her fourth heart attack, Mom will be living
with a rotating roster of full-time aides (strangers in the house!), who
take her to the doctor and sometimes to visit a friend. She will then no
longer drive but also will not ask her caregiver to take her to church on
the thirteenth of any month. One of her caregivers tells me that Mom
often likes to read the newspaper on the patio with a glass of lemonade. If she realizes these are the very things about her husband she
often complained about, she never says so. I don't either. People do
what they have to do.

I get a call from Silvio's daughter, Carol, one fall afternoon about a year
after her father's wedding. She lives two hundred miles west of me, in
Pennsylvania, and we have not seen one another since the wedding
where we had snickered together, half-admiring the old coot. Imagine getting married at that age, we'd mused, when they already live one
floor apart in the same subsidized senior citizen apartment complex
and could have gone on collecting more from Social Security if they
remained single and simply moved in together?

Carol had shrugged. "He can't be alone. She's a good woman."
What I heard behind those words, what I was thinking, was, *she seemed
like too good a woman for a man who had openly "dated" another woman
for nearly the entire thirty years of his first marriage.*

Now, it's Carol on the telephone on a weekday morning. Although
we like one another, and are chummy Facebook friends, we never call
one another on the phone.

"I know this is a long shot, but have you seen my father?"

My uncle and his new wife live five miles from me, and Carol
knows that even after my father died, he'd occasionally drop over. He'd

also sometimes drop in at Frank's business, show up unannounced to have a cup of coffee and chew the fat.

But I haven't seen Silvio much in the past year. Once, he and his new wife pulled into my driveway, but when they saw I was planting flowers they only stayed a few minutes, saying they were on their way somewhere, passing near my street. I'm sad that I don't see him anymore; I've gotten over the jolt of visuals at his wedding and want to behold across my kitchen table that nose, that hair, hear his guffaws, pour him espresso.

Carol explains that her father's new wife, Helen, called first to say that Silvio packed up some boxes, put them in his old car and said he was leaving her, moving to Florida, where two of my father's remaining sisters live. Then her father called her, only a half hour ago, from a phone booth in the parking lot of the Hot Grill—to say yes it's true, he was leaving Helen, and don't try to stop him. I put Carol on hold and call Frank, whose office is two blocks from the Hot Grill. He drives over, but Silvio is gone.

Silvio is not supposed to drive in the dark. Carol is worried that he won't have anywhere to stay along the way, that he might not even have any cash, because Helen was firm about budgets. I tell Carol I'll drive around the small nearby city of Clifton, where he and my father grew up and where he still lives, and check his usual hangouts—Gus's Luncheonette, two different Dunkin Donuts shops, the Hot Grill again.

First, I recruit Laurie, who knows all about my father's sometimes dippy relatives, and together we canvass the hangouts and press on the usual suspects. Someone must know something. An assortment of old Italian men, perched on counter stools or sprawled around tables, call us "doll" and "honey" and give us donuts and buttered rolls, but no one knows anything.

For two days, Carol and I swap cell phone calls and texts and emails, and we strategize. Laurie and I drive around some more, the same route, asking counter clerks and more old geezers if they know my uncle, and some do, but no one has seen him. I know this is not my problem. I know that I am doing this for my cousin, who works full-time and has several kids and an ill husband and cannot drive to New Jersey in the middle of the week.

I know I am doing this for my father.

Carol and I reason that her father is a resourceful guy, always land-ing on his feet. Maybe he had a plan of some kind; maybe he's stay-ing on a buddy's couch. What I don't say is, what I learned from my father is, that Silvio is crafty and selfish and often dishonest and has probably squirreled away chunks of cash here and again, that he always knows where to go for a hot meal or a little sympathy. But Carol, I think, already knows this about her father, and slowly, reluctantly, she tells me there may be another woman in the picture, improbably named Helene, this one also widowed and living a mile from where Silvio lives with Helen, the wife.

I am amused but can't say I am surprised. I can't wait to tell this to my father when next we talk, and when I do, he shakes his head and laughs and then calls his brother a clown. Until Dad was no longer trusted with cash, he had sent Silvio some money every month. He always said his brother needed the dough, even though Silvio had an army pension and spent a fair amount of time at the race track.

When my parents visited me in New Jersey for weeks at a time, Silvio always arrived in his noisy, ancient, rickety blue Oldsmobile every day at mid-morning, had a cup of coffee, and then he and my father headed out for lunch. Once, the last time my father was ever at my house, Dad and Silvio came back after only five minutes, my father running through the kitchen to the bathroom, and not making it in time. Silvio stood in the kitchen with me while my mother handed my father a new set of boxers and clean trousers. "Hey, it happens. We're getting old," Silvio laughed. Then they were gone, shuffling down my driveway and laughing, and all I could think of was the way my two sons rip up and down that same driveway, hockey sticks in hand, and I recall not minding so much about the money or the soiled boxers now waiting for me in my laundry room, and wondering about the bond between brothers.

When Carol tells me about Helene, I'm surprisingly relieved: Silvio has a place to go and is probably not driving a thousand miles alone in an unreliable vehicle. Finally, Silvio calls his daughter, tells her he's not happy with Helen (the wife), they are just too different, and that at eighty-eight he deserves to be happy with Helene (the girlfriend).

"That's when I lost it," Carol tells me.

As a teen, Carol had been rebellious and not an infrequent recipient of Silvio's harsh discipline and ultimatums.

"I told him, he made his bed, and this time it's *his* turn to lie in it," Carol explains. If not, she would not speak to him again, and he could not come visit her. "It's his turn to take the consequences," she said. And he does. He goes home to Helen.

I go back to thinking about my father, and how unfair it is that he's gone and Silvio is still causing trouble and acting up. Still, I think about calling Silvio, inviting him over for coffee, serving it in my dining room, where I have hung the photo collages we made for my father's wake. Would I be able to stop looking?

Growing up in our New Jersey suburb, I believed we were rich. We were, for that place, that time. We had what nearly everyone else couldn't afford, and I knew it. Only one other kid in school flew first class and stayed in suites. Until I traveled the horse show circuit later on, I didn't know anyone else who had a weekly engagement with a seamstress and also shopped in the most expensive clothing stores. We had restaurant meals three nights a week, and I began to think it was normal to jet off, regularly, to Las Vegas, Bermuda, Puerto Rico, Europe. At Christmas Dad often hung Mom's new diamond jewelry from the tree, like tinsel. There were new Cadillacs or Buicks or Lincolns for each of them every two years.

But Dad refused to move from our small split-level house to the tony suburb next door, Montclair, where gracious, sprawling houses whispered my mother's name. They fought about it. All the things and trips, he always said, or the bigger house. Not both.

Each time I'm in my parents' house, I raid my mother's huge collection of vintage postcards that she'd buy wherever she traveled, and keep for herself, the backs empty of scribbled notes. "Greeting from Las Vegas" is printed in an old-style red script, over a photo of the pool at the original Frontier Hotel, which survived until a year after Dad died before being razed and rebuilt in sleek modern style. The old Frontier is where we often stayed on trips to Vegas, and when I scrutinize the postcard I get a little weepy.

A man in a poolside lounge chair under an umbrella is reading, old style, a newspaper in his lap balanced on slim long legs. It's not my father, but it could be, on one or another visit. Sometimes, we'd stay in Vegas on the way to somewhere else—Disneyland and more conventional vacation spots. But Dad loved Vegas. By the time I was eight, I did too. My mother was partial to the more elegant strip hotels—the Desert Inn, Dunes, Sahara, or Sands. I loved any room, anywhere— the International Hilton, MGM Grand, the Flamingo, Riviera, Bally's, the Tropicana, and more I've forgotten. Yet it's the Frontier I recall most vividly, where I felt comfortable at a time when young girls could cavort about on their own, even in Sin City. Dad liked the size and scale of its casino—small enough to be known, big enough to disappear in—and the slightly scruffy down-home western motif. He knew it was a manufactured theme, but it appealed to his corny side.

Each evening, we dressed—sometimes in gowns—for dinner at a luxe restaurant in our own or another hotel. Our two favorites, both in the Dunes, were Sultan's Table, where a dozen tuxedoed violinists circled our table and serenaded us while we ate delicate frogs' legs, and the Dome of the Sea, where a harpist floated on a platform on a tiny waterway, the domed walls and ceiling dotted with sparkly stars in a velvet ink sky. Dad also liked to discover what he called hole-in-the-wall eateries, away from tourists and casinos. "Let's go to a local place," he'd say after five nights of dressing up, of ordering lobster and filet mignon, of pressing bills into the hands of room captains, of cherries jubilee and bananas foster. Occasionally, he'd even call for a couple of pizzas and have to phone down to warn the bell captain about the delivery.

Most nights after dinner, Dad and any men on the trip gambled, while Mom and I and any other females who were along—my sister, sister-in-law, or Laurie—spent money in the lobby shops. Other evenings were spent at hotel showrooms: Sammy Davis Jr., Liza Minnelli, Don Rickles, Ann Margaret, Robert Goulet—mostly entertainers more of my parents' generation, though once in a while, they'd agree to see someone more contemporary, like Mac Davis, George Carlin, Cher. We would tell Dad what show we wanted to see that night, he'd have a discreet chat with a pit boss, and that night, a prime center booth was ours. Often, Dad escorted us in, assured we had good seats, and then retreated to the casino, protesting the loud music hurt his ears.

I learned Vegas slang: comps, markers, the pit, off strip, the west side, book (sports, not library). I learned that *comps* weren't really free, that *markers* weren't magic, and—because I always appeared older than my age—long before I could legally do so, learned when to hit in blackjack, when to stay.

Breakfast in the hotel coffee shop was always accompanied by keno. Room service carts rolled to our suite doors regularly. Anything we wanted from a hotel store, we simply showed our hotel key, signed, and forgot about it. Laurie and I figured out how to sneak into celebrity parties, sneak onto Elvis's hotel floor, sneak back to our suite at three in the morning, mostly undetected.

The idea of early retirement in Vegas took root during those trips. My parents liked the weather, the nightlife, the sun, the relaxed pace and low cost of living off-strip. It felt comfortable, but still smacked of adventure. Reasonable building costs meant Mom could finally have her dream house, custom built. I was about to graduate college. They were only fifty-five when they sold everything in Jersey and headed west, full of good health, a fat bank account, wanting maybe to spoil themselves a little for the decades of work, childrearing, duty.

Dad was friendly with a dozen men who were executives in various hotels and casinos; Mom got to know some of their wives. It may have been through these acquaintances, plus his voracious appetite for business news, that he began to study the city's shifting tourism demographics, think about how to make a second fortune. By then, Gary was interested in moving to Vegas too, and they started to hatch an idea to build a small hotel-casino aimed at local residents, on the outskirts of the city line. Gary and his wife moved first, he completed dealer school, and was working in a downtown hotel when my parents moved into the sprawling house I'd learn to call home, as I ping-ponged from there to Orange County, California, where I'd flown out my best show horse. My father and I made a deal: I could travel the horse show circuit for a couple of years, competing on my own horses, writing freelance for equestrian magazines, trying to figure out a way to make a full-time living one day doing what I loved. Plenty of young women on the circuit were doing some variation of that. The trainers called it a "parentship."

The Frontier postcard reminds me of all of this, of the many gin rummy games we played poolside, ordering fruit punches from the bar and running up debts I'd never pay, but playing cards for money anyway because that made it more interesting to Dad, who I suspect was only relaxing long enough to get over his latest losses and get back to the tables.

I liked being the rich kid.

The kid whose father may or may not be in the mafia.

My father was not in the mafia. I always knew this. But as a kid it was fun, and often useful, to pretend, or feign innocence or sworn silence; to talk about uncles and second cousins and goombahs with names such as Carmine, Johnny the Jet, Fredo, and Fat Frankie—all real people, but not Mafioso, my father said.

On a trip to California when I was ten (the summer after the one when we'd spent seven weeks in Europe because my mother was grieving her mother's death), my father hired a stretch limousine and driver to thread us all—my mother, me, Cathy, now one year past college graduation, and her friend Hillary—along the coastal highway from San Francisco to Los Angeles.

"Take your time, the women want to see the scenery," my father told the driver, Carl, who I recall thinking was cute, but old. Probably, he was thirty. I pretended he was my boyfriend.

When we ate in nice restaurants, even for breakfast, my father invited Carl to join us; mostly he said he'd sit at another table, but my father paid. At every overpriced hotel we slept at—it took us five days to make the 350 mile trip, stopping at everything, anything of interest (huge trees! a museum! great stores! an outdoor theater! the beach!)—I remember my father saying things to Carl like "Call home from the room if you want" (this when most people feared long-distance call charges); "Go to the barber shop, get a shave if you want, sign it to the room"; "We're going to the pool in the morning before we leave, so sleep late if you want."

In Italy, when I was nine, a private driver who had chauffeured us for two weeks through Switzerland, Austria, and Italy, cried when he said goodbye to my father. But Carl mostly grunted, shook his head. Probably, he hated us. He didn't even flirt with my sister, and everyone flirted with my gorgeous sister. Once, he complained that the trip was taking so long, and my father raised his voice.

"The deal with your company was: anywhere we want to go, any route, as long as it takes." Then he winked at Carl. "Don't worry, it will be worth it."

Each day when our plans shifted, Carl reported back to the limousine company over some kind of two-way radio, and each time the dispatcher said something like "Whatever Mr. Chipolone wants."

When, finally, we arrived at the gilded hotel in Los Angeles, "the women" waited just inside the glass lobby door, while Carl opened the limo's trunk. Before he got around to unloading suitcases, shopping bags, my mother's wig case, I watched him hand my father a small yellow piece of paper, the bill I supposed. My father reached into his pocket, extracted his money, a thick wad of it, held with a discreet gold clip, and began reeling off bills, hundreds I think, or maybe fifties. He put them in Carl's hand, put away his roll of bills, and was just reaching for his wallet when the bellman asked him something, and for a moment he stepped away but held up a finger to Carl: *wait.*

Instead, Carl slammed the car trunk, narrowly missing my father's wrist, grazing his hand just enough to make it bleed. Then he hurled a string of vulgarities Dad's way, jumped in the car, and drove off so fast he left skid marks.

Later I'd learn the cash was intended to be Carl's tip, in the exact amount of the bill, while the check to pay the limousine company was in my father's wallet, which he didn't get the chance to pull out. Poor Carl, thinking he was getting stiffed.

Poor Carl, he didn't know that sometimes, only once in a while, and precisely when it suited his purposes, my father liked to pretend.

In minutes, we were up in our suite, and my father was on the phone to the limousine company.

"I was going to give your bastard driver a big tip. But he drove off with our suitcases, and almost cut my hand off. I'll say this once. If he doesn't get back here in twenty minutes flat, I'm going to make a phone call back to the East Coast, and then my brother Silvio is going to make a phone call to someone here on the West Coast, and by dinnertime, your driver is never going to be able to drive again. Understand?"

We were all watching Dad on the phone, listening, shocked, amused, confused.

He winked at us.

"Now get my stuff back here," he said very calmly into the receiver. "The women need their bloomers," he added, and we all giggled.

In ten minutes, the bell captain called up to say our driver was back. By the time my father got to the front drive, the suitcases, shopping bags, and wig case were all neatly lined up. Carl was gone.

There was rarely anything fake about Dad, and he took a lot of pride in his ability to help people, to make people feel at home, feel important.

Years later, I would overhear him in my own kitchen, laughing with Silvio over cannoli and espresso, about how rattled that limo company owner had sounded on the phone.

I ask my father about the story once after he's gone—not really about the story itself, because I was there, but about the pretending, the "family" phone threats. A grin slices his face open.

I decide when I see Silvio again, I will ask if he too remembers that story. But when I do see Silvio again, it is first at the emergency room, where he's gone because he's having trouble breathing (another phone call from Carol, but this time I know where to find him), and then it's at the nursing home a quarter mile from my house where he's rehabbing. I am surprised to find that I like having him close by, like knowing I can drop in on him.

When I need a walk, I bring Silvio the Stella D'Oro Anisette cookies he likes, and once a week or so when I need a break from working alone at home, I sit by his bed for an hour as he tells me stories about his time in the army when he was assigned to build roads in the western United States. They're actually interesting and funny, his stories, and he doesn't repeat any. As I listen, I regret having criticized my father for taking care of his brother so dependably.

During this time, a Jewish friend will tell me I'm performing a *mitzvah*, a good deed, a blessing. But I wonder if it's just me being selfish, me trying to steal time. My father was never in the military, but I'm sure there are other stories of him as a young healthy man—dozens of them, even—he could have told me if I had been willing to listen, to show up, to sit still long enough without making an excuse about all the work I had to finish.

Silvio eventually tells *me* the story about the California limo driver, and it's different from my version of course, but I can't be sure if it's different from what actually happened. I picture and hear the two of them, my father embroidering the story, laughing into their espressos.

I go home and call Carol and say that her father is fine, just fine. Then, I go hunting for, or should I say, listening for, my father. But he's silent this day, not visiting, not thanking me for visiting his brother as he's done other days. I'm quiet too, until my sons burst through the back door, home from school, joke-punching one another and laughing, sounding different and alike, sounding like something I've heard before.

Thinking about my father and his brother, I want to know what I can't know, about what it was like before he became my father. I know, or I think I understand about his business, because I listened (or at least, absorbed) when he explained. And I was there sometimes, when some big deals were conducted across dining tables at restaurants, in New Jersey, Miami, Dallas, at meals with the families of his suppliers and customers. But I want to know more about what came before all that.

As a child, my father started out poor, and then just getting by and then doing well, but not yet rich. I don't know much about those days, though I know he talked about it from time to time. I tuned it out mostly, and now of course I wish I hadn't. This is what I know. He had five sisters and two brothers. His parents were born in Italy, got married as teenagers, and were first cousins. (Oh, the jokes we made about how that may explain some of our odder relations.) Dad was sickly for a time as a child, and his gastrointestinal problems began as a teenager and young man. He worshipped his mother, feared and respected his father, and loved his siblings but was always wary and perhaps disappointed with his much older brother Vinnie, who moved away early. I try to ask him a few times, about those early days, during his ethereal (unearthly? otherworldly?) visits, but he shushes me.

So I try to piece together a sense of how things were in his childhood home, from small pieces of conversations, old stories I remember my aunts and uncles telling. But I know I am only remembering less than half of all I heard with only half-interested ears. I'm troubled by why he had to quit school to work and wonder if it was really because they needed more money, or because his father needed an assistant and didn't want to share what profit was generated with a worker who was not related. I know that in the thirties and early forties his parents owned their own house, a small rental building next door, a horse, a barn, the scrap metal business, and, eventually, a car and trucks. Yes, there were ten mouths to feed, and five of those were daughters who needed to dress nicely enough to attract good husbands. But I never understood why all of the daughters were allowed to graduate from high school and went on to secretarial school, nursing college or book-keeping courses, while the sons were made to quit and work physical labor jobs.

By the time my parents met in 1942, he was fifteen and she was sixteen, and they were both working full time. She was sewing night-gowns in a Silk City lingerie factory in her native Paterson. When she was seven, her mother, Josephine, had tossed out her father because he had another family, kept hidden across town. Noni Josephine, on the dole, her three daughters working menial jobs and a son at war, got by by keeping records for the neighborhood numbers runners.

At first, Mom thought the handsome boy she met was just as poor as she, based on where they'd met, at a dance at St. Michael's church near her Paterson neighborhood. He was handsome, flirty, cocksure, but also gentlemanly and sweet. She was lithe, a spark plug of a girl ten months older. She realized that his family had money, after eating dinner at his house (they had a whole house!) and noting that there was meat on the table. In her home, a fourth-floor two-bedroom cold-water tenement flat, the daily evening meal was always pasta. Pasta with beans, pasta with peas, with cheap greens, with tomato sauce or oil, pasta occasionally with egg or eel or meatballs made mostly with breadcrumbs and raisins; perhaps, once a month, if her mother flirted just enough with the butcher, there was some cut of rather undesir-able meat.

She tells me my father's parents never liked her, and I believe her; I could detect a cold air in my grandparents' kitchen even twenty years on. She was from the wrong kind of family, the wrong neighborhood, and for some reason it seemed to matter to them a lot that she was just shy of a full year older than their youngest son. But there he was, at a church dance in her neighborhood, just another working-class guy with an Italian last name who knew how to wear clothes and asked her to dance and dance.

When I'm a teenager, I do the math, and eventually Mom tells me the rest of the story: I picture her, at twenty-one, engaged and pregnant, facing his parents, then her mother, explaining the need to move the wedding up a few months. My mother told me his parents openly accused her of trapping him, their golden smart son, that if he wasn't getting married, he could have done something with his life. But what did they mean? Hadn't they already closed that door themselves when he wasn't allowed to finish high school? They yelled about how he'd be handing his paycheck to her now instead of them, how it all had to have been her idea (Mom says it was really his, a constant shared drama, "We're getting married anyway!"). It must have never occurred to them that they had a role in it, putting out heaping plates of brasciola.

Many years later, when I eavesdrop on my parents' late-night conversations in an attempt to understand what seems to me then—not yet married myself—a kind of deep love and volatile dislike dynamic, I hear my mother yell about why my father was "still, after twenty years, still" paying for things his parents asked for, like a new television, when there was "a couple hundred grand" in his parents' bank account.

"Don't worry about it," he'd said. "There's plenty to go around."

There was. Polyester was hot, for a good while, and Dad was smart about diversifying, about investments and real estate and collecting rents and about stocks. Not doctor-smart, but scrappy-smart. I never heard my father say he regretted not becoming a doctor, only that we kids were so lucky to go to college, even though it was costing him, wink-wink, "an arm and two legs." When my brother quit midway through his sophomore year, moved back home and began working full time at the textile factory, I saw how happy my father was to have his son around again, but I also think I saw a kind of prescient worry, that years later his son might feel stuck in a place where he might not want to be.

Even before my father dies, my brother, who worked beside his father in various businesses and varying degrees of agreeability and tension, sometimes seems bitter about it too, about not having done something different.

I don't ask my dead father about these complicated things; mostly I don't ask anything, but wait for his lead, his questions, his advice, his tone. He never mentions my siblings, and I don't volunteer any information. If he wants to, I suppose he could "visit" them, too, and who knows maybe he does, but they don't say. He does tell me to be more careful about money, which I think is funny coming from someone who could lose thousands at craps, blackjack, or baccarat and smile and say, "C'est la vie."

He could lose gracefully, but Dad never liked getting something for nothing. If a waiter brought an extra thick slice of cheesecake, that waiter would get an extra generous tip. When the gardener came by on a Sunday to reprogram the malfunctioning sprinkler timers, my father gave him a six-pack of beer along with some extra cash. But kids asking for donations so their soccer club could go to Disney got nowhere with him. Others, offering to stencil house numbers on the curb, or shovel snow, usually got hired or at least a couple of bucks and a suggestion of what other neighbor might be interested. "At least they're working for it," he'd say about those kids.

Once, on a writing retreat, I had a partial grant, and agreed to settle the rest of the fees by working two hours a day in the kitchen. Dad disapproved.

"How come they aren't paying *you*, kid?" he asked.

I tried to explain about the value of time away from home, and uninterrupted creative hours, and being among other artists, and he said "Oh," and we leave it there.

I want to ask my father if he ever regretted how we spent his money, how he lost some of it, how it came to draw a certain shape around his life, our lives. I don't though. I want him to be proud, even in death, that he'd showed his children something about money, even if he thinks that what he showed us was not what we learned.

12

Crossing the Midline

SHORTLY before my father dies, Sean completes eight years of therapies to address developmental delays. Physical therapy. Occupational therapy. Sensory integration therapy. Speech therapy. Vision therapy. Auditory processing therapy. "Don't worry about labels or a diagnosis," we'd been told. "Just get him what he needs." He needed a lot. But by twelve, he is all caught up; *intact* is the buzzword—meaning more "neurotypical."

I am not convinced the timing—of my father's demise and Sean's emergence from the grip of whatever the hell he had/has—is coincidence.

One of Sean's symptoms of multiple developmental delays was that as a toddler and young boy, he couldn't "cross the midline." If he was coloring with the crayon in his right hand, and needed to color in a section of paper to his left, he had to switch the crayon to the left hand. When holding an object in his left hand that had to be put at the right end of a shelf, he'd need to transfer it first to his right hand. It was almost as if he couldn't see anything as belonging to a continuing whole, as if everything existed only in its parts. Watching a tennis game was torture, because the tendency was to watch only one side, then the other, but not both at once, back and forth. Moving both feet in sync to inch along his little plastic Cozy Coupe car was agony.

As my father slipped from life, and my son's life began to open up, and as my grief progresses and I sense some unspoken edict that I'm not moving on fast enough, I feel like a child who can't cross the midline: handcuffed, frustrated, and unable to understand what I'm doing wrong, since what I'm doing is working for me. That it's what I know and how I cope. I begin to see my grief as my inability to cross some kind of invisible but important midline of my own. I can't see the whole, only one part at a time.

One thing I do think I see in full is that my father and my son share more than blood.

My son, with his rigid behaviors and his quirky ways, who constantly asks for help then bats it away, reminds me of the father who infuriated us all with his rigid behaviors and his quirky ways, who insisted he never needed help.

When Sean first hooked his right hand into the waistband of his pants, I started to see. And now, here is my father in the shape of my son, sitting here in my living room, watching sharks on television. When my father told a nurse to do something exactly the way the other nurse had done it the day before, there was my son, in the hospital bed. Why did it take me so long to see these two, sharing something stronger than blood, strangely true like fiction, moving steadily in their orbits: I am amazed, ashamed, not to have seen it sooner.

By the time I can make sense of them both, my father is living only in my memory.

As I get to know my gone father better, I learn more about my corporeal son. As I watch my son grow and thrive, I find more ways to comprehend my disappeared dad. When I worry that it's too late for me and my father, I know it's perhaps perfect timing for me and my oldest boy.

Sean seems to share not only his grandfather's brain wiring and sensory dysfunctions, he takes after his PopPop in other ways. He pretends to know answers to things he has no idea about. He likes a tall glass of orange juice every morning. He thrives on predictability, expected results. For a long time, I am not happy about this. One day I notice Sean on the patio, his long legs crossed one over the other, a book in his lap, the sun setting just beyond the line of tall evergreens along our back fence. His posture is so much like my father's, squinting because he refuses, like him, to wear sunglasses. One day, when I get some unpleasant news, this manchild hugs me with one arm, rubs my back with one hand. Whenever I express any lack of confidence, it's this child who tells me how great I am, how I should believe in myself. If my father visited upon his grandson some of his more infuriating tendencies, at least he's also passed along a few of his most endearing. Sean seems proud when we say he's "just like PopPop."

Only now I see something—or maybe I mean I imagine something—I could not before: that my father, when he was a teenager, might very likely have been just like my son. That idea—and I may be wrong in a clinical sense, but it feels right—makes a difference. Dad: I wish I could have told you before you died in a way you could have understood, that I think I get it now. I think I get *you*. But if I had told you Dad, that I think you have some kind of neurological quirk, you probably would have grimaced and glanced away or walked away, and it would have been just one more time when I felt misunderstood. I don't trust myself to put this into words with my father during one of our unearthly conversations.

When my father was far away and dying and scared, I'm told it took massive will and energy for him to sit up in bed, severely curled by kyphosis as he was, like a comma. At that same time, talking to me in our quiet house, Sean, who is twelve and smiling, energy in his every hand wave, telling me elaborate stories of school and friends and bullies, can't get the words out fast enough, can't sit or lie down for three seconds without shifting, kicking out long (and when did they get so hairy?) legs. On the corners of his mouth are dark hairs, his underarms smell musty each evening now, he combs his hair only on occasion and talks in code to his friends about girls. He has my father's body, the lean legs, thin arms. He has my father's mannerisms and manner of speech and hands.

The midline has disappeared.

About eighteen months after her husband dies, my mother has her first of what will be four heart attacks. She calls me at midnight in New Jersey, where I am doing what I do every night—watching TV, writing in a notebook, and trying to overcome the driving need to binge on junk food. I am in one of my frequent but inevitably short-lived periods of gradual weight loss, of eating in moderation, regular exercise (mostly walking), and fitting into the smaller-sized clothing from the attic.

Mom is yelling on the phone about how I don't care, how I don't come to Las Vegas enough, despite her calls scolding me. This is only partly true, but I know that when I'm home in New Jersey, I want to stay put. Here, I'm oddly comfortable with my father's ghost bumping around my house, which may be one of the reasons that I've not dealt more directly with her mounting distress, her widowhood. But we have all been to Vegas. And she's visited us twice in New Jersey. She's been driving around Vegas, meeting Tessa for lunch and shopping, showing up for her weekly bowling league games, zipping over to CVS to pick up this or that and spend thirty minutes at the slot machines just inside the store door. There's been no particular health scare, no mental dysfunction, no reason to make an unscheduled emergency trip. There has been only loneliness, which I've rationalized wouldn't be relieved in any substantial way by more frequent visits from me, though perhaps this is just what I want to tell myself.

Yet, tonight something in her tone is off; she's weak and thin voiced when normally she'd be full bodied and bold in her guilting accusations. I call my sister, and we compare schedules and figure out which one of us can make a visit soonest, but for both of us it's weeks away. I call Gary, and he says he was there earlier, that she's fine.

The next morning, she dials him at 5:20 a.m., just before passing out on her bedroom floor. No one knows how long she may have had pain down her arm, or felt her chest tightening, or how long she waited to call. I only know that when I arrive there a week later (Cathy will swap with me in two weeks), her sink is full of dishes, days' worth of her soiled underpants are tossed in a corner of the bathroom. Her bed is unmade. I can't think of anything—not the deepest sadness, only perhaps the worst pain—that would cause my mother to neglect keeping her house tidy.

I go to Vegas first because writing freelance articles and completing graduate school assignments are both portable. I make camp at the kitchen counter and undertake the final revisions on my graduate school thesis and run to coffee shops for internet hook-ups and to Kinko's to print out pages. It's inconvenient and costly, and my brother grouses that I should be at the hospital more and at the counter working less. I call Cathy daily with updates and my frustrations, and she is sympathetic and, always concerned for my mental health, suggests I defer a semester or two.

"I did that, when I was in graduate school and had a miscarriage," she reveals.

"But that was about you and your body and you were only thirty," I growl. "I've waited twenty years to do this, and I'm not delaying, not for anyone."

This is a lie, of course. If my children were ill, or my husband's business was failing, or my own health was compromised, I'd be filling out the deferral forms without regret. I work and I shuttle to the hospital and back, and I defrost and cook (or inspect and discard) most everything in my mother's freezer, and I eat alone at the smooth counter, feeling my father's absence, new and sharp and differently than in New Jersey. I wait for him, but he doesn't show up to keep me company.

I remember back to the first time I was in this house while one of my parents was in the hospital.

In 1999, a week after my mother had quadruple bypass surgery at age seventy-two, I'd left four-year-old Sean and fifteen-month-old Paul home with Frank and flown out because my father was an uncharacteristically shambling mess, Cathy couldn't travel for another few weeks, and Gary couldn't handle her transition from hospital to home without help.

I was in the early stages of having lost around eighty pounds—again. I was shaky in my new body and my new eating habits and new daily exercise patterns. Although I did take a thirty-minute walk around the perimeter of the hospital's large parking lot that first afternoon, it was more out of claustrophobia and frustration.

When I arrived at the hospital, the first thing I heard from my mother, whose weight surely contributed to her heart disease, was "Oh I see you're getting skinny now." She wasn't pleased by my appearance. My mother refused to perform the respiratory exercises designed to make her strong enough to go home and was complaining about the food, nurses, discomfort, thrice-daily blood draws, the light streaming through the blinds, the too-few television channels, being constipated, and more. In the way of all adult children who return home—even if that physical place is not the house in which we grew up but only the place their parents now call home—I reverted to my immature, known teenage child-self.

That first week, I could barely stand to talk to my father, falling apart at the prospect of her not recovering, and it hurt to see how shaken he was by the possibility that he'd be widowed at seventy-two, that his wife could leave him to face a world grown impolite and strange. We shared rides to the hospital, shared meals, decisions, awkward silences.

I had no intention of sharing myself.

That week, though, was the beginning of my early (and then easily forgotten) suspicions that maybe he and I were, after all, the similar ones. As much as I understood that I loved shopping with my mother and all our long phone calls, and tried to emulate her sense of style and admired how she brought beauty into a home, I could see some glimmer that at my core, perhaps I was more like my twitchy irritable father, that his desire to spend hours or days reading and thinking and making plans and lists felt more familiar. But I wasn't yet ready to do anything with this information, and with her in the hospital, I longed to please my mother, to reinforce the idea that we were simpatico. Anything else might have seemed disloyal.

That first night, when my father and I returned to their house from the hospital at around nine, I broiled him a steak and steamed myself some frozen vegetables. We talked in broad philosophical terms about illness and recovery, and by 10:30, drained, he went to bed. Jet-lagged, anxious, missing home and not sure what *this* home meant to me, I wandered, read, paced. There was plenty of space: giant great room, luxurious living room, welcoming dining room, den, guest rooms, more. Although I'd lived in that house for a few months after college, this was the first time I was "home alone" there, for after my father retired to his expansive master bedroom—the one whose square footage equaled half of my own house—behind the double oak doors at the far end of one of the house's ell wings, it felt as if I were very alone. Since becoming a mother myself, it was also my first time there without my own little family, without sticky hands, folding cribs, car seats, and overtired children. I had no idea what to do with myself, and I hadn't yet learned to listen to myself, to accept the idea of not doing anything with myself, of just going to bed, of seeking restoration in preparation for what I already knew would be long, frustrating days ahead. My father found solace in the newspaper and his patio breezes, in TV and pacing and complaining about arthritis, in straightening towels. I sought motion, the distant lure of what used to feel comforting: shopping, and overindulging.

I grabbed my mother's keys and drove around the corner to the twenty-four-hour Walmart, grinning at the tone-deaf zoning laws in Las Vegas that allow large discount stores a half mile from a neighborhood of sprawling, custom-built ranches half the size of football fields. I told myself there were things we needed, that I had to find a comfort bra for my mother and a pair of flip-flops for me, having forgotten it could be summer-like hot in Vegas in April.

At Walmart, I tossed the comfort bra into the cart and lingered over the bin of flip-flops: pink with a silly flower, or utilitarian black? Then I was wandering around with an XXL basic white comfort bra and impractical pink flip-flops in my cart—why did I get a cart for these two small, light items?—and it yawned empty, as empty as I felt in my new body, as desolate as the store, as deserted as my parents' house, as vacant as my own reaction to my father's inexpressible fear.

And so I did what I always do in times of extreme stress. I ate my way to a temporary relief, which morphed into compounded stress.

Three times before that, I'd lost somewhere between 60 and 100 pounds. Each time, my mother's grudging notice and razored remarks ("You've lost your curves") reminded me becoming slimmer made us different, while my father usually reassured me: "Good for you. You'll be a lot healthier now."

I snuck back into the house from Walmart (though the door from the garage to the kitchen is of such an upscale design that it's virtually silent, and he was sleeping fifty yards away). I had a big bag, and inside was a bra, flip-flops, two magazines, a bag of Doritos, a box of Chips Ahoy, a couple of candy bars, a cheese Danish, and a box of Pop Tarts. I don't remember what else, but there was more. I tiptoed across the deeply padded carpeting to my father's study, where I selected a predictable mystery novel I'd read before (I needed to turn pages and not think). I could have sat at the expansive kitchen counter, but instead I put on my nightgown and sat up in my queen-size bed, reading, and eating. And eating. Self-medicating.

I read and stuffed myself, crumpling wrappers into the thin white plastic store bag, which I took directly to the trash barrel in the garage. I remembered just as I was drifting to sleep, that my father, an early riser, would be bringing the barrels to the curb the next morning, and it was his habit to pick up the barrel lid and push down on the top of the trash even if he didn't need to fit any more in.

Back home in the house two days later—identical days of hospital waiting and sparring with my mother about how she had to breathe into the blue plastic tube and why she had to take walks round and around the nurse's station, and why they need to take blood every few hours, and why she couldn't go home yet—my father and I were clearing up after a meal of Chinese takeout, when I said I was going to Walmart to get my mother a new pair of sneakers with easy fasteners.

Dad nodded and said, though not unkindly, "And this time, don't go getting any of that other garbage, okay?"

I swung around, too quickly and with too much sarcasm in my voice. "Why are you digging in garbage anyway?"

He mumbled, "Never mind," and slunk away, like a dog after laying a tennis ball at your feet that you've snatched up and hidden in a pocket.

That night, worn down, I returned from Walmart with only sneakers, a magazine my mother likes, and a box of Slim Fast protein bars, and went to bed early. The phone jangled around five in the morning, both of us picking up the extensions near our beds. It was Mom, adamant. "I'm dressed and I'm checking myself out. You better come and get me." Click. Over the extension, I asked my father what we should do.

"I'll go," he said.

I said I'd drive.

In the car, he chewed his fingernails, smoothed his hair a dozen times, crossed and uncrossed his legs.

"She has some nerve," I said, "making us get up at this hour to deal with such theatrics."

"She's scared. You don't know what it's like."

"Oh Dad, please!" I moaned. "She acts like this all the time. Don't you know her well enough to see that?"

"I know her pretty well," he said. "But you don't."

In the moment, I overlooked the nuance. Of course I knew her; of her three kids, I knew her best, didn't I? Hadn't we spent decades shopping, talking, eating? Hadn't we driven across the country together seventeen years before when I'd moved my horses from California to Florida, giggling and stopping off any place we wanted? Hadn't I listened to her complain about *him*? About his controlling edicts, his lack of understanding that besides taking care of his kids and cooking his dinner, she also wanted to work part time but he wouldn't allow it.

Even then, it had begun to occur to me that while she may have been misunderstood in one aspect of their marriage, it was a marriage of its time, and not my responsibility to right perceived wrongs. Holding a grudge against him because of something they chose, even if by default, was silly as well as bad for our relationship; I'd inserted distance even beyond the solitude he naturally craved. I began to see that looking at someone else could teach me something essential about a part of myself, and that when this happens, I'm likely to flail away in flight.

When I was a teenager, I sporadically treated my father terribly, making nasty remarks about anything and everything he said. I refused to engage in a civil conversation with the man who bought me overpriced horses and who once had offered to send me to expensive private high schools in New England or Gstaad. I was bratty and doled out teenage arrogance and flippant pretentiousness. Once, while he was driving and I had impaled him with another one of my rude smartass summations of his clearly unenlightened ideas, he said, "You treat me like a dog."

I didn't argue.

What fueled my mistreatment of the parent who never criticized my choice in friends or boyfriends, is still unclear, though I suspect it was my way of deflecting what I didn't see myself as worthy of receiving. While my mother loved me fiercely, affectionately, grandly and steadily, she also disciplined me with her hands, and made me a kind of co-conspirator in her annoyance at, among other things, not getting the bigger house she longed for, venting a kind of bitterness in my presence and sometimes, on me. Dad kept his frustrations, and his hands, to himself, and he treated me with a detached adult-like respect I certainly hadn't earned but which was proffered in the same way, the only way, he knew to treat anyone—with politeness, deference, and a sense of equanimity, if not warmth and effusive devotion. I never felt coddled by him as a child, and he, in a bid to instill independence and self-reliance, sometimes expected me to act too soon like a grown-up.

When I was about ten, and wanted to take horseback-riding lessons at a rather fancy stable a few miles from home, he insisted that if I wanted to ride badly enough, I should "pick up the phone," speak to the people at the stable, make the arrangements. Another two years went by; he wouldn't call, and Mom, for some reason, didn't feel something like that was in her purview. I didn't ride until "Aunt Marion" invited me along to her daughter's lessons.

I learned. I learned to make the phone calls, speak to the right people, and whenever after that, I failed to speak up, or did speak up or out, or complain, I've heard his voice in my head. And I've tried to become that voice in my sons' ears: make the call, say your piece, speak.

Dad didn't agree with everything I spoke up about either, but he let me know that my judgment was acceptable if it was in line with my beliefs. This last became clear when I brought a young black man home to our street of split-level houses where only white families lived.

Brant was one of the barn managers at the stable where I kept my show horse, in charge of keeping the right stocks of grain and hay, driving and packing the show van. He was twenty-three to my seventeen. The age difference alone was not even part of the reason for my mother's outrage. I'd already always dated older; she'd watched me dance with young men in their twenties, on cruises, at resorts, family weddings.

Dad was a registered Republican who often voted Democratic, a business owner whose employee roster had always been rainbow colored. I only announced Brant's imminent arrival minutes before he rang the bell, explaining that Brant was now more than a face in the crowd of stable buddies. Dad shook his hand, led him to a spot on the living room couch, brought him something to drink. While my dating rules had never been strict, still I took this to be my father's clever way of defusing my interest: accept the boyfriend or else risk her secretly sneaking around. But when I remember my mother's horrified expression, her whispered urgent pleas to my father in the kitchen "to get that colored guy out of here before the neighbors see," I also remember his response: "We know him. He pulled our car out of that snowbank last winter, remember? Anyway, she likes him."

I did like him very much, and though I didn't invite him home again except for one Christmas party, I saw him off and on for a few years while home between college semesters. Dad sometimes knew, but we never talked about it. When I was twenty-one, on our last night in New Jersey—Dad and I were staying in a hotel before a morning flight, while Mom had traveled ahead to their new retirement house in Las

Vegas—Dad shook Brant's hand once again, asked no questions, and went off to have dinner with Silvio.

I didn't appreciate any of these gestures when they happened, but not long after Dad died, they all came flooding back. How could I have assumed, even for a brief time, that I'd been left with the one parent who knew me better than the other? As I came to understand it was the other way around, I think my behavior changed, subtly, slowly. It no longer seemed possible to hide anything about myself that revealed where I stood, on anything. I believe Mom saw that as a betrayal, another loss. Yet, even before all that, within days of becoming a widow, my mother seemed to go away from me. By two years later, when I told her I'd voted for Obama, she was appalled, and I felt her go cold on me. I like to think Dad would have voted that way too. When I ask, he doesn't answer.

When I begin writing about my father, not long after he dies, it isn't because I now claim to know him best. I begin writing about my father because I want to know him *better,* because I'm hoping that a reunion of sorts might be possible, on the page, in our conversations.

I turn again to *The Invention of Solitude,* where Paul Auster writes: "I had lost my father. But at the same time, I had also found him." I don't recall a profound sense of recognition when I'd first read those lines around the time Dad died. But later, I am shocked to see that I had highlighted, underlined, and circled them. There's an easy explanation, maybe: the first time, I needed notes for a grad school assignment.

By the second time I find those heavily notated lines, I'm scared that Dad's visits may stop, that my sons are going to forget their PopPop, that my husband is no longer sympathetic to my loss because I've lived up to my reputation as a strong, resilient, pragmatic person.

I want to tell everyone that I too had, finally, found my father, but I also want to keep quiet, keep this big, pounding truth to myself, and mostly, I do.

Meanwhile, my own life pulses on.

I put on weight again, learn that I am heading toward diabetes (like my maternal grandmother, aunts, and my brother). As I'd long suspected, I learn I've inherited my father's weak bones and vitamin deficiencies, and Mom's family's heart and metabolic issues. Despite having seen how ignoring his health issues contributed to Dad's death, and how Mom's inattention to her own problems is worsening her condition, surprisingly, I ignore it all. I binge-eat, I don't exercise, I skip medical tests. I lose weight again but gain it right back. I even break a new dining room chair. The pain in my right knee is a combination of arthritis, osteopenia (pre-osteoporosis), and—a condition I've never heard of—osteonecrosis: some bones are dying because enough blood cannot flow to the area to make enough new bone to replace old bone.

Frank and I begin to argue about anything, everything, agitated quarreling that erupts then settles into bouts of multiday silences. My freelance work isn't bolstering our finances in the way we need. One child is in high school, the other four years behind; college tuition is a certain future nightmare we don't want to face, and so we don't. I pretend to seek enough work to bring in a full-time income, but secretly am satisfied with my half-time cash flow. Bouts of *why-can't-my-husband-be-more-like-my-father?* resurface, and I sense that Frank resents the time and money spent on my graduate degree. He loses a customer who accounts for half his business the same day I secure a plum assignment. I have to reconcile the role I can and cannot play in managing my mother's worsening, weakening heart and kidney problems, with her desire to move back to New Jersey but refusal to sell her expensive home. Together, Frank and I decide our sons must come first, before anyone, everyone else.

When I've had enough, of almost everything, I announce that I—we—have to *do* something. I tell my husband our marriage is slipping, that we don't seem like each other's biggest admirers anymore. He doesn't agree, but we talk, about how much of it is because of motherhood, or my mourning, how much is midlife. He jumps in with me to fix it. I accuse him of not being supportive of my writing, so he—a lifelong nonreader—begins to read more of it. We buy me a new car, big and powerful. He starts to cook dinners. We go out more, alone, talk more. I go after more and better-paying freelance opportunities, easing the financial worries a bit. Desire wins out, the flame ignited when we met on a bus trip to a New York Giants game when I was fifteen sparks again.

Cathy and I continue to make tag team visits out west, but I don't think it is ever enough for Mom or for Gary. We all go on.

I find only one through-line: if I write a little bit, every day, about the father I fought, I find peace.

I still want to know more.

When in Vegas, I study a certain item on the family room wall. When my mother turned eighty, I asked my siblings, and all her grandchildren and friends, to write down a few things they liked about her and some of her hallmark characteristics. Between them all, they came up with thirty-five notes, so I wrote the rest. I titled the resulting document, "80 Things We Love About Mickey," typed it up in a fancy font, and framed it.

I wonder if I could have come up with forty-five things about my father.

I want to know more about him, so I paw around in memory for moments that perhaps passed by me too quickly, with too little notice. I want to know if I ignored meaning, missed opportunities to ask him about his life before me, assigned motives where there was only love.

When I did something, or said something cruel, and he said, "Forget it, kid," I used to think it was in response to that one thing. As we communicate more in his afterlife, I come to think he meant it more globally, as in *forget it all*, no need to apologize about any of it: all is forgiven, maybe even forgotten. Move on. "Forget it, kid."

I am thinking about this one night when I wonder if he'll drop in for a chat. It's been a while, and I don't know how I feel about the visits dwindling—relieved or worried. I only notice, as I might not have when he was alive, that it's been a while since my father and I had a conversation.

I'm at my dining room table, where I often work into the night, the soft whir of the refrigerator behind the wall in the kitchen, the sharp occasional ping of the hot water traveling through the baseboard heating pipes in our old house, the odd creak of our old mattress upstairs as Frank rolls over in sleep.

Something seems suddenly off in the room. A shadow or quickening falls across my computer screen but so briefly it could have been the moonlight, or the patio lights shifting through the thin gauzy cream curtains. My father is standing near the window, one hand looped in his trouser waistband, flat against his abdomen, the other arm straight and leaning on the back of a chair. He seems to be waiting for something. Maybe he does not want to interrupt me, or is he, again, simply waiting for me to pay attention?

"There you are," I say. "I have a big deadline. Hang on."

"I'm going now," he says, as he sometimes does when we're done talking, though we haven't even begun tonight.

I mutter, "Okay," eyes still impaled on the computer screen, not so much because I'm concentrating intensely, but because something about the way he's standing triggers a memory of him in his best I'm-the-father-I-have-spoken mode. I can't look. Anyway, he has politely said goodbye all the other times when we have talked in the night, alone in my hushed house, boys and a man sleeping above us, unaware. But I have the clear and vivid sense that this is a different kind of leave taking. I think about asking why, or even where he has to go, or trying to talk him out of it but quickly (and I think, wisely, but who can say?) decide against it.

"Dad, I'm sorry," I say, finally turning from the screen, an urgency rising in my chest. "I'm so sorry . . ."

"Forget it kid," he says. Then he waves a small goodbye with his big right hand, his face resolved and mostly calm, save for a little twitch I think I detect in the chin.

He leaves, then, dissolving into the curtains. I do not know if I will see him again, and for many months I don't, except in dreams—the real, nighttime ones that follow me around like a hangover until past lunch the next day. Many times when I'm replaying the dreams over my morning coffee, my mind drifts to that bittersweet film *Yentl*, in which a confused and yearning grown-up child sings to ask her gone Papa: *can he hear her, can he see her?*

Once, I dream that my father has died, and in my dream I go to the local funeral home to make arrangements.

The funeral director seems confused. "I'm sorry, Lisa, but didn't we have your father's services here already?" Bill asks. He speaks slowly and with kindness.

"Yes, of course," I answer, slightly amazed someone in his line of work could be so obtuse. "But it's happened again."

"Oh, I see," Bill says, nods, and opens a file. "Well, then."

———

Although my husband is quick to remind me that it may not have been technically necessary each time, I've performed the Heimlich maneuver four times—three times on my own kids and once when a friend's four-year-old son choked on a big bite of Italian bread. I would love Dad to have seen me with the friend's boy, like to think he'd be proud.

But I'm relieved he wasn't around to see my own boys' choking. Not that Dad was paralyzed by medical crises—in fact, the opposite. I remember him dislodging an apple chunk stuck in my throat once when I was five and lying on the floor in our living room watching cartoons on a Saturday morning while everyone else was in the front yard raking. How did he know to come in the house at that moment and haul me upside down by the ankles and dig his strong fleshy finger in my little mouth?

When I was ten and my mother found me bleeding into my pillow (I'd hit my head on a cabinet door an hour before bed but it hadn't hurt), he'd whisked me off to the hospital and watched while I got stitched up. On Thanksgiving Day when I was twelve, I fell down our brick front steps and broke my front tooth, and it went through my lip. Dad roused a doctor and dentist.

But action was different from worry, from anxiety and fear of loved ones getting injured. Dad was the one who taught me to instantaneously jump out of my seat, spring across the house any time I heard anyone cough, or a loud sound that could have been a fall, or a screech that was probably laughter but could have been pain. He taught me to yell, "Are you okay?" up the stairs, or down the stairs, or across the yard. My father taught me to worry, to fear losing someone or something because I couldn't get there in time enough to do something about it.

I don't think he meant to teach me those things, but he did.

My father taught me how to walk with my feet pointed out, "like a duck" on icy steps. He taught me the difference between clear and yellow and green phlegm, and when to go to the doctor for a sore throat and when to just sip juice and eat fruit. He taught me to watch the way any man I dated treated his parents. Is there an end to the list of things a father teaches his daughter?

————

I'm not sure if membership is restricted to daughters without fathers, but I decide that I've joined a club without rules: we do what we can to continue to conjure up those fathers, no matter how surprisingly flawed or exquisitely fine we after all find them to be. We understand that it's preferable for parents to die before their children; we may explain as much to our own children. But we are not whole; we are not intact. We ache. We mourn, but not always in the traditional sense. Our mourning, our grief, works in ways that make sense only to each one of us. We begin thinking we will keen, but most of us don't; or if we do, it's only when we are alone when no one will hear, no one will see, no one will pat our back and tell us *it* will get better in time, that *things* will settle down soon.

I am sure it is the same with motherless daughters, but I will not find this out for years.

From what I can extrapolate from my own first few years without a father—and I do know that it is my experience only and not perhaps representative of anyone else's—it seems to me that fatherless daughters think and feel and do things others might judge as strange, in the name of things we cannot even accurately label. Grief? Mourning? Loss of security? The cavitating sensation of falling out of my own life. The comforting idea that time heals, taunts. It. Things. Get better. Pass. The idea slips wet from my dried-out hands.

About two years after my father dies, I read an article that analyzes the distinction between what Medicare will pay for and what is in the best interest of aging, frail human patients. The article notes that taxes are paying for operations such as hip replacements for elderly people who for significant other health reasons cannot even attempt the requisite physical therapy rehab.

I read this and many other things.

I read an article in another newspaper describing an atmosphere, in the pharmacy of the hospital where my father spent weeks prior to the nursing home admission, of chaotic mismanagement, slipshod procedures, incorrect drug labeling, malfunctioning calibration machinery. My father had had pneumonia and was taking between six and nine medications daily. He was allergic to penicillin.

I wonder, I worry, I wish for—I don't know what, not a way back exactly, but that I had been more able to speak up across the miles. When I dream one night that my father is slowly limping along next to me on a precarious walk around his Vegas backyard, I apologize for not speaking up, not picking up the phone more often, as he taught me.

"Nah," he says, placing his warm hand on my forearm. "That wasn't your job."

But I think it was.

I wonder more about things that we never discussed.

My father quit smoking cold turkey one day in late December 1993, after being hospitalized in Las Vegas for severe chest pains, described as "only" angina. It is on the same day I give birth to Sean in New Jersey. I'm told the angina incident scared him enough to stop what by then had been, for a few decades already, a two- to three-pack-a-day habit. I like to think that my son's birth had something to do with it as well, something along the lines of his wanting to stick around to see the boy grow up. But by then he already had four other grandchildren, so I may be kidding myself.

In the late sixties, when I was a child of about eight or nine, I frequently hid my father's cigarette packs in the tiny kitty-corner shelf tucked under the belly of the white baby grand piano in our living room. I was afraid he would get lung cancer, of course, afraid he'd die and leave me and my mother alone, afraid his lungs would be as black as those we'd seen in a scary filmstrip at school. I didn't know then all the other ways smoking so heavily would deteriorate his health, but Laurie had already pestered both of her parents into quitting, and now it was my turn. Remembering the charade, I have to question my resolve or at least my level of commitment: I hid the cigarettes in the same place each time.

I did want him to quit, but at the same time, the crush I had on my father—that crush I think almost all little girls develop—was somehow connected to how he dressed, how he looked when he was going out on a Saturday night with my mother, and in that memory, part of that vision, was the way he held a cigarette in his hand. The photos from that period bear me out. In every picture, he is inhaling or exhaling, or holding his cigarette poised between the long fingers and buffed nails. He resembled a movie star. Movie stars back then were smokers.

Sometimes he'd ruffle my hair and teasingly ask for the hidden packs back, and other times he'd demand, curtly, that I return them, depending I guess on whether or not he had another pack in his car, or a drawer somewhere I didn't know about, and maybe on how many unsmoked cigarettes remained in the pack always in his shirt pocket. Funny that I can't recall him ever folding his long strong legs and tucking his winsome head under the piano and snatching the packs back himself. I don't even recall that he ever pointed to the piano or in any other way indicated that he knew where I stashed the boxes. But I did not make any show of waiting until he was out of sight to retrieve them, always from the same spot. I wonder today what game we were playing with one another back then, with ourselves.

Mildly to me, he'd say, "Okay, very funny young lady. Now give them back." Or, less mildly to my mother, "Why do you let her keep doing that?" Sometimes to me, "Get them. Right now. And don't do that again."

Then I'd crawl along the green shag carpet, scrape the packs from the shelf, and go find him, sometimes by then already out on the patio smoking and reading the *Wall Street Journal*. I might sheepishly hand them over, or slap them down on a table, depending on my mood. If one of the pilfered packs was already opened, I sometimes pulled out several cigarettes before returning the pack. These I sometimes crushed and tossed them in the kitchen garbage can, edging them underneath that morning's coffee grinds. Other times, I secreted them away in the back of a drawer, behind my green school uniform knee socks, or zipped them into a compartment of a fake leather purse. I don't think I wanted to smoke them, but I wanted to have them.

There they would sit for a day or two until I grew panicky my mother might find them, and then I threw all these away too, buried deeper in the kitchen trash, wrapped inside a wadded tissue. Once, I buried them in the backyard while digging up dandelions, wondering idly if a tobacco plant would rise up the next spring. I dropped them in the toilet and then was a little anxious they might not flush down, but they did, after first spreading their insides across the bowl, the paper tubing softening and disappearing. I peed on top of them first.

Dad was smoking heavily by the time I was old enough to understand the differences between addiction and social posturing. He once told me he had his first cigarette at nine and was smoking regularly, openly, by twelve. A boy smoking as a preteen in 1938, in the Italian immigrant neighborhood where he'd grown up, was nothing shocking or unexpected. Boys were regarded as young men by that age then, already able—expected—to help their fathers with matters of earning money, doing the heavy work, using their bodies as a wedge against the possibility of even a family's fall into poverty, hunger, homelessness. By twelve, he was already working alongside his father "the junk man" after school and on weekends, hauling broken-down furnaces and other metals from residential basements or old factories, heaving them onto a wagon pulled by a horse.

When my father told me these stories when he was alive, I tried to picture this elegant man, who liked to neatly turn up the bottoms of the sleeves of short-sleeved shirts into a neat crisp cuff, as a gangly adolescent in torn dirty pants and too-tight shoes and soiled sweaty shirts, tried to picture the wagon, the horse (old and often lame, he said), the streets, the occasional motorcar, a housewife holding open her door for the boy and his panting father, as they maneuvered out hulking broken-down and rusted radiators, boilers, utility sinks, pipes, pulling from her apron pocket a few pennies or a nickel for a tip, him taking puffs between stops.

I want to be mad at my grandparents for letting him smoke and must remember that little was known then about smoking and cancer, heart disease, emphysema, brain cells. Idly, I wonder if my own sons' future children will one day want to know what my husband and I could have been thinking, allowing our boys to do something that, in twenty-five years, may become the smoking of its day—using a cell phone, keeping a flash drive in his pocket, drinking milk from antibiotic-medicated cows.

I try to picture my father, puffing from a cigarette dangling inelegantly from his lips, a young man against a tableau of cropped low houses, noisy streets, stickball games, laundry hanging in dirt backyards. He is the smart polite boy who everyone thinks can go far but went only to work, at thirteen, setting bowling pins (where he was allowed to smoke while working) and at fourteen in the Nabisco factory (where he wasn't). This handsome boy, who wanted to be a doctor, smoking cigarettes and thinking about Walt Whitman poems, is the same crush of my childhood, inhaling deeply and blowing smoke rings on the patio behind our suburban split-level, the day's problems at the polyester factory behind him, the newspaper in his lap.

On a chilly winter day, my father and I are talking about nothing in the kitchen while I clean up after dropping the boys at school, when he gets up from the stool and disappears. Next, he's sitting at the patio table, and lights a cigarette. I grab my jacket.

"What are you doing out here?" I ask. "And by the way, you quit smoking long before you died. So what's up?"

He waves me off. "I don't know, kid. Maybe I didn't quit soon enough for it to stick."

"Dad, you're funny."

He flicks the ash in the air, and it floats away, and in a few seconds, he does too.

Much as I may have hated it, my father's smoking habit was also part of what made him irresistible. It was also a dirty habit that made his teeth yellow and my mother's custom living room draperies smell. My half-hearted attempts to get him to quit when I was a child did nothing. When I was older I simply forbade him smoking in my bedroom, in my car, and later, when I had my own home, I banned smoking everywhere inside, and when he visited he sat in a lawn chair smoking on my patio, in the heat, in the chill.

Improbably, I smoked too, for a while, on and off (mostly off) for about two years. It was just after college while I was traveling with two ridiculously overpriced Thoroughbreds on the horse show circuit, supported by my father's money and easygoing nature. I hated the way cigarettes tasted, how their smoke made my clothes smell and, when I caught a glimpse in a mirror, how I looked with a cigarette in my hand and how it felt in my mouth. But I started as a way stave off the nearly paralyzing anxiety I had in social situations with fellow horse show competitors whose fathers made fortunes while wearing elegant suits

behind desks on Wall Street or in executive suites at major corporations, not grimy textile mills. I stopped the day it became clear that even
when I felt relaxed, I still had nothing in common with them except
an ability to buy pretty horses and swipe credit cards with our father's
names on them. Not once did I ever let my father see me smoke.

In 1993, no one tells me about my father's angina scare until my mother
arrives in New Jersey to help with my newborn. By then, I am already
teetering on the edges of an abyss we'd learn to call postpartum depression, which would stick around for nearly two years. My reaction to the
news that he'd quit smoking is a mix of resigned acceptance, fear, and
I-told-you-so and also admiration and respect, picturing him—in the
way it was described to me—tossing out his cigarettes right in the emergency room and then not taking another.

But I don't share any of these emotions. Not joy or relief or gratitude. All those years, I had raged, and he always said he couldn't quit,
that the addiction was too powerful, the chemicals too strong, the need
too great. All those years I'd pleaded, "But can't you do it for us? For
me?," and he said he couldn't, and *now* he could? For what? For whom?
For himself? For fear of dying, of no more afternoons with the newspaper? It should have been enough. I should have been happy, grateful.
I know that the next thirteen years of mostly good days, when he got to
play with my sons, were likely possible only because he did that, he quit,
and while it may have been selfish, it was also very good for all of us.

But at the time I felt something else. I felt like a child hiding cigarette packs and only half-grudgingly handing them back, scared but
also infatuated by an image, when the real culprit was not the cigarettes
I once watched floating in the toilet, but something else, a boy who
at age thirteen already knew that so much else was out of his control.

As my sons grow beyond what their PopPop can witness, I watch Sean
move slowly, but passionately, toward his life's dreams: to study meteor-
ology at college, to work in forecasting. I watch Paul discover what
makes him excited: the internal workings of computers and all electronic devices. And I continue to think about my father again at those
ages—how he had dreams but no resources, professional ambitions
unrecognized in a milieu that valued only the ability to put a meal on

the table, honor one's parents, make a sacrifice. I didn't ask him, ever, if he regretted or was bitter about leaving school, abandoning those goals, and so it's presumptuous of me I know to think I know his heart. He made a living, a life, respected by industry peers and community members. Maybe at some point along the way, the old dreams left him, and he didn't mind. So I don't ask.

I leave it there.

As his visits ebb, it matters less that I ask him anything at all. The further I move from the day he died, the visits become less talky, more a quieter communion, opportunities to observe and listen. Each time I am afraid it will be the last, and I am less willing to tread any trail I cannot navigate without stumbling, hurting myself. As I see Dad less, I see others more.

13

A Country Full of Old Men

ON A TOO-WARM fall morning in 2008, just before the second anniversary of Dad's passing, I am moving tables and chairs into place in the small township library two blocks from my house. I am going to teach writing to adults. The library has secured a grant, and I am being paid to teach creative writing for the first time. Since the library cannot charge participants for the class, it is with halting trepidation that I await my first students: who signs up for a free memoir-writing class on a weekday morning? Will any of them even be able to write— anything? Are they coming because they are bored, lonely, unemployed? Just like to read? I do not know what to expect. Sixteen names are on the list, but I'm pessimistic that people will show up and so I arrange only ten chairs, figuring that if six or eight show up, it won't look so bad. *I* won't look that bad.

I am worried about so many things, but mostly that they will want someone younger, someone less care-worn or who is more obviously optimistic, someone who believes that everyone who writes can write well and all those who want to be published will be. But I am not feeling optimistic. It has been a difficult year, and I feel old.

Since completing graduate studies in the summer, I have been interviewing for part-time and even full-time writing-related jobs. Twenty- and thirty-something managers regard me as though I am their grandmother, and they ask about my "energy level" and whether I'm "comfortable online." I'm forty-eight and some days, feel seventy.

There has been accumulated change, worry, and loss of other kinds. Our church parish has sent away Father James and the other Franciscan Friars, who were interesting, engaging sorts, "liberal" priests, people I respected and liked, and in their place sent dull Diocesan replacements who are doctrinaire, who are apparently uninterested in getting to know their parishioners, and have trouble looking me in the eye. My sons have moved on, from middle school to high school, from primary school to middle school. Laurie and her husband are considering moving away. My mother's heart attacks are piling up. Even trivial losses conspire to shake me: someone steals the decorative grillwork that was on the front of my big SUV when we bought it, the grill I at first didn't like, but grew to love for the way it made me feel—fierce and fearless. And there have been a record number of rejections from editors, and even though there have been acceptances too, it is the rejections I focus on.

I am loose with all this change.

Then. Something wonderful happens as I make photocopies of the handouts and pull my dog-eared books from my canvas bag. I notice that I do not feel old this morning. I feel energized, excited. I have something to say, and, I hope, people to say it to. Decades of writing have toughened me, softened me, to their plight. Maybe age is an advantage, here.

Then. Another wonderful thing happens. Fourteen people arrive and take seats, pulling up extra chairs and angling in to fit around the two tables I have matched together. And the next wonderful thing happens: though I am older than a lot of them, I am younger than a few. Much younger, in fact, than one in particular.

We go around the table and share info: one would-be writer was laid off the week before from Lehman Brothers, one is a stay-at-home dad, another is a former copy editor. There's a nurse, an attorney, a genealogist, and a wedding cake baker. There's the former library director from when I was a kid. A few retired folks. Then there is Gregory Maxwell, who is old. Very old, ninety. This makes me feel younger, and I must ashamedly admit—upon his self-introduction, learning that he is hard of hearing, and a wiseacre—impatient. Here is yet more evidence of a pattern in my life of late, which I do not understand, but cling to.

In the last two years, I have been collecting encounters with old men, stalking them. Or, perhaps I've been seeking them out. Everywhere I go, there is an old man I am certain I would not have noticed before. I watch their gait, gaze at their age-spotted skin, smile at the familiarly stained cardigans, recognize the way they clear their throats, cough, and shake their heads. I watch, transfixed, as they unfold dollar bills from a neatly folded stack, remove hats the moment they walk through a door, neatly fold their trench coats over the backs of restaurant chairs. Once, an old man at a Red Lobster stirred his coffee with a butter knife, and I cried into my crab legs. Do all old men do that? I thought it was just my father.

About seven weeks before, we are at a diner eating breakfast on a lazy Sunday morning, my husband, our two sons and I, when I notice an older man a few booths away, who sharply resembles one of my father's old textile business cronies. I contemplate wandering over to introduce myself. I would say, *Excuse me, but you look so familiar. I'm Tony Chip's daughter,* and he would smile immediately and say something like *Good old Tony, how is your Dad?* This has happened often enough in my life, though much less frequently in recent years than it did a decade or so ago. Still, when it does, I warm.

Only this will not happen because, I remind myself, we are on vacation in Maine, hundreds of miles from New Jersey, the only place where my father lived and worked when he was in the textile business. But even if we were home, I'd have to stop myself. The odds that someone I remember from when I was a teenager or young adult, some thirty or so years ago, would still be recognizable to me today, would even be alive now, are getting slimmer. I am not good with numbers, but I can add and subtract. I know that any middle-aged man my father was likely to have done business with in the 1960s or '70s is by now likely quite old or, like my father, dead.

For some reason, this man's demeanor reminds me of the protectiveness among my father's mid-century textile associates—mostly Italian or Jewish men with strong ideas about family and especially daughters. As a teenager, I found it irksome and patronizing, even condescending. What right did they have, I silently raged (and sometimes vocally ranted), to watch over me, for example, during a convention in Miami Beach? Why right did they have to tsk-tsk and smile and shake their heads and warn my father about the boys who would be soon coming around? Why did they think it was okay to protectively watch as I crossed a hotel lobby to the restroom to be sure I got there and back okay simply because some odd man had paused a moment too long in my path?

The man I see in the diner is too young, maybe only in his early seventies. As I push pancakes around my plate, I think about what it will be like to never again see one of my father's old business friends, one of his old Moose Lodge brothers, one of his third cousins, and have them greet me with nods and wide grins and sloppy handshakes and awkward hugs, and say nice things about my father and ask if he's enjoying his retirement out in Vegas, or offer surprised belated condolences.

In fact, maybe the last time this will happen has already happened.

When I was twenty-four, I moved back to New Jersey after a few years boomeranging between Vegas and Southern California, and between Florida and Central New York, and all over the East Coast horse show circuit, riding and writing. I moved one town away from my childhood suburb and worked as an account executive in a public relations agency in Manhattan. During those years, I had these encounters more frequently, and I bridled under the men's affectionate embraces and warm words about my father. Then, I wanted to be myself and not just Tony Chipolone's youngest daughter. What I might give now to have one of these older gentlemen look into my eyes and see in them a bit of my father, have one of them gaze at my nose and see a hint of my father's big familiar schnozzola. To hear even one of them tell me, with a slightly reverential tone, "I loved your father; he done a lot for me," or "Your father is a prince of a man." These praises made me wince, once.

Once, I was on a dinner date when I spied one of my father's business buddies several tables away. By this time, some people were surprised to see me in New Jersey again and not living in the Southwest near my parents. The man glanced in my direction a couple of times before I waved, and finally he rose from his table, slid a napkin across his lips, and approached.

"Aren't you Tony Chip's daughter?" he asked. I said yes, and we had the usual conversation about how my parents liked living in Vegas (they love it) and how was my father's health (the desert agrees with him) and what was my brother doing now (dealing blackjack). Then this gentleman, shifting nervously, kept glancing from me to my date, who was twenty-three years my senior, and whom I introduced as "my friend, Andy," though he was clearly more than a friend. My father's old crony raised one eyebrow, pulled a card from his wallet, and placed it in my palm, cupping his entire hand around mine.

"Say hi to your Dad. And honey, you call me if you ever need anything, you call me, understand? I know what it's like to have a daughter living far away." He squeezed my hand.

I miss hearing someone say that I am "Tony's daughter." I miss who I was allowed to be when he was in the world.

I suddenly, hungrily want this other older man in the diner in Maine to tell me what a good man my father was, to hold my hand in his and offer to slay an unsuitable suitor, to be anyone who knew my father, to look my way. I keep watching him. I know it can't happen, but I continue my fantasy that it is someone who knew my father. I want this man's familiar slow gait, and the BAND-AID twined around his eyeglasses (do all old men do that?), and his old coot's mischievous and familiar-sounding laugh to mean something. I want him to tell me stories about when my father could dance until three, negotiate a better restaurant table, fix a stalemate, make a big loan and keep it quiet.

I see my father. This particular old man does not see me.

That night, Paul tells me he has had a dream. "PopPop and I were jumping on a trampoline. He was old on the outside, but he was still young on the inside." My son repeats this last sentence twice.

I tell him that's often how old folks feel, that no matter how old someone is, they may still feel inside the same way they did when they were much younger. I hope this is true, and I am also fairly sure I'm lying. My father looked, in his final months, old inside too. But, I hope.

These old men, the ones I fixate on, the men who are strangers, I wonder about how they might see me. A pleasant middle-aged woman, maybe the age of their own daughter? I always exchange a greeting with every old man I notice, whose eye I catch. Can they know my secret, that because I ache for my father, I yearn for their watery eyes to rest on me, for a minute, a lifetime?

There are plenty of eighty-something men about, men the age my father would be. Not all of these octogenarian men interest me, however. The ones who smell as if they have not showered in days, they do not remind me of my father, who gave off always an unforgettable mixture of Dial Soap and Old Spice aftershave. And the men who have grown mean spirited or who are rude to strangers—these men do not hold my attention, being nothing like the pre-Alzheimer's father I knew who said, to busboys and clerks, to taxi drivers and to executives, *would you please* and *thank you ever so much* and *if you would be so kind* and *I certainly appreciate it.* These men who mutter, *damned right* and *you better believe it missy* and *hurry up* and *it's about time*— they are not worthy to occupy any of the space in my mind reserved for my father.

Of course, I am forgetting. Forgetting about the times my dad was a curmudgeonly bother, when he put on a self-righteous face and thunder leaped from his eyeballs at a hapless service person, or at me. But in these cases—or perhaps in the way I remember these situations—the anger seemed justified, the ire earned. I am forgetting when it was not. That is all right, as long as I know I am forgetting, and I do.

One day over a school winter holiday, Sean goes "on the road" with Frank, helping make deliveries of shoe polish and laces and waterproof spray to shoe stores. As they are carrying boxes from Frank's van down a sidewalk to a mom-and-pop shoe store, a bent-over old man falls on ice only yards away. They both drop their boxes and help him up, Frank hoping the man needs only a minute or two to settle, because there are many deliveries to make that day. But the man has cut his hand and is shaking, and sobbing and shivering. Frank bundles the man into his van, drives the old man a mile back to his house, and calls the man's son. Sean fetches a blanket from the man's living room, and in the man's kitchen Frank boils water for tea. They don't leave until the man's son arrives. Later, Sean tells me two things. That, as a Boy Scout, he's performed an extra special good deed of the day, and that the man reminded him of his PopPop.

While I am in a book store buying large-print mysteries for my mother-in-law, waiting for a prescription at the pharmacy or a pound of sliced turkey at the deli counter, when I am at the eye doctor picking out new frames, my gaze settles on old men. Men with neatly combed gray hair, with button-down shirts tucked smoothly into belted pants in "easy care" fabrics, the ones with canes or eyeglasses with lenses that distort their eyes, the ones who smile at strangers for no reason other than to be polite, who begin statements with "I'm an old man, but in my day . . ."

These are the old men I need. I wonder if I am going to need older and older men all the time, if I will continue to calculate how old my father would be if he were still alive.

I wonder if my interest in old men will last until I'm old myself, and there will be no men around anymore who are old enough.

I'm curious that these old men seem endearing to me, someone who, when her father first became befuddled, thought of old men very little at all. I began to bypass my father's muddled attempts to stay in a conversation. I talked around, over, and down to him. When he began having trouble following the plot of an hour television drama, I did not explain it to him, slowly, during a commercial. When he was at my house once, about six months before he died, and was trying to work the TV remote, after three aborted attempts, he eyed me plaintively. "I can't do it anymore. Can you do it for me?" I shot back, "You can so. Just try." Even as I said it, I was thinking what a little shit I was.

Maybe I figure these old men, if I smile at them nicely, they won't think I'm a little shit.

In the library at my first class, with his shuffling, *I've got-time* walk and tendency to repeat himself, nonagenarian Gregory Maxwell's presence in the room, reminding me of my status as the daughter of a dead man, rattles me. I am also aware that to maintain order, I need to temper Gregory's perhaps unintentional attempts at taking control of the agenda with his self-deprecating humor. But I have no idea how to do this, either as a teacher or as a woman who could be his daughter.

Gregory has come to class without, he explains, his hearing aids, and *could I please speak up.* I ask him to sit next to me, and he does, and he smells like aftershave and stale crackers. When I ask if everyone uses email, he pontificates, in a not annoying way, about why he has no use for a computer and asks if he can recite a poem he's written about how his brain is better than a computer. I tell him I would be delighted to hear it when it is time for sharing toward the end of the session. His long blink makes me wish I had responded differently, but how? Allow anyone to recite any poem at any time? We have work to do.

I begin a discussion about reaching back in our lives for stories, and I notice Gregory's big brown-flecked hand resting on a small diary, the once-black leather worn to dull brown on all edges. I ask him about it.

"This is my diary from when I was a boy, in the 1920s. Oh, there's a lot of stories in here, you bet," he says. I expect him to say more, but he quiets, nods, and taps his fingers on the book. For a second, I want to reach across and push open the clasp (does it still lock, I wonder?), but of course I do not.

"I hope you're thinking of writing about some of those times?" I ask, no I *instruct*, stupidly impressed with myself.

"Oh, I don't know. It was all so long ago. I'm pretty old, you know," he says, his hand stroking the book, his eyes averted.

"Well, that's okay," I say, not knowing what else to say.

Gregory throws his arms up in the air and smiles. "It's okay that I'm old? Well thank you very much!" The lightheartedness is back in his tone, the tease returned to his watery eye.

Everyone laughs. I notice he has crossed his stilt-like legs one over the other at the knee the way my father used to, and that on his eyeglasses is a frayed BAND-AID. I am glad to have my notes to concentrate on, printed out, slid into plastic sheet protectors, in a neat three-ring binder, because I don't know what will happen if I keep looking Gregory's way. As I discuss writing, I glance at each student and try to ignore Gregory's slow nods, the way he raises an index finger in the air and dips it slightly to signal his agreement, in precisely the way my father did.

I can't look, and I can't look away.

Later, when others are reading aloud from the writing exercise, Gregory doesn't volunteer. And I forget to remind him to recite his poem. After class, I'm packing up notes and books and chatting with a seventy-something woman who wants to write about once being a "women's libber," when Gregory leans my way and explains again, interrupting, about his hearing aids and how he won't forget them next time, and when I ask him to remember about the assignment, he answers that he won't forget because it's already in his "computer" and then he begins to quietly recite the poem about his brain, and at first I think I will have to feign being charmed, but instead I realize it's actually quite good.

"I like that poem, Gregory. Will you write it down so we can all read it next time?" I ask.

"I don't need to write it down, I can say it out loud again next week," he says.

"Yes, but I'd like everyone to see the words on paper. You can write it in long hand. Or do you use a typewriter?" I realize that I am exasperated, that I am nearly shouting, and though the man is hard of hearing, he is also standing only inches from me. I realize, but too late of course, that the exasperation is not about his hearing aids but about how frustrating it was to communicate with my father in the last few years of his life.

Before he capitulated to all of our entreaties and got fitted for hearing aids, Dad misinterpreted much of what was said to him. "What would you like to drink?" I would ask him at dinner. And he would answer, "What? What do I think?"

His hearing aid was either always malfunctioning, or forgotten (often on purpose), on his dresser, left behind in part because he could never get the hang of adjusting the volume. Once, on the phone with my husband, he kept asking Frank to repeat himself, which my patient husband did.

Finally, Frank said, "Maybe you need to adjust your hearing aid?"

Dad said, "Good idea. Hang on." When he returned to the phone, my father asked Frank, "There, is that better?"

It occurs to me that getting through to Gregory might or might not be the same experience, but that I had better be careful—this man came to me for advice, and even though he may, like so many students in so many classrooms, at first be suspicious of or cavalier about the advice he's being offered, I could do real damage here if I assigned to him all the unresolved business between me and my father. I need to keep our interactions between us, me, and Gregory.

Gregory says he might write his poem down, and I say thank-you and I remember to look him in the eye when I say this. Later, when Frank asks how my first class went, I tell him it's an interesting group of students, most with a high level of interest, but that I am still a bundle of nerves, even hours after class has ended, and that I think it's connected to Gregory.

"He's an older man, really old, and he's sort of annoying, but also charming in a way," I explain. "He can't hear, he interrupts, he makes bad jokes, and I'm not even sure he wants to write. I think he's there just because he's lonely."

"Or maybe he wants to write and just happens to be old," Frank suggests.

"Maybe."

I think about Gregory's diary. Why would he bring it along if he did not want somehow to share its contents? I wonder if I should have asked him to read from it, if I should have asked, politely, if it was all right for me to peek inside. Is that what he wanted? For someone to open that old book, to travel backwards seventy-five years, to nod, to know?

As part of their assignment, I've recommended they choose one of three different books to read over the course of the eight weeks. I invite my students to email or call me if they have questions about the books, or any questions. I know I won't get an email from Gregory, and I hope I won't get a phone call; I remember how in his final years, when I was trying to talk to Dad on the phone, I'd be shouting and rolling my eyes in my empty kitchen, and he'd be saying, "what" and "how's that" and "say again." I know how often I gave up. I have no idea how often my father wanted to give up.

Then, on day three, the phone rings, and my younger son reads from the caller ID. "It says, Maxwell, Gregory. Who's that?"

I take the phone. "Hello, Gregory."

"Oh, you know it's me! How clever, these new phones! Listen I have a cold, it's not that bad, but I don't want to give it to anyone and it's chilly out so I won't be coming tonight, I'm sorry," he says.

I am momentarily confused; tonight, I teach the first session of a different class. I suddenly realize he's signed up for that one, too. Now I decide he is more interested in social contact than writing.

"Gregory, you take care of yourself. Don't worry about it at all," I say, pronouncing my words slowly and with care. I wonder for a moment to whom I am actually talking.

"Well, I wanted to ask you: I wrote a play a while back and I wondered if you'd read that. It's about my life."

Immediately, I am embarrassed for treating him as a prototype, a lonely old man, not a writer, and worse, as a stand-in for my father, for all old and seemingly sidelined men. I feel stupid, for thinking his age might have any bearing on his ability to write, or to think. Hadn't I just recently become acquainted with the other end of that kind of thinking? And I realize I have mistaken my job here; it's not to make a nice old man feel he is still vital, or to give him something to do and somewhere to be a few times a week, but to figure out what he needs as a writer.

"Of course I'll read it," I say.

"Good. I also have a story I want to write, about the time I found my best friend kissing my girl. You know back then, a kiss was a big deal, so catching them kissing, that was a major thing for me—I was about nineteen. Would that be the kind of true story I can write?" he asks.

"Yes, that's perfect. Does that come out of your diary?"

"Oh no. The diary—that's other stories."

I am beginning to feel better, as though I am the teacher, he the student, and age doesn't matter and that I have clearly established the boundaries we both need. Then Gregory tells me again that he has a cold and is not coming tonight, and could I read a play he's written, and that he has a story to tell about his best friend and his girl.

During this time, I'm also editing other writers' self-published books. Many are family histories and tributes. One is by a woman in her six-ties, a short but loving biography about the artistic life of her father, a respected watercolorist whose Florida landscapes, which will be printed in color in the book, remind me of so many childhood vaca-tions, of walks with Dad along Florida parks and reserves. She's in a bit of a hurry because her octogenarian father is losing his eyesight.

I rush the work ahead of other projects and cut my usual fee in half when she explains, "He can feel it slipping away."

She meant his vision, I think.

Gregory only comes to the morning memoir-writing class twice more, and the last time he shows up, he hands me his play script. When he doesn't come back, I decide it is my fault, my clumsiness. Did I push him away? Did I try to get too close? When he had asked if I would take his diary home and read it, and I'd declined, graciously I'd hoped, was he offended? What happened was, I'd glimpsed the slanted script inside, and feared tearing the dry tea-colored pages. I also didn't want to be responsible for taking it home where I routinely lose books and my eyeglasses and treasured old recipes from my beloved dead aunt Antoinette. I suggested that he photocopy it first and give me the photocopied pages the following week, and when I left that day I saw him at the copy machine with a stack of dimes, studying the row of blinking buttons, perplexed. In a hurry to get somewhere, I didn't stop to help him. Guilt resurrects a day when my father phoned, telling me to go out and buy that day's *Wall Street Journal* so I could read something "very interesting," and my asking him to have my brother email me a link instead.

I think about whether I should phone Gregory, or find his address and mail the likable play back to him, marked up now with some encouraging notes, or maybe drop it in his mailbox, even ring his bell. But I do not phone him or ask the librarian (the one I noticed he seemed friendly with) if she knows whether Gregory is okay or if she has an address. Then I think Gregory may be absent simply because he has another cold. I picture him in a doctor's office where the young internist slaps him on the back and says, "I hope I'm in as good a shape as you when I'm ninety."

I do finally ask the librarian if she knows if Gregory is okay, but she says only that he hasn't been in for a while but sometimes he does that, and then shows up again. Weeks later, I will try to locate his name in the community phone book, but I will not find it. Two years later, I will ask someone in town who seems to know everyone else over age eight-five, and she will nod and say, "yeah, I remember him but I don't know if he's still around."

On week six, as I'm juggling my heavy tote and switching my sunglasses for the new bifocals I can't get used to, I momentarily think I see Gregory when I first enter the library. But I'm wrong. When I get closer, it is a new older man I see, already at the seat furthest from where I will be teaching, a walker parked beside him, a yellow legal pad and a black fine marker on the table. He has not been here before and I wonder if he's in the wrong place, or expecting something different this morning— the historical society meeting maybe, or the geologist scheduled the next day to discuss the centuries-old boulder some Cub Scouts found in town decades ago.

I smell him first and it is the combination of that, plus the sight of his walker, his stooped seated posture, the sparse hair littering an ear, his wool sweater vest over a flannel shirt, and the smooth cold curve of a hearing aid seen from behind, which pulls me closer. He smells like too many cigarettes, too little mouthwash, and too much espresso, a little cologne and antacid: in other words, my father has come again to call.

I introduce myself and learn his name, Joe, and I suggest he come sit right next to me so he can hear. Joe takes the seat at my left hand, closing in on me with a question in his rheumy eyes. It turns out Joe is the person I spoke with by telephone a few days before, when he asked if he could join the class even though it was already underway. I had pegged him to be maybe sixty, but I undershot by at least twenty years. As I unpack my handouts and water bottle, Joe tells me he is deaf in his left ear but the hearing aid in the right works great; likewise his left eye can see nothing. By happy coincidence I have directed him to a chair from which he will, I hope, be able to both hear and see me.

He wants me to know more: He writes slowly. He must leave five minutes early to walk the library path to the parking lot where the senior citizen bus will be waiting. He recently had a ministroke and is always cold.

All the while, all this while, I am responding with what I believe to be a civil demeanor, nodding and smiling (but only really listening with one ear myself, listening as my father might have), and I am hoping that Gregory will come back today. I think of Joe as a possible buddy for Gregory, the way I used to point out men my father's age around his neighborhood and urge him to introduce himself, which he never would do, the way I once scouted out playgrounds and sandboxes watching for potential playmates for my sons. But Gregory does not arrive, and I am glad because how will I cope with two old men repeating themselves, waiting through the seconds while they form a question, tell an anecdote, precious class time falling away?

The first day Joe shows up, I spend ten minutes talking about prying loose details from stubborn memories so we can write about past events, then I ask if there are any questions. Joe is first to raise a hand, tautly wrinkled and bulgy with arthritis.

"I would like to read something," Joe says, his left hand smoothing the flat top page of the legal pad, which was empty when we began and is now three-quarters filled with deeply angled script.

I repeat my mistake, responding with *my* need, with what *I* think is important—maintaining order, being fair—and already I know I am wrong, but I cannot stop myself. In my head, I am talking to my father, explaining why I can't come out for Thanksgiving, because my husband has a family too, because one kid has a double ear infection, because finances are tight, because, because.

"We always have some time at the end of class for people to read, so will you hold on to it till then?" I ask. Only I don't really ask, I tell, and of course I expect that Joe will quietly nod and smile and say he understands. Only he does not nod and smile, but nods and goes quiet, and just before I turn toward Betty, whose hand is in air, I see something in Joe's gaze, something in the way his right hand leaves the air and scratches his temple, which saddens me.

Forty-five minutes later, when it is time for those who wish to read, Emily volunteers and I neglect to turn to Joe and to say, *now's a good time, would you like to read first?* Already, he's standing, adjusting his walker, and begins the journey to the senior bus.

That night, my husband and I are driving somewhere alone together. I try to explain why Joe, and before him, Gregory, cause me so much worry, consternation, guilt. Why I cannot seem to get either of them to play by the rules, how I probably will not ever be able to help them as writers if they will not at least try to do things as I wish.

"I guess I'm just not cut out to teach senior citizens," I say.

"It's not that. I think you just see your father every time you look at them, and you miss him," says my husband. "You could never teach him anything new either, remember?"

Months later, at a minor league baseball game in northwestern New Jersey, Frank heads down to the concession stand for ice-cream, and I watch him move aside to allow an old man in a bright Red Sox jersey make his slow way up. The man stumbles, nearly dropping his pretzel, and Frank reaches out to catch him so that the man won't fall on the concrete steps. There's gratitude on the man's face, understanding in my husband's eyes, a tear in mine.

There is so much to learn, but the old men, the ones who follow me, are teaching me—about still being young in an old body, about what we owe those who are truly old. I'm learning something too about what we shouldn't try to repay.

The old men are not really following me; they were there all along, but I see them now. I recoil from their beseeching gaze. I move toward it.

14

At Home in the World

BECAUSE I WANT to teach from it, I reread *The Woman at the Washington Zoo*, a book of essays by Marjorie Williams, a journalist who died of cancer at age forty-seven. In one passage she tries to explain how, in her childhood, her self-denying mother dimmed her own career desires to support her husband, a luminescent standout in his professional field. The author admits, in an essay entitled "Into the Sun," that even at a young age, she knew she would follow her father's path, seeking not just a career, but to be accomplished and successful in her field and that she knew this would eventually cause her mother discomfort, even jealousy, and erupt later in a not well-cloaked anger. Still, she knew she would choose "the sun," choose to move into the bright open world like her father, leaving her mother, once again, in shadow.

I sometimes think that is what I began to do myself as my father was dying, moving on from the mother-advocate self who had put everything aside while my boys were young, moving on from the temporary homemaker role I think my mother was happy to see me in, not only because it meant less stress for me, but because for a time my adult life mirrored the one she'd lived. I think she also resented that my grad school enrollment and my attempt at revitalizing a career meant I had to get mentally and physically busy in a way that precluded long, lazy visits to Las Vegas where she and I would hang about, talking and shopping. It meant I also wasn't always available to linger so long on the phone with her, to spend entire days when she visited New Jersey watching old movies. My father—the little of this he could witness before he died—took in my new busyness without much comment. But my mother saw it perhaps as a betrayal, especially after he was gone and she wanted more of me and I had less time to give.

It wasn't so much that my father directly lit this sunny path for me, though he was, always, moving straight ahead into new ideas for another business, more investments, ways to expand, increase, improve, learn, earn. Certainly it is his example of self-determination and entre-preneurial spirit that I carry, but the scurrying, in my mid-forties, just as his life dimmed, into my own version of the sun, was propelled more by a realization of how diffused my life might become if I didn't push through. I could easily have let myself repeat my mother's self-deny-ing stance, sacrificing another dozen years not for an ambitious hus-band but for the needs of my sons. I could easily imagine a brownout, the second half of my life shadowed by sons' flights. It scared me how close I came to doing this, hovering in my children's silhouettes, peck-ing at my husband's activities, neglecting my own desires.

It was Sean who jolted me, one day in the car after I picked him up from fourth grade, and he asked his usual daily question, "What did *you* do while I was at school, Mom?" I answered, in a sad tone, "Oh, the usual," and he said, "You have to find something to do."

And so I did.

I didn't exactly tell my father—but he could figure it out, or maybe he already wasn't able to think it through—that once in grad school, Frank and I would be spending our vacation funds on tuition instead of trips to Vegas. I still often mailed him things I wrote, just like before, and just like before, he read them and folded them neatly and put them in that file drawer in his den.

One afternoon not long after the Maine vacation, Paul wanders into my office one day, and fingers a bookmark I keep on my desk that says, "It is never too late to become what you might have been"—George Eliot.

"You know Mom, that saying sounds true," Paul tells me.

"Yes, I suppose it does," I say.

Paul rubs the bookmark's cord with his grimy thumb. "I guess George Eliot was a pretty smart guy."

"Girl," I say.

"No kidding!"

One summer, Frank, Sean, and I—courtesy of accumulated credit card points—spend a few nights at The Greenbrier, one of the country's oldest, grandest resort hotels, the kind of place my father would have loved, where the air is perfumed with gentility and old-world charm, but that also includes the most modern amenities.

We're only in West Virginia because Paul is on a nearby adventure—twelve days at the National Boy Scout Jamboree—and Sean, who is an Eagle Scout, and Frank, an Assistant Scoutmaster, and me, a nervous mother, want to visit. The morning after we arrive, when we're planning to make the fifty-minute drive, a Scout leader we know who is already there texts to tell me it's ninety-five degrees and humid at the site, it's been raining, mud everywhere, and there's not much shade. He tell us this because he knows that under those conditions, I'll be miserable.

All this way—435 miles in the car—to see my son, and now I won't. Normally, this might upset me, I'd feel guilty and annoyed with myself for not being a go-along-get-along kind of woman, but instead being the I-need-air-conditioning-and-a-flush-toilet kind of woman, and I know whom I have to thank for that: Mom and Dad and a childhood and young adulthood spent in luxe hotels. But I'm nearing a point in life when I begin to understand that certain things about me—quirks and knowing what's necessary to feel right in the world—are something I can choose to accept and like, and not bemoan. More important, having an appreciation of why I'm particular (okay, spoiled), that the people and experiences that have made and formed me, aren't a problem; maybe, in fact, it's a blessing.

I stay behind, and I'm glad. It turns out, I have ghosts to consult.

I begin by taking a slow walk, "getting the scope of the place," something my father always did when we arrived at a new hotel, a new city or country, while my mother unpacked and I read the room service menu or stood out on a balcony, dreaming. My walk has me exploring the first three floors of the hotel, a sweeping gracious accumulation of connected sitting rooms, parlors, and lobbies, some designed for conversation, others for relaxation, for solitude, tucked in corners with fireplaces and potted trees. I notice things that would have pleased my father: the height of the ceilings in all the public areas, the fine fabrics and vibrant colors on the sofas and windows, healthy soaring plants. A feeling, in the airy gathering rooms, of going on and on, a sense that, even though a couple of hundred people are about—engaged in everything from hoisting a Bloody Mary, to having quiet conversations, or reading—no one area seems crowded.

To use up my day, I decide to spend a little bit of time in every public room, and that includes the side hallways where I linger at framed photos of important men from the decades of the twentieth century—presidents, royalty, authors, movie stars, business tycoons. Many names are familiar. My father could tell me stories.

Instead, I tell myself a story.

I come upon a small alcove equipped with several grand writing tables, leather blotters, old pen-and-ink stands, and a copious supply of hotel stationery. By hand, I write a letter to my father, because I want to tell him about this place, and how being there reminds me of so many other places we've stayed, in Zurich and Nice, in Wiesbaden and Vienna, how it reminds me of him strolling across a dozen other lobbies, one hand in the pocket of a summer suit. Memories bubble up, of days, times, a life gone by. Me at thirteen, in Miami or Puerto Rico, with braces, thighs that rub, frizzy hair, unshaved legs, and a suitcase of new clothes. Me dressing for dinner and a show—we wore gowns with our tans and jewelry—and he waiting in the lobby for "the women," and then me coming out of the elevator, and feeling as if I'm emerging from a cocoon, ready to flit and fly, then there's Daddy, striding toward me, whistling and shaking his open hand, and saying, "VaVa Va Voom young lady!"

I write and write, in the foreclosing shade of a long afternoon, about my mother and I glide-crossing the wide floral carpets of hotels just like this one, us both pretty in Lily Pulitzer pink in a cream and green world of hushed luxury. I write of my Italian off-the-boat grandparents, our scruffy New Jersey textile factory money, new money. But it was money just the same, and with it my father could buy an American fantasy, family memories, time, days, meals, the world.

I fold the letter inside an envelope and lick it closed, gently rub the flap, wishing I could mail it, happy that I cannot, that I can keep it. Later in the day I will carefully reopen the flap, reread what I've written, and think it is so very silly of me to make a kind of religion of good hotels and elegant lobbies. I chide myself too for insisting to Frank that sometimes when we travel, we don't scrimp but splurge; but then I remember it isn't silly—it's my way of re-creating a little bit of what formed me, of revisiting that feeling of being at home in a hotel.

I know my father wanted to give me that feeling, of finding myself at home wherever in the world I land. He himself learned the confidence to treat himself well, to savor luxury, to know its value, how it can be balm and retreat. He wanted me to treat myself well too, though he made it clear luxury wasn't a reward. I wish my father also knew that when he was gone, I carried with me—in a Greenbrier or a Comfort Inn—that peace of traveling lightly, traveling both within myself and in the world. I wish him to know that every time I venture out, I find it there, on the road, in almost any hotel.

When I get home to New Jersey, I place the envelope containing the letter in a spot in my office where I'll see it from time to time. I slide the envelope into a funny little piece of bric-a-brac, something I have that used to reside in my father's office as early as the mid-sixties—an eight-inch-long gold paper clip, mounted vertically upright on a small round black plastic base engraved with the name of an industrial metals company in Newark, probably one of the vendors to which my father's scrap-metal-buying company sold its inventory. The company name, the paper clip even, has little significance, but the memory does.

I saw it first in my father's rough-built loft office where he over-saw his businesses. He used it as a paperweight, holding down pieces of paper he called "bills of lading." Later, it lived on his marble desk in the spare bedroom (Gary's former bedroom) in our split-level New Jersey house, keeping household bills in place. The paper clip traveled to Vegas, where it moved from the marble desk to a side credenza, and then later when he could no longer write checks, someone moved it to a bookshelf.

Eventually I find the paper clip sticking up from a box in Mom's garage. Inside is an old half ream of creamy business stationery, and my father's scrapbooks from his early days in business, articles about his community service and the one about the fire that once destroyed his factory. A photo with that article shows my father walking through the burned-out rubble in the early morning, hours after the fire, his coat pulled around his pajama top, his hair sticking up. It is the saddest photo of my father I will ever see. I was eight that day, cuddled under the covers with my mother since the call from the police came at 3 a.m.

I take the paper clip back to New Jersey, to my house three blocks from the one where it once rested on his marble desk, and place it next to my collection of poetry books, in honor of my father, who worked in the dirty, grubby world of fabrics and scrap metals and who occasionally read poetry on weekends. Now it lives with his youngest daughter, who never worked in any kind of dirty place (high-priced equestrian centers don't count). I keep it there, just within sight when I'm at my writing desk—well, if I lean and cast my eye to the right—because I like to remember all the choices I have always had that he never did. I like to remember the way it once gleamed in the sunlight that streamed through Venetian blinds in Dad's humble office that no longer exists, where for the first time I came to know my father as someone who thought big, stayed humble, and who made and took chances.

It reminds me to do the same, to mind the sun.

15

Exit Zero

Sometime between the two- and three-year mark, I start to question my outsize reaction to my father's death, and my lingering insistence that we could talk our way to a new relationship after he died. Then someone sends me the text of a sermon about grief, in which a clergyman posits that the work grief is not about forgetting, but finding ways to remember. That grief is how we work out what was wrong in the pre-death relationship.

I'm further buoyed when I learn that Freud once asserted that the death of a loved one with whom you once sparred might rock you more than the death of a loved one by whom you felt well loved. In *Tuesdays with Morrie,* Mitch Albom quotes what the playwright Robert Anderson once wrote, in *I Never Sang for My Father:* "Death ends a life, but it does not end a relationship."

Does it matter that I feel closer to my father in death than I did during his corporeal life? That we "talk"? (It certainly seems to matter to some others: watch someone's face when you use the present tense to talk about a dead person.) I used to think so, that it mattered, that it all had to mean something. Then I listened to a few Buddhist friends who recommend I try not to attach meaning, but simply to watch, listen, wonder. So, I gradually stop dwelling on the idea that our post-death conversations are either my own ego (or guilty conscious) or that I am indulging myself as a way to pretend all the hurt I may have caused him in life is now absolved.

As I try to learn more about the odd way my grief unspools, I learn that in some Asian cultures, talking to the dead is commonplace, expected even. In *Generation to Generation: Family Process in Church and Synagogue,* Edwin H. Friedman writes "grief is always proportional to the un-worked-out residue of the relationship that was lost." Surely my continuing relationship with my elusive father comforts me, but that's not the point. A soothing hot bath, plenty of rich dark chocolate, poetry, or sex could do the same (and does). What it does do for me (for the two of us maybe?) is to bring back into life (well into *my* life anyway), something that went by too quickly, unnoticed, unappreciated, the first time. It brings into my life something that didn't happen before: a particular kind of bittersweet father-daughter reunion.

What's more American than a second opportunity to get it right?

More times than I can count, my father clarified his forgiveness of a debt, giving a disgraced employee his job back, agreeing to help finance another business venture, with the same simple explanation: everyone deserves a second chance.

We do too, he and I.

It seems I wasn't ready, during his lifetime, for the kind of relationship I find it possible to have with him following his death. Maybe that's an easy way out for me, naive. Anyway, it feels more natural now. I talk, and when he talks back, it is in the way I'm mentally ready to hear. And this is true: I'm clearly in control. Someone must be, though I'm intensely aware of the need not to lie to myself.

The relationship I had maybe been (unconsciously?) seeking in life is perhaps the one I re-create from the post-death experience. But perhaps not. Maybe, like an unsure girl in sparkly red shoes, I already had it all along—that it was on offer all my life. I just never took him up on it. When he was here, I must have spent so much time trying to diminish him in my mind that it is only in death I recognize him as—then and now—my biggest influence.

I don't think of our grief-fired relationship as "making peace," though I know that's what others may make of it since it's what we're all urged to do with the dying. To my mind, I "made peace" with my father the day I walked into his hospital room after his stroke and decided not to try to talk him out of his half-out-of-his-head ramblings. I wasn't any kind of angel or any smarter than my brother or mother. I was just doing what came naturally in the moment. All my life I'd been wanting him to be wrong, me to be right. That day, it all stopped.

I'm glad in a sense to be able to recall our earlier discord clearly, to label my own cruel, mean-spirited actions and words that come back to me with a clarity others might imagine would get clouded by time, conveniently "forgotten" by embarrassment. I'm glad too that the opposite, the manner in which we now interact—because we do, bodies or not—after his demise has been the opposite: full of compassion and understanding, curiosity and respect, examination and, occasionally, delight.

Though not always: a few times when he visited (What are we talking about here, I still wonder, my imagination? A dream? A daydream? Or him, *him*?), I was rushed, disbelieving, angry at myself—for what, for calling him forth? Conjuring him? Thinking him into existence?—when I should be doing something more productive. But mostly I'm grateful for the experience, the ongoingness of whatever it was, whatever it *is*.

I'm thinking about all this when I read Gloria Steinem's memoir *My Life on the Road,* part of which measures her parents' strong influence on her adult choices; her mother was a retiring, depressed woman who put aside professional career aspirations to follow Steinem's free-spirited, fun-loving father around the country carving out a carefree, sometimes unreliable living as an itinerant jewelry and antiques salesman. Early in the book, Steinem laments things never discussed or acknowledged between father and daughter.

She writes that like many children, she was drawn to the parent who seemed to need her most, in her case, her mother. But she had a clearer understanding of what drove her father and herself—an interest in reshaping their own futures. "There wasn't time or place to explore what I think we both knew: that in our small family, we were the most alike," Steinam writes. "For reasons of work and geography, we saw each other less and less in the years before he died. I never told him that I could see myself in him, and vice-versa."

I didn't have any of those conversations with my distant father, either. I'm sorry for that, but I'm not sorry that, eventually, I too realized that what drove us both might have driven us closer in life, had I slowed down to notice.

When I read more about how adult children react to a parent's death, I learn that while there has always been robust interest on the part of researchers about how the death of a mother affects daughters, and how the passing of fathers impacts sons, it's only relatively recently that some have turned to what happens emotionally to adult daughters upon the death of their fathers.

Now, when I see a movie Dad would have liked, I don't for an instant think to mention it. I only think, *Dad would have liked that.* Sometimes I say just that to whoever is there—my sister, kids, husband, even a new friend who never knew him at all. I like to talk about him, even in a country, even in company that doesn't easily talk of the dead.

I'm often sad about how Americans disown dying, how we're so hands-off about all the details and rituals of death, funerals, grief, mourning—even remembering. I'm also heartened that I see a new interest in death; online, I hang out online at sites like Modern Loss, Death Café, Good to Go. As my father was dying, and then more vigorously after his death, and finally, passionately, in the first years of his postmortem *existence,* I begin reading about death, about losing a loved one, and why, in convoluted and inexplicable ways, losing isn't the worst thing. No, worse is not examining that loss, not holding it up to the light, and not asking, in the reality of that loss, what was the reality of what came before? If an unexamined life isn't worth living, I come to believe an unexamined grief is a bigger loss.

I notice with curious detachment that death itself seems to be ascending in popularity, if *popular* is the right word, among Baby Boomers in particular, the generation that regards even natural phenomena as unique to itself. I was born at the tail end of the Boomers, so I don't find it odd. Although death and grief have come to billions before us, apparently Boomers are "re-creating" death rituals, co-opting grief as something previously unexplored. We are fascinated with the question of what will happen to us and how we behave after death comes to those we love. Death doula has become a profession. "Complicated grief" is now a recognized psychological disorder.

I don't care if I'm part of any new label.

I talk about my dead father as if he's here, because he is. I'm not talking about ghosts, restless wandering spirits who can't move on. I come to believe all the dead are here, but mostly we don't see them because we've been somehow taught not to think of them.

At some point between the two- and three-year mark, I stop thinking about how long it's been, nor do I forget anymore that he is dead, in odd moments, as I once did. But neither do I "get over it," though

I have always been a big fan of moving forward. I dwell, I linger with the idea that one can carry on a *relationship* with someone who has died. My father seemed more alive to me in the first few years following his death than during his lifetime. Maybe, I think, relationships don't end, as lives do, and I'm pleased to read one day in an article that I'm not the only one.

Susan D. Block, chief of Psychosocial Oncology and Palliative Care at Dana-Farber Cancer Institute in Boston, is quoted in a *New York Times* article explaining that often people continue relationships with those who have died. "The relationship evolves," she says. Relationships are mutual though, and I have come to understand that what I have with my father is a one-sided relationship. Or is it? All in my mind, this ongoingness, a way to cope with his gone-ness? Maybe it's just my way, in a life ruled by unrelenting workaholism and the belief I must do everything myself—to indulge just this once? It may be the small and single kindness I show myself.

My friend Laraine, who writes a category of fiction called magical realism, asks me to read and offer feedback on her novel draft and I demur (*I'm a nonfiction person,* I say); but she insists, and I'm surprisingly swept up in her fictional story of—what?—spirits, ghosts, dead people still having relationships with their left-behind loves ones. Later she returns the favor and reads some of my work, and when she gets to the part about my father's postmortem visits, she writes in the margin: "Magical realism triumphs again" and inks in a smiley face.

When finally (I knew there would be a finally) Dad stops showing up in my days, at first there is a terrible sadness, a feeling of not knowing any longer where I am in space and time. Then, a kind of odd relief. That is a surprise.

16

Epilogue

I AM ACCEPTED for a residency at a far northern artist colony, a place where many writer friends have told me they've made surging progress on manuscripts, reenergized stalled projects, been able to write and think with clarity among the evergreens and quiet. I'm excited to get away. My boys, by now fifteen and eleven—and after two years of my graduate school residencies and five years of my flying to my parents' sickbeds—are not only okay with my leaving, but they seem to relish the idea of more guy time with Dad, my checking in only once a day via email or a quick phone call, if I will have any cell service at all.

My writing studio's one large window faces a small frozen river, and I gaze out at the daily swirling snow for hours. I'm stuck, blocked, unable to write a word about anything other than my father and am still convinced I should be writing about something else. The four things in closest visual range as I gaze out the window are a rustic old red barn, which serves as the artists' dining hall; a remodeled yellow barn, where the visual artists work; a cluster of small snug houses, where we all sleep at night; and a plain steel reinforced cement bridge connecting everything to the beautiful modern new studio building.

There, in my private studio, I feel too isolated, and I learn something about myself as a writer: I don't want or need to get away from the hubbub of my everyday life, the sloppy imperfection of my family, the noise and routine. It's not so bad that when I close my office door two boys and a man who loves me open it anyway.

That winter, in the middle of my failed writing residency, I sit each day in a green velvet wing chair next to the lovely oak writing desk I hardly touch, and stare out the window. I stare and stare. I think, on that other side of the bridge are meals and rest and community and my car (and escape), and on this side is stillness and my notebook and too many words and not enough of the right words, and it's all about my father, though I don't want it to be. It's the bridge's fault, I decide, and the fault of all the hidden stress in me. When I learn there is a plan that coming summer to replace the cement bridge because of hidden structural stressors, I begin to dread the idea of it disappearing, just as I dread I will disappear inside myself if I can't begin to write about anything else but my dead father.

I keep thinking: it's okay now to move on. Move past the mental bridge, cross that midline.

The days are long and cold and quiet, and that feels right somehow, even though I'm disappointed that I don't do what I imagine most of the other writers on retreat here are doing—writing steadily and easily for four-hour blocks between scheduled meals. I read. I write emails to my kids. I call Frank and tell him everything is great, that the studio is modern, spacious, warm, and soundproof. I procrastinate. I reorganize my electronic recipe file. I write poetry of quite questionable quality.

I make lists: Books to write. Books to read. Things to splurge on.

A few days, I do write a little. No matter what I do, I do it for only about an hour at a time, and then shrug into a long down coat that grazes the top of my sturdy boots, an oversize scarf, hat, and gloves, and I take a walk across the bridge. I gulp cold air, eyes down at the path my feet make. I don't go anywhere else, just across the bridge, a distance of about thirty yards, and then back, then across and back again. So that I don't appear too silly to anyone else who may also be staring out their own studio window, I make a ridiculous point of stopping, stretching, lifting, and bending and unbending my elbows above my head, lifting and bending and unbending my knees, so they might think my bridge walking is part of a thought-out plan to exercise and breathe fresh air between productive writing sessions. This is almost precisely what my father did on long airplane trips to ward off the danger of blood clots—walked from his first-class perch to the back of the plane, stretched, bent, then walked back to first class, repeat.

I do this about three times in each direction, and then head back inside, mix a fresh mug of instant hot chocolate or another salty noodle cup in the communal kitchenette that smells like popcorn, then to try to write for an hour, a half hour. Sometimes, I succeed. Otherwise, I catch an episode of a TV drama on my computer (in a way another writing resident showed me and I don't think is quite legal).

By the fourth day, the bridge walking has taken on major meta-phorical significance, first without my noticing, then with my avid com-plicity. I reason that it symbolizes connection and choice and a reluc-tance to move past a certain important but lingering period of grief and reconciliation. I can choose to cross over and back any number of times, and as long as the bridge does not fail me, I don't have to decide just yet. I could choose to complete what I intended when I first arrived. I could choose not to. And in not choosing, I choose. Those weeks, I keep trying to get away, and trying to get back, and trying most of all, to be still. To listen to myself and to pay attention to whomever or what-ever else I should be paying attention to.

One day I stop to read the sign posted by the county public works commission that explains the bridge is scheduled to be demolished in spring, rebuilt over the summer, open again to foot and vehicle traf-fic in early fall. Suddenly, a panic rises in my throat. Although I will be long gone from this place, I wonder about the writers who will be here during the time the bridge isn't there (I even have a friend scheduled for a late spring residency). How they will manage the divide? I read on: a shuttle bus will be provided, taking the long way around over another bridge, a couple of miles up (or is it down?) river. That seems awful to me, somehow, that they won't be able to traverse the bridge under their own power, whenever they want.

At some point during my timekeeping watch out that window, I under-stand two things: First, that I will soon turn fifty years old and—not to get too Oprah-esque—maybe that means it's time for something, a change. I've made so many new friends in the last two years who have launched or relaunched careers and vocations and passionate hobbies in the creative arts, women mostly, well into their fifties, sixties, and sev-enties, that I have retrained my brain to think of aging as not only nat-ural, but as a doorway to possibility, maybe even as positive. Second, I understand, maybe even hope, that an ending might precede any new beginning.

Since my father died, it has felt as if he were still *here,* on one side of some metaphorical bridge or line, still sometimes with me. Noth-ing felt final, but still unfolding, the present-day visits a continuation of the past. The time between death and present day, a kind of bridge I've been able to tarry on.

My time at the artist colony is drawing to a close soon. One dark afternoon at the window, I am transfixed by the image of the soon-to-be-gone bridge, the bridge I love and don't understand, a bridge whose days are numbered.

I know that I'm running out of another kind of time.

One day I think I see Dad through the twisting snow and treacly fog, but it's another man, not even an old man, whose carriage and step only remind me of his.

But the next day I *do* see him, from my studio window, on another dark afternoon, in the middle distance. It is for only a few seconds, and my eyes are struggling with the glinting sun's low horizon this far north.

He seems to be moving further into the distance, approaching the red and yellow barns and the houses, though not so far that I can't see if I squint. He's looking back over his shoulder and whispering something across the still waters. Eventually, he stops and turns, first at the opposite shore, then from the back of the red barn, from the shadow side of the yellow barn. Each time he pauses and waves. Then, he simply begins walking away, and away, rounding the rural snow-packed road, slipping between the towering evergreens. Finally, he's a shadow between the barns and houses, between the buildings and the hills beyond. The last thing I see is his back, and his hand, raised above his head, fingers spread and waving ever so slightly. I can't tell if it seems like a big hand or not, only that it is open.

Postscript

The day I am making final revisions to this book, I ask Sean, by now twenty-three, to pick up some things for dinner. When he returns, he tells me something odd happened at Foodtown.

"An old man who looked like PopPop was on the check-out line right in front of me," Sean says.

This isn't the first time one or another of my kids, or my husband, has reported a PopPop "sighting."

"He was wearing the kind of shirts PopPop always wore. He walked stooped over, and he was paying with a fifty-dollar bill. The cashier was fumbling with the change, and he was telling her that he wasn't in a hurry. He even *sounded* like PopPop."

"That's interesting," I say. We smile at one another. I think the story is over.

Sean continues, "He had only one item in his cart. A loaf of Italian bread."

Acknowledgments

Writing is singular. Moving writing out into the world involves others. Many generous, intelligent, kind (and sometimes helpfully tough) people have lent expertise and support. If I've left anyone out, it is only because I have been hugely blessed in the *help* and *friend* department.

Christina Baker Kline read a pile of essays, told me the hard truth of what had to be done, and waited patiently until I was ready to hear. I'm forever humbled and grateful for her sunny belief in my writing, and her friendship.

Laraine Herring's lovely, strong, no-nonsense input on an early draft was what I kept returning to as I rewrote.

Ideas for this book first emerged while at the Stonecoast MFA Program at University of Southern Maine. There, I benefitted from the interest of faculty members Joan Connor, Richard Hoffman, Ann Hood, Barbara Hurd, Debra Marquart, Joyce Maynard, Leslea Newman, and Suzanne Strempek Shea; and fellow students including Sheila Boneham, Kathy Briccetti, Christin Geall, Florence Grende, and Nan Steinley, who continue to create community.

I'm grateful for support from my teaching colleagues, including Leanna James Blackwell, Susan Ito, and Kate Whouley, in the Bay Path University MFA program; David Galef at Montclair State University; and Michelle Cameron and Judith Lindbergh from the Writers Circle.

I appreciate others who helped in small or large ways: Liane Kupferberg Carter, Christine Corso, Erika Dreifus, Janice Eidus, Vincent J. Fitzgerald, Suzannah Windsor Freeman, Sonya Huber, Nancy Davidoff Kelton, Peggy Lavake, Jennie Nash, Judith Pepper, Karen Rile, Candy Wechsler Schulman, Sue William Silverman, Sheila Squillante, Kate Walter, Ryder Ziebarth—and so many online writer pals.

I treasure the wise counsel, spirited confidence, and endless listening gifts of Deborah Lerner Duane; at our monthly breakfasts, every time I cry into my eggs and she orders us bacon, I feel loved and held.

I fondly thank Judith Merz, who once said, "Lisa, you are a writer." I chose to believe her. The late Bill Glavin taught me there's always more to the story.

To all the editors who've published and supported my work, I owe heartfelt appreciation for seeing something. To those who hire me to edit and guide their writing projects, thank you for providing important scaffolding in a writing life.

I'm grateful to my lovely agent Joelle Delbourgo, who appeared precisely when I needed her.

I'll always be glad that my feet hurt at a writing conference, which made me slow down enough to meet Justin Race at the University of Nevada Press booth. I couldn't have asked for a more enthusiastic champion of this book; thanks also to the rest of the team at UNP.

I appreciate the generosity of the poet Brian Henry, who allowed me to showcase his gorgeous poem in the front of this book.

Memoir exists only because life happened. The closest people in my life contributed first by living these experiences with me.

All her life, my mother, Domenica ("Mickey") Marco Chipolone, wrote the most beautiful letters. Watching her compose them at the dining room table, from long before I could read, planted a seed. She read everything I ever wrote and told me it was great, even when what I wrote stung.

This entire book is a thank-you note to my father.

I'm grateful to my sister, Cathy, who bought me my first typewriter, and brother, Gary, who may not always like what I write but so far hasn't stopped liking me.

Laura Granata Rode is a constant reminder that lifelong friendship makes me rich beyond measure.

There is no way to fully thank my husband, Frank, for his unstinting and steadfast support, for reading the *final-but-not-final* pages and giving no-B.S. critique, and for always making me laugh—always. So much gratitude goes to my two sons, who are now men: Sean, who read drafts, told me truths, and generously allowed me to write with candor about his early life; and Paul, who reminded me that this book was not going to write itself.

You three are my heart.

About the Author

LISA ROMEO is a writer, editor, and creative writing teacher. She's part of the founding faculty of the Bay Path University MFA Program and has taught at Rutgers and Montclair State Universities in New Jersey. She works as a manuscript editor, ghostwriter, and editorial consultant and also teaches with The Writers Circle.

Lisa's nonfiction work is listed in Notables in *Best American Essays 2016* and has been nominated for a Pushcart Prize. Her essays have appeared in many anthologies and are published regularly in popular and literary media, including the *New York Times, O The Oprah Magazine, Under the Sun, Brevity, Hippocampus, Under the Gum Tree,* and others.

A former horse show competitor, Lisa developed careers as an equestrian journalist and public relations specialist before completing an MFA degree in the Stonecoast program at the University of Southern Maine. She also holds a BS degree in journalism from the Newhouse School at Syracuse University.

When not writing or reading, Lisa can be found in the kitchen or taking a long walk around the northern New Jersey suburb where she was raised and where she and husband, Frank (her high school crush), continue to live with their college-age sons.